Communicate
to Inspire

Inspire

Verb:
Fill (someone) with the urge or ability to do or feel something. Create (a feeling, esp a positive one) in a person: 'inspire confidence'

Definition:
Encourage, stimulate

Synonyms:
Affect, animate, arouse, be responsible for, cause, elate, embolden, enkindle, enliven, excite, exhilarate, fire up, galvanize, give impetus, give one an idea, give rise to, hearten, imbue, impress, infect, inflame, influence, infuse, instil, invigorate, motivate, provoke, quicken, set up, spark, spur, start off, stir, strike, sway, touch, trigger, urge, work up

Antonyms:
discourage, dissuade

Communicate to Inspire
A guide for leaders

Kevin Murray

LONDON PHILADELPHIA NEW DELHI

First published in Great Britain and the United States in 2014 by Kogan Page Limited

2nd Floor, 45 Gee Street	1518 Walnut Street, Suite 1100	4737/23 Ansari Road
London EC1V 3RS	Philadelphia PA 19102	Daryaganj
United Kingdom	USA	New Delhi 110002
www.koganpage.com		India

© Kevin Murray, 2014

ISBN   978 0 7494 6814 9
E-ISBN   978 0 7494 6815 6

British Library Cataloguing-in-Publication Data

A CIP record for this book is available from the British Library.

Library of Congress Cataloging-in-Publication Data

Murray, Kevin, 1928-
   Communicate to inspire / Kevin Murray. – 1st Edition.
      pages cm
   ISBN 978-0-7494-6814-9 (pbk.) – ISBN 978-0-7494-6815-6   1. Leadership.
2. Communication in management.   3. Chief executive officers.   I. Title.
   HD57.7.M86797 2014
   658.4'5–dc23
                                                         2013044129

Typeset by Graphicraft Limited, Hong Kong
Print production managed by Jellyfish
Printed and bound by CPI Group (UK), Croydon CRO 4YY

CONTENTS

07   Engage through powerful conversations: how to use conversations to drive culture, and why culture delivers goals   84

PART III   Connecting to the emotions that drive behaviours   109

08   It's all about them: how to become more effective by being more focused on people and behaviours   111

09   The listening leader: why you need to listen louder   129

LIST OF FIGURES

FOREWORD
by Peter Cheese, CEO, Chartered Institute of Personnel and Development

Leadership in today's world is more demanding and leaders are being more challenged than ever before. We live in times of great uncertainty and rapid change, with a need for adaptation and innovation on an almost continuous basis in order to ensure our organizations survive and thrive.

Old rules and boundaries are falling away, and disruptive business models, competitors, technologies, and ideas abound. We are seeing new organizational forms and business models; the growth of the network, the wisdom of the crowds, the collaborative and social enterprise. Young people in particular have different expectations and, instead of a job for life, they now talk about a life of jobs, where they have more control of their environment and destiny. Loyalty to the organization (or seemingly remote top leaders) is diminishing, and loyalty is transferring to ourselves or to those closest to us. Diversity in every sense is the norm, with diverse ways of working, diverse teams and individuals, diverse aspirations and expectations.

This changing context means that leadership at all levels becomes harder as we seek to understand and manage these trends, whilst working with more volatility and uncertainty in the economy than most of us have ever encountered. Leadership, as Kevin Murray explains in this book, has never been more tested, nor more important and valuable.

Yet, as the environment for leaders has got tougher, basic trust in leadership is being severely tested, with regular revelations and scandals that have engulfed the banks and other sectors of business, the media, the public sector, politics, and even sport. It's a fruitful time to be a finger-wagging newspaper columnist. It's not quite so great if you're looking for consistent leadership or moral fortitude among the senior ranks of organizations. Sadly, but perhaps not too surprisingly, The Institute of Business Ethics has recorded a 10 per cent drop over the last year in the proportion of the public who believe businesses behave 'very' or 'fairly' ethically, a view now held by only 48 per cent of people.

The wider concerns are echoed through to internal organizational views of trust. The CIPD has recently released research on trust which found that one in three employees rate their trust in senior managers as weak. The research also found that trust ratings increase with an employee's seniority, with senior managers far more likely than non-managerial staff to report strong trust between employees and senior management. But then they would, wouldn't they?

Building on this theme, Kevin's research on what makes for inspiring leaders and whether leaders themselves are inspiring found similar levels of concern. As he reports in this book, only one in five employees rated their boss as really inspiring, with one in three rating them as uninspiring or worse!

These findings are of real concern given the central importance of trust and engagement to performance, as Kevin amply illustrates. Much more visibility has been given to these themes in recent years, and not before time. Motivated and happy employees, aligned to the purpose and value of the enterprise, will always be more productive. It shouldn't take much science or data to convince us, but it seems we need to be reminded. Latest research on neuroscience and the newer areas of psychology such as positive psychology and behavioural economics has now started to hit the mainstream – even the UK Government and Number 10 have been talking about national happiness quotients and created a 'nudge' unit to focus on how to make large-scale behavioural shifts.

No surprise, then, that senior business leaders themselves point more and more to their concerns about having the right leadership capabilities and talent at all levels, but are also becoming more and more aware of their own role in creating the right cultures, living the corporate values, and engaging their people. Tone from the top and how this is communicated now seems to be the common mantra. Indeed, as Kevin points out, communication is now a top three skill of leadership.

What then is the answer? Well, one thing is for sure, there is no lack of advice. Leadership is a topic that has been more written about than any other theme in business. Amazon shows over 20,000 books currently available on the subject!

In the end, leadership is in large measure about people. About creating and communicating a common sense of purpose, about engaging, about influencing and inspiring, but also about trusting and empowering your teams to work effectively – to succeed, but also at times to fail. We have moved on from a single view of leadership that is about the leader, to one that is about devolved leadership everywhere in organizations. The charismatic leader still exists, but we can see many other types and models that are highly effective in creating a real sense of engagement and empowerment in those around them. But how do you do this in a way that is compelling and effective?

In Kevin Murray's research and experience, what he has consistently found and points to is that it takes excellence in communication. In this and many other pieces of research on trust, when employees are asked what they looked for in building trust in their leaders, communication rings through with common observations such as being more approachable, consistent, and speaking and acting with honesty and integrity. And in particular the recognition that communication is a two-way process, that and good leaders are also great listeners.

Creating inspiration through communication, and building a consistent voice for leaders that inspires confidence and trust, must now work through many channels and forums. There are so many new ways of communicating and connecting, with multiple channels to speak through, and importantly to listen through. Twitter has only been around since 2006 and yet has over 500 million users tweeting 1 billion thoughts, comments, jokes and observations every five days. It is now a regularly accepted forum for leaders to talk through and engage. We have blogging, LinkedIn and a host of other ways to express and expose ourselves.

Employees, customers, shareholders, and other stakeholders all now expect to see and hear leaders through these channels. They expect leaders to be 'open', 'authentic', to reveal the whole person or 'be themselves better', and to listen more, not be just a scripted voice box.

This is particularly true for the younger generation, so called Gen Y, who are highly active themselves in these channels and communities and expect their bosses to be too. I have found that myself, and despite my belief in all these forms of communication, had to be somewhat dragged over the threshold in to Twitterland. Once in there it was fine, but those of us not born in to a digital world are more likely to find this daunting and unnatural, at least to start with. Kevin's chapter on why leaders need to engage with social media is a particularly helpful and important reminder for all of us.

What, then, should we communicate? Let's start with communicating our meaning and purpose and our values, at a personal level, but also of course at the organizational level. Without this understanding and employees' alignment to these at all levels, we lack the golden thread of engagement. As Kevin has so often found, the best leaders bring these to life with stories and examples and they visibly celebrate behaviours and actions that reflect the purpose and values.

This book then is a great insight on how leaders should communicate and how to inspire. It builds on the success of his last book *The Language of Leaders*. There was much in his first book for us all to use, learning from many diverse leaders in diverse organizations. They all shared many common perspectives, but also reflected their own personal way of communicating, of inspiring and of engaging. In this follow up book, *Communicate to Inspire*, Kevin has been able to pull all these learnings together into models that frame the good practices for us to digest and build from.

If trust and inspiration really are in such short supply, then this book is not only extremely timely, but critically necessary.

Peter Cheese
Chief Executive
Chartered Institute of Personnel and Development

The CIPD is the professional body for HR and people development. Having over 130,000 members internationally – working in HR, learning and development, people management and consulting across private businesses and organizations in the public and voluntary sectors.

Introduction
The inspiration gap

Inspiring leadership communication is about getting others to believe in your cause, believe in themselves, and then achieve more than they thought was possible. We've never needed it more. Yet research shows there is a growing gap between bosses and employees when it comes to perceptions of inspirational leadership. How good are you?

To be successful, leaders must inspire others to achieve great results. How ironic then that few leaders are taught the critical communication skills that enable them to be inspiring.

The simple truth is this: How well you perform as a leader, will depend on how well as a leader you communicate. You can have the best plan, the best resources and the best people, but if you don't communicate well, you won't persuade people to your cause, and you will fail. It is that simple.

Yet any leader can easily derive competitive advantage by learning how to be more inspiring. It is much easier than you might think.

To do this, you need to be more authentic, more empathetic and more engaging. You need to learn how to tell stories and how to truly listen. You need to understand why you should stand up for your point of view, and be hyper-aware of the unconscious signals you send. You need to learn how to articulate an inspiring vision and how to lead the critical conversations that change everything. Together, this mix of communication skills can provide the super-fuel that will enable you to be hugely effective.

There has never been a more demanding environment. Today, leaders are living in a fishbowl where they are under more scrutiny than ever, where every action is transparently obvious and where the people they depend on for success have greater expectations of leaders than ever. Capturing hearts is now more important than capturing minds, though both still have to be done. But how do you achieve this?

Answer: through more inspiring communication. By being more inspiring, you can positively influence people, change their behaviours and achieve results. That is why communication is today one of the top three skills of leadership.

My aim in this book is to share some practical tools, and give you some tried-and-tested guides to being a more inspirational leader, and a more effective communicator.

Is all this really necessary?

Yes, undoubtedly. There is a significant inspiration gap that exists between leaders and followers, one that must be bridged if we are to grow and prosper.

I recently asked many hundreds of leaders from around the world to rate themselves on their Leadership Inspiration Quotient. They gave themselves – on average – a mark of about 7/10, which is less than brilliant but still a fairly good assessment. I guess no leader wants to be thought of as less than inspiring.

What mark would you give yourself?

If, like the hundreds I have surveyed, you give yourself 7/10 (or more), you may be unaware of your biggest challenge.

Here's the problem. Most employees, when asked how inspiring their bosses are, give them a significantly lower mark. On average, they give them just over 5/10. Only one in five says their boss is inspiring. Why? Because most leaders do not really know what it means to be inspiring.

Since the publication of my first book, *The Language of Leaders*, I have given dozens of talks in many countries around the world. At many leadership conferences, I see the output of brainstorming sessions where people have been asked to name leaders they have found most inspiring. Often, they are asked to put up photographs of these leaders and name a characteristic about them that they found inspiring.

As I walk around these rooms, I see the faces of President John F Kennedy, President Reagan, Winston Churchill, Margaret Thatcher, Gandhi, Nelson Mandela, Indira Gandhi, Martin Luther King, Mother Teresa and many other prominent political and religious leaders. These people were more than inspiring. They were awe-inspiring. Most commanded a world stage and were commanding orators. But, if this is the concept we have in our minds when we think of being an inspiring leader, it is entirely the wrong concept on which to model our own leadership style.

After all the work I have done with leaders over the past two decades, after all the interviews and all the research, I have come to believe that the best definition of leadership to which we should aspire comes from Lao Tsu, a philosopher of ancient China, best known as the author of the *Tao Te Ching*. He said: 'A leader is best when people barely know he exists; when his work is done, his aim fulfilled, they will say: we did it ourselves.'

There is a huge difference between being seen as inspiring and making others feel inspired. If you take only one thing away from this book, I hope it is this: inspiring leadership communication is not about great oratory or great charisma; rather it is about getting others to believe in themselves and believe in your cause, and then achieve more than they thought was possible.

If you stop for a moment and think about your role as a leader, there's nothing more important than inspiring others. To achieve your goals, you have to get others to perform. How well they perform will be a function of how you make them feel. It is all about how you make them feel.

What influences the way they feel? At best, a powerful and uplifting speech will provide transitory inspiration. To be constantly inspired, they need something else. This 'something else' comes from how well you listen and how much interest you show in them.

It comes from the stories you tell, the behaviours you exhibit and, thereby, the signals you send. It stems from the beliefs you hold dear and make clear. It comes from their belief in your integrity and your values. It is delivered by the meaning and context you provide.

It is in the passion you dare to put on display, in the words you use and the subjects you focus on. It is in the possibilities you see and speak about and the conversations you stimulate and lead. It is in your point of view and in the call to action that you use to rally people to your cause.

Most of all, it is in the way you make followers feel whenever they talk with you.

Here's the question I most often get asked: Are leaders born or can they be taught? I believe that anyone can lead. All you have to do is want it enough. You have to want to achieve something, to make a difference. It could be something relatively small, like wanting to improve a process or to make a small change that will improve the customer experience. It could be to lead a global organization.

Anything you set your heart and mind on. If you want it enough, your passion will act as a magnet to the like-minded, and you will be able to inspire the support of a team. So yes, you can be taught!

Today, leadership is everywhere, and must be everywhere to cope with the incredible speed of the modern world. In a radically connected and transparent society – where everything moves at the speed of light – the only response is to build more agility into our organizations. And that means more leadership, everywhere.

As you will see in the following chapters, value today increasingly comes from intangibles: 'soft assets' such as relationships, culture and values, reputation and trust, knowledge, skills, processes and systems.

Perhaps, though, the greatest intangible assets of all are leadership and communication, because they deliver all of the above.

This is why I have written this book – in order to help make leaders more effective, by making them better, more inspiring communicators.

If you want to become a more inspiring leader, you have first to become more audience-centric, so that you can connect better with the people you need to influence, and build and maintain relationships and trust.

You need to learn how to more effectively bring the outside world into your organization in order to drive positive change.

You have to be clear on your own purpose and values so that you can be more passionate about what matters, and be more authentic. You have to learn how this is integral to trust, which is the bedrock of leadership.

You need to understand the compelling power of a shared purpose and shared values. And you need to understand how to combine this with the precision of a clear vision of success.

You need to learn how better to engage your employees, by holding more powerful conversations, more systematically.

To do that, you have to learn to become a better listener, so that you can relate better to people and get more relevant, more timely information, in order to make better-informed decisions.

You have to become more conscious of the inadvertent signals you send that can overwhelm your words and sabotage your plans.

You have to learn how to articulate a powerful point of view, and how to tell more inspirational stories. At the same time you have to understand the persuasive impact of a single word. The more senior you get, the more effective you have to become on public platforms. You need to learn the power of social media in modern leadership.

You need to become more conscious of the need for great communication throughout your organization, and the need to strive constantly to become better at it.

You need to learn the language of leaders.

The dictionary defines language as 'a system of communication used by a country or community'. I believe there is a system of communication used by the community of people who describe themselves as leaders.

The system has 12 principles, with one underpinning essential, and this book is designed to show you how to deliver effectively against each of these. There are many books available on how to be a good listener, or how to tell stories, or how to be better at leadership conversations. This, I believe, is the only one that integrates all of these into a single system.

Are you an engaging leader who can create and engage followers and, through them, a super-performing organization? Do you understand the difference between employees seeing you as inspiring and actually feeling inspired themselves?

I know that the outstanding leaders in my life were the ones who inspired me to be my very best. They liberated me to achieve results beyond the goals I had set myself. They connected with me on an emotional level and made me feel appreciated, talented, responsible and accountable. I trusted them and could predict how they would behave and how they would react to issues. They loved hearing my thinking on challenges we faced, and that influenced their decisions.

They guided me, encouraged me and supported me when the going got tough. I knew what they were trying to achieve, why it was important, and what my role was in helping them to achieve their goals. Most of the time, they achieved their aims. They communicated brilliantly and selflessly and I – like other members of the team – felt inspired.

These bosses learned how to create outrageously successful working relationships. This book is designed to help you do the same.

PART I
Leadership in the age of transparency

The new leader

> *As the traditional model of leadership changes, the biggest obstacle to leaders is not a lack of expertise, but rather a failure of relationship management. In the new world, talk is work, trust is a strategic asset, and relationships are the engines of success.*

Are you in a new leadership role? Or are you a leader with ambitions to achieve even more? Either way, your challenge is to achieve your goals through others.

So, how are those people feeling? Do they know exactly what needs to be done? Do they know enough about what their colleagues are doing to be able to collaborate properly? Do they have the resources they need? Do they have the right incentives to motivate their behaviours, and the right sense of purpose and values to guide their actions? Do they feel valued and respected? Do they know how you would like your customers to feel after every interaction with them? Do they know why what they are doing really matters? Do they truly care?

If you can win the emotional commitment of the people who follow you and inspire them to achieve more than they thought possible, then you really will be a new leader. A new-age leader.

To be a great leader today you have to be a great communicator. This is because leadership is all about relationships and conversations. Relationships are all about trust, care, concern, understanding and constant communication. Whether those relationships are with people inside or outside the organization you lead, the same rules apply. Nothing is more valuable to leaders than the quality of their relationships. Those relationships can only thrive on constant and excellent communication.

Conversations drive change

By 'great communicator', I don't mean you have to be a great orator or a charismatic speaker. I mean that, in today's world, you have to be a great conversationalist. You have to learn to have the conversations that matter, the conversations that drive change, the conversations that encourage people to support you or that inspire them to great performance. And you have to have them many times a day, every day, if you want to succeed. When you aren't having them yourself, you have to ensure that all other leaders in the organization are.

You don't have to stand up on the stage and be amazing. Even if you did manage to inspire from the stage, such inspiration would only be transitory. Inspiration that transforms everything, that gets people to change direction and commit with their hearts and souls, only comes from constant conversation.

The radical transparency of the modern world has radically changed leadership over the past five years, and has placed huge emphasis on the management of intangible assets such as trust and relationships, which in turn places such a huge emphasis on excellence in communication.

For my first book – *The Language of Leaders* – I interviewed more than 70 chairs and chief executives of a wide range of global private sector companies, global charities and more than a dozen public sector organizations. Loudly and clearly, I heard that modern leaders have to learn to be much more focused on relationships, inside and outside their companies, and communicate better within those relationships in order to build trust, the essential prerequisite of successful leadership. Organizations that want to survive and thrive in the age of transparency must place the building of trust at the heart of their strategies.

Talk is work

Conversations drive change, and relationships are the engines of your success. These are two such simple but powerful thoughts: Put another way, *talk is work* and *trust is a strategic asset*. It is for these reasons that all the leaders I spoke with said that communication was now a 'top three' skill of leadership… but they worried that too little training and emphasis is placed on developing this skill in future leaders.

Indeed, a recent study by the Marketing Society and Accenture, after in-depth interviews with 40 CEOs, also identified communication as the third most important attribute of leadership, behind strategic thinking and customer focus. 'In an age when more people "like" videos on YouTube than vote in elections, it is easy to see how the digital world has empowered the consumer on a mass scale. Increasingly, organizations have less and less control of what is being said about them,' commented the Marketing Society. Faced with this, it said leaders had to communicate clearly with customers, shareholders, analysts and the media as well as with their workforces in order to motivate and energize.

But, remember this: whatever you promise to people outside your organization, will never be delivered unless you are able to convince and inspire the people inside your organization.

Why? Because employees retain a level of effort and commitment that they give at their own discretion, and only if they are inspired to do so. That 'discretionary effort', however, can be the difference between an adequate performance and a great performance – and can be the difference between success and failure for a leader.

In one way or another, every leader I talk with describes a new world of transparency and scrutiny where their reputation is their single most important asset. In a world of 24/7 news, always on social media, of viral storytelling and instant global access to information from anywhere on any device, speed is the new currency of business. Under these conditions, being a leader – wherever you sit in the hierarchy – is a demanding, intense and risky role.

Speed is the new currency of business and leadership

A growing alliance between the public and the media, aided by the ubiquity of the internet, has been the catalyst of the speed that defines our world today. This, in turn, has forced on leaders the need to revolutionize their organizations in order to try to deliver far greater agility within them. And this is another factor that has placed a huge emphasis on more, and more effective, communication.

Consider the following factors:

- the sheer speed of modern communications on a global scale;
- a staggering increase in channels of communication, especially digital;
- rapidly shifting patterns of influence and the rise of citizen and consumer power;

- the elevated expectations of all stakeholders, especially for speedy response;

- new and rapidly changing communities of interest, enabled by digital technologies and a new sense of empowerment;

- increased regulation and all of the consequent communication requirements;

- the aggressive pursuit of information by journalists, and the tabloidization of business reporting;

- declining levels of trust in business, institutions, politicians and the media, with rising levels of trust from peers, family and friends, often including strangers connected by the internet.

A new kind of leadership is key to prosperity

Good leadership is the key to organizational effectiveness and social and economic prosperity. But – because of all these forces – the traditional model for what constitutes a good leader is changing. How we develop our leaders must change too. The Institute of Leadership and Management, Europe's leading management organization, recently conducted a survey of HR professionals from global businesses, who emphasized a distinct set of personal characteristics that future leaders need to possess. They now seek visionary, motivational and inspirational people who are emotionally intelligent, trustworthy, natural leaders and communicators, and who are also driven and ambitious.

Said the ILM: 'HR professionals want leaders who can understand, inspire and motivate people. The ability to motivate and inspire others was the characteristic most commonly cited as important when recruiting senior leaders.'

Power, title authority or even competency are no longer enough to make you a great leader. Rather it is the ability to earn and then keep the loyalty and trust of those whom you are leading that will make you great. That means adding value to their lives, constantly, in order to build the bond that can survive mistakes, downturns, obstacles and intense competition that inevitably will arise.

Followers won't care about how much you know until they know how much you care. Rational argument and intellect will not compete with strong emotional or philosophical positioning. Great leaders are able to provide common purpose and meaning to all sorts of people. Great relationships take a huge amount of energy and commitment, but it is trust that binds all of those different people together – and trust takes a long time to build and can be lost in an instant.

Emotionally intelligent communication is a key leadership success factor. I am persuaded that by far the majority of leadership effectiveness is related to emotional intelligence such as authenticity, integrity, openness, empathy and listening skills, and much less is related to IQ or technical competence. The biggest obstacle to some leaders in shaping the future is not lack of expertise but rather a failure in relationship management and poor communication.

True communication emerges from your being

I have spent a career helping leaders to be more effective in the messages they give, and for a long time I mistakenly focused on the content, sometimes to the exclusion of authenticity. True communication emerges from our being and is most powerful when it gives expression to our values and emotions. How leaders learn to be more emotional in the way they communicate is therefore a critical factor in their success.

The Work Foundation, part of Lancaster University in the United Kingdom, is a leading independent authority on work and its future. A recent two-year study by the Foundation entitled *Exceeding Expectation: The principles of outstanding leadership*, showed that outstanding leaders combined drive for high performance with an almost obsessive focus on people as the means of achieving this. It showed clear differences between good and outstanding leadership.

It says: 'There is now strong evidence to support a systemic, people centred approach to high-performance leadership. This is a paradigm shift for most leaders who remain focused on the numbers and has implications for all organisations seeking to improve their performance.'

The results showed some fascinating differences between leaders who are good and leaders who are outstanding. For instance, all leaders talked about the importance of engaging others in the vision, but outstanding leaders conveyed a greater depth and higher purpose when speaking about vision, seeing it as a clarion call that affected employee commitment and engagement.

Good leaders were more likely to see vision only as useful in aligning people through a cascade of objectives. When it came to creating the right working environment, all leaders understood the need for trust, respect and honesty. But outstanding leaders understood how they combined to create the conditions for exceptional performance.

Create space for meaningful conversations

Outstanding leaders are much more likely to see the link between behaviour and outcomes and are more likely to provide the space for 'meaningful conversations'. 'Outstanding leaders are deeply people and relationship-centred rather than just people oriented,' says the Work Foundation.

> 'Both good and outstanding leaders seek to create a compelling vision, live their values and focus on the individual. Outstanding leaders however, place less emphasis on charisma. While they recognise that being positive is important, being consistent in creating purpose is more so. They recognise that how they are with people hinders or helps to galvanise others behind the vision.
>
> Outstanding leadership depends on trusting and positive relationships that are built over time for the long-term benefit of the people and their organisation. Outstanding leaders spend a significant amount of time talking with people to understand what motivates and how they can support and boost enthusiasm in others.'

They also spend a great deal of time building buy-in to company direction, and a shared set of values.

Personal connection to organizational goals is critical

Creating a sense of shared purpose is all about ensuring employees understand exactly what to do, and linking their daily work with company success. Inspiring people is about encouraging people to develop their own ideas, find new solutions to problems and try new things – in pursuit of organizational goals.

Trust, however, remains probably one of the single most important factors in success. Organizations with high levels of trust enjoy clear economic benefits. Trust has a direct link to the subject of ethics and what leaders are doing to embed ethical values into the culture of their organizations.

Adopting a strong stance on ethics is not just the right thing to do but offers performance payoffs too.

This is because trust is an essential component of effective leadership at all levels. Trust drives engagement and motivation and is critical in enabling higher organizational performance.

Trust by employees for leaders is rising

The Institute of Leadership and Management has conducted research on Leadership Trust. The trust index reveals the extent to which leaders and line managers are trusted by their employees. The good news is that for the three years from 2009 to 2011, trust by employees for managers and leaders has been rising.

However, the more distant employees felt from their team boss or their senior leaders, the less likely they were to trust them. The more visible leaders were, the more they walked the talk, the more open and understanding they were, the more they were trusted. It was clear from the Institute's study that leaders were making much more effort in these areas. The report notes that:

> 'There is still plenty of room for improvement, though. Trust is the ultimate leadership commodity; you can never have enough of it. And the index highlights several areas in which leaders can focus to further build their trust capital. In order to continue to close the distance between themselves and their employees they would benefit from even greater visibility and stronger relationships with the workforce. By continuing to focus on good communication, visibility and accessibility, leaders must try to maintain the progress they have made.'

The ILM worried, however, about the trust marks that line managers were receiving. 'Line managers are invariably more visible to employees. As such we would expect line managers to be significantly more trusted than senior leaders. However the latest index shows that managers have not kept pace in improving their trust capital.'

Line managers need help to improve trust

The ILM says that one of the chief reasons for this may be the relative lack of support and development line managers receive in the field of communication. CEOs and senior leaders are likely to have access to a support network of executive coaches, public relations and brand advisers, and communications specialists to guide and inform their behaviour. Managers at lower levels generally receive far less support and development, while any weaknesses in their competence and capability are far more visible.

In the aftermath of the banking crisis, the BP oil spill, the phone hacking scandal and so many other events that have destroyed trust, the ILM also explored the importance of ethics in building trust. It said:

> 'Ethical considerations are increasingly important for employees and we expect this trend to accelerate. It was very clear to see that those managers and leaders considered more ethical were also considered more trustworthy. This highlights a clear trust benefit attached to improving the ethical attitudes and approach of the organization, the workforce, its managers and leaders.'

Earning a trust dividend

> 'Our research suggests that organizations which drive ethics into the hearts of their operations can obtain the additional bonus of a trust dividend. It is a dividend that feeds into employee engagement and workforce commitment, and thus improves organizational performance.'

Ethics, relationships, trust, reputation – even leadership itself – are intangible assets, and are sources of incredible value to any organization. They are the sources of competitive advantage and above-normal financial returns – where even some of the basic economic rules seem to break down.

For example, the more you use tangible assets such as machines or buildings, the smaller is the marginal return. However, for intangibles such as brands, reputation and relationships, this can be exactly the opposite. So, the question is: how should leaders now think about, measure, monitor and manage such valuable but 'soft' assets?

Leadership
The greatest intangible asset of them all

In the new economy, value isn't where it used to be. Intangible assets are hidden gold, and leaders who concentrate on them will outperform their competitors. What, really, are they – and how do you measure, monitor and manage these intangibles? Why do these 'soft' assets require different, and better, communication skills?

How do you measure the value of employee emotions? Does it even matter how employees feel? Is the culture in your department or your organization collaborative and supportive? Are all the key relationships in and outside the company in good order? Do your customers value your support and services, and do they keep coming back to you? Can you count on the support of your local community if you want to expand your factory? Do people widely recognize and favour the name of your business and regard you as a force for good?

Strange questions, you might say, but increasingly crucial to leaders because of the powerful influence – both positive and negative – that the answers have on leadership effectiveness.

The answers to these questions reveal a lot about the state of your intangible assets. Those assets that cannot be seen and weighed and accounted for in conventional ways, like factories, plant, machinery, stock, equipment or real estate. Intangible assets are the basis of competitive edge and long-term growth and wealth creation – and are the 'worryingly' emotional side of leadership. I say worrying, because at any moment people's perceptions of these assets could change, and a vast amount of value could be destroyed as those perceptions get worse.

In the new economy of a radically transparent world, I have seen it said that more than 65 per cent of global market value is determined by intangible assets. I have seen reports that the total value of all listed companies all over the world is estimated at more than $50 TRILLION (million million). This means intangible assets are worth more than $30 trillion – and that is not including all the private companies in the world. *Immense* financial value! The problem is that leaders do not spend a proportionate amount of time managing these soft assets. Even if you are a leader in the public sector or a charity, these intangible assets are key determinants of whether you will succeed.

Organizations that outperform their rivals usually do so less on the basis of competitive advantages such as market share, product differentiation and price, and more and more they achieve it through leaders who value and nurture intangible assets.

Positive emotions drive better performance

I often hear from leaders I work with that you can't account for or measure intangibles like employee emotions. How do you do that? Yet all the research shows that positive emotions are much more prevalent in higher-performing workplaces. Where people have a strong emotional connection with their workplace, where they feel valued, empowered, encouraged and supported, they are more likely to be cheerful, proud and high performing. Workplaces that don't do so well are characterized by more negative emotions and have higher levels of depression, anxiety and lack of trust.

So, in the new economy, value isn't where it used to be. Those solid, quantifiable assets like plant and equipment are now often far less indicative of a company's value – or even its future performance – than intangibles like ideas, relationships and knowledge. Because intangibles are so hard to measure, they're rarely managed with the same rigour. Yet the return on investment in these areas is likely to pay significantly higher dividends.

Very few executives would say their companies are proficient at monitoring critical non-financial indicators of performance, let alone managing them effectively. In my experience management and boards have tended to focus their energy on budgets and operational performance, taking the value of intangibles like brands, relationships and human knowledge and talent for granted.

Increasingly, however, leaders are recognizing that intangibles may be hidden gold. And that the most valuable intangible of all is the talent in their own organizations. They talk about how people are their only asset, but it's a glib line that makes a terrible mistake. Not everybody in your organization is an asset. Time wasters, work shirkers, toxic colleagues and active resistors of change are most certainly not assets. Committed, passionate people who give of their discretionary effort to help achieve goals are the real assets.

When leaders create an environment where those people can flourish, they can impact competitive edge in a thousand different ways – by being much more productive, by being more efficient and by delighting customers, for example.

Reputation is increasingly acknowledged as not only a crucial intangible asset but also a wealth generator. Total shareholder returns of the most admired companies tend to greatly exceed those of competitors that are less well thought of. A positive reputation generates higher sales, more referrals, key relationships with suppliers and partners, and the ability to attract the best people. Positive relationships with government and regulators can have a huge impact on business, and on its costs.

The reason is that a strong brand or reputation, allied to positive and supportive relationships, *greatly* improves your operating environment and your chances of success (see Figure 2.1). That translates into better performance, which delivers higher financial returns and better growth potential. In turn, that improves reputation, which improves valuation – particularly of your intangible assets. This leads to greater financial value, better shareholder returns and the Holy Grail: sustainable success. A very virtuous circle.

Intangible assets demand extraordinary communication skills

Intangible assets provide potential competitive advantage, but as assets they clearly demand focused leadership and extraordinary communication skills. As a leader, your ability to deliver your strategy is dependent on customer relationships, your brand and reputation, and most importantly the relationship you have with your employees. And all of those depend on excellence in communication.

FIGURE 2.1 SUSTAINABLE SUCCESS: THE VIRTUOUS CIRCLE

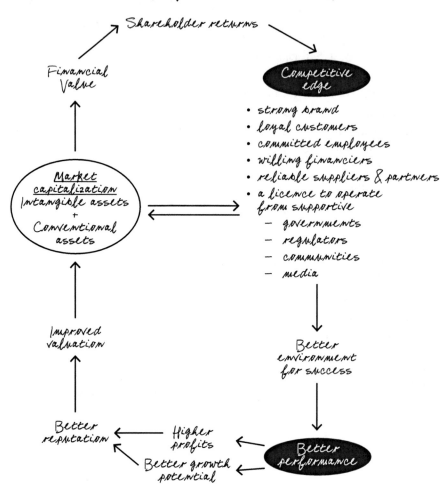

In May 2001, the UK government's Department of Trade and Industry published a special report entitled *Creating Value from Your Intangible Assets*. It was, I believe, a report ahead of its time. It is still available on the internet and is still an invaluable resource for any leader.

It says: 'In practice, there are few sources of competitive advantage that cannot be duplicated and matched by competitors. Ultimately, a company's ability to flourish in this environment will depend on its ability to create value from intangibles.'

Future success depends on identifying, developing and making best use of such intangibles. What are they? The report identifies seven:

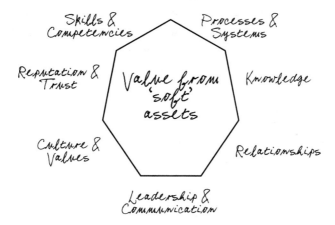

FIGURE 2.2 INTANGIBLE ASSETS BUILD COMPETITIVE EDGE

*Government Report

- skills and competencies;
- processes and systems;
- knowledge;
- culture and values;
- relationships;
- reputation and trust;
- leadership and communication (see Figure 2.2).

The value of people is a theme running throughout the report, but it majors on the crucial importance of people having the right skills and competencies – crucial to the ability of any organization to meet and exceed customer needs and realize full potential. Attracting, developing and retaining the right mix of talented people, and then liberating them to perform, were all crucial to sustaining the organization.

How those people behave, and whether they are supported by the right processes and systems, is the next key intangible. How organizations set about using knowledge to design the right processes to deliver value to all of their relationships is often a massive competitive edge.

'Most knowledge in today's information rich world is not unique. Good ideas can be copied and ways of working replicated. Having knowledge is only half of the equation, having it within the organization where everyone who needs it has access to it is what creates value in the context of relationships.'

The speed with which new ways of working could be identified and replicated made culture and organizational values vital. A key component in any company's ability to achieve its goals is its ability to inspire its people, create outstanding products and services and connect effectively with the aspirations and values of all of the important internal and external relationships.

'Successful companies are those which recognise culture and values are valuable resources that help them to get things done in the right way at the right time with the right result.'

The report paid close attention to reputation and trust as special intangible assets. It noted that whatever sector of the economy, whatever organization you are in, the fact that you had the best product or service would count for little if your reputation with all of your stakeholders, and the trust they had in you, was low.

Competitive advantage through quality relationships

It was for this reason, said the DTI report, that only by developing an effective strategy for managing and maintaining excellent relationships with all stakeholders could any organization hope to achieve its full potential.

'A successful company is one that looks constantly to build on its existing relationships – be they external or internal – in a quest for competitive advantage.'

It said that whether internal or external, sustainable relationships relied on each party continually providing value, or at least the prospect of value, to the other party.

'For your company to reach its full potential in this area, it is essential that you not only consider how you can develop and improve your current relationships, but that you also carefully consider how you can develop and improve the relationships necessary for your future success.'

For all these reasons, it was clear that leadership and communication were perhaps the most important intangible assets of all.

'If companies are to achieve their full growth potential it is essential that clear goals and aims and values are set and embedded throughout the organization. This can only happen with strong leadership and effective communication. This is not just about people understanding what they are supposed to do, it is also about commitment because they believe that it is the right thing to do. This goes further than simply understanding mission statements and targets, but requires a much deeper understanding of context.'

In 2012, the Association of International Certified Professional Accountants and the Chartered Institute of Management Accountants published a report entitled: *Rebooting Business: Valuing the human dimension*. The world's two most prestigious accounting bodies questioned more than 280 CEOs on the subject of current global challenges and what they saw as the priorities in leading the way through them.

The finding of this research was that it was the human dimension – relationships with customers, employees, partners and communities – that would be key to getting things moving again and sustaining success over the long run. It notes that:

'Most of us sense that we are caught up in something big and uncertain. Much of what we have known – the paradigms that have guided business and government – have been disrupted by a dizzying pace of change brought about by globalisation, innovation and the fallout from the global financial crisis.'

The first challenge is to understand intangible value

The accountants' report concludes:

'Our 280 CEOs consider that the first challenge is to understand value – where it comes from and how much there is of it. They see people's ideas, skills, knowledge and relationships representing the unique value of their companies. The need to measure and manage the human dimension, although difficult, has never been greater if companies are to achieve long-term sustainable success.

One thing we can be sure of in this uncertain world is that people – their ideas and relationships – will be more important than ever before. There is value to be gained by being open and transparent in that it will help organizations build better, more valuable relationships. But, we will have to improve our ability to measure and promote the value that comes from people – because it takes longer sometimes before the value coming from people becomes apparent, and we have to overcome the current emphasis on short-term leadership.'

Interestingly, the accountants drew special attention to the value of the radical transparency of the modern world:

'Transparency comes in two guises. First, companies can choose an open and honest approach to reporting their activities and may be repaid by winning more trust among investors and other stakeholders. Transparency permits stakeholders a better understanding of the firm's operations, though it places greater pressure on the firm's management to produce acceptable results in all facets of their operations.

Secondly, organizations are finding that, despite their best efforts to do so, it is becoming increasingly difficult to keep confidential or damaging information out of the public domain, with the outcomes being as damaging to corporate reputations as they are unpredictable. In an age where it seems that nothing is private, CEOs see transparency as a critical driver of growth. But it is also a juggling act as it is not always easy to find the right balance between openness and protecting commercially sensitive information. But ultimately, relationships are built on trust and openness.'

Transparency has changed the nature of leadership

Radical transparency was also a major theme of all of the interviews I conducted for my book *The Language of Leaders*. It was why many leaders felt that they were operating much closer to the precipice.

Reputation has always been important but today, they say, you can lose your reputation in seconds. Lord Mervyn Davies (Baron Davies of Abersoch), former Chairman of Standard Chartered plc, Chairman of Chime Communications plc and a former government minister, argues that communication has assumed crucial importance in a world where:

'news travels so fast; where bad and good news can move across continents in milliseconds. This has changed the nature of politics and changed the nature of business.

It means that whatever you're doing wherever you are, there is a chance that because of CCTV, YouTube, cameras on mobile phones, somebody is watching you. We live in a world where a small action can cause a big result.'

Kevin Beeston, who is Chairman of Taylor Wimpey, one of the largest British house building companies, and a former Chairman of global support services group Serco, says:

'These days, everybody's got a camera with them. Everybody's got a mobile phone with a voice recording system or a video camera, so you cannot drop your guard. Make one mistake and you will not get away with it.

But the opposite is also true – if you manage this environment well you have more ways of getting your message over and building your brand. And a strong brand is probably one of the most significant competitive advantages a company can have. So if you manage it effectively, it could be a big driver of shareholder value.'

Graham Mackay, the immediate past Chief Executive of SAB Miller, one of the world's largest brewers, says that the modern world places much greater demands on leaders:

> 'Businesses are much more like open democracies. People expect to be communicated to much more and see themselves as part of a democracy where they consent to being led. As well as the need to communicate more with employees, there is increased regulatory scrutiny, the rise of global NGOs and 24/7 media. You have to represent yourself and explain your company and your actions all the time.'

Learn to embrace transparency

Leaders must embrace transparency and work with the raised communication expectations of a digital age. This means they have to put reputation management at the top of their agenda, right up there with the need to build relationships of trust. To do that, leaders must communicate more clearly, more often and with the idea firmly embedded that communication today is about rapidly evolving stories and conversations.

The communication demand on leaders is far greater today, requiring them to address a wider array of audiences and use an ever wider array of channels. But, if you manage this environment well, you have more ways of getting your message over and building a great organization where everybody wins.

Leadership is about trust

Sir Stuart Rose, former Chairman of British retailer Marks & Spencer, and new Chair of internet grocer Ocado, says: 'For a leader, building reputation and trust *is* the day job, which makes communication the day job too.'

Communication, along with other supposedly soft management skills, has too long been neglected. It is an issue that affects not only the fortunes of businesses but also the prosperity of nations.

Says Sir Stuart:

> 'All of these changes call for more open leadership. There is a definite need for more open dialogue, for more social engagement, for more social responsibility and for more accountability... Leadership is not just about producing the right results. Leadership is about setting the right tone in the organization. It's about ethos, it's about what you stand for, it's about trust.'

Every day, it seems, we read about further declines in levels of trust. As a result, business leaders increasingly pontificate about the need to restore trust, and they're right to be worried. Trust is money. It delivers improved cash flow, higher valuations, faster times to market, competitive edge. Without it, everything takes longer, is more complex and often vastly more costly.

Paul Zak, Director of the Centre for Neuroeconomic Studies at Claremont Graduate University in California, says that personal trust is a strong predictor of a country's wealth and prosperity.

> 'High-trust countries tend to grow much more rapidly than low-trust countries. Trust really is a kind of economic lubricant, resulting in a government sector that works well, a social sector that works well and an economy that also works well.'

he says.

So trust matters, and is essential to progress. And it starts with employees. Restoring trust though is misleading as a concept. It is very hard to think about what to do with that concept. The thing we forget about trust, is that it only occurs in relationships. A better concept is that relationships are the engines of success, and we need to focus on the health of our key relationships. We can do something about that. Building a climate of trust in relationships requires emotional intelligence. Knowing how to create a positive relationship with employees, customers, suppliers, the local community, society and shareholders is becoming the fundamental element for long-term success.

The biggest risk is the destruction of relationships

The worst risk is therefore not in the loss of reputation but rather in the consequences of a bad reputation – the destruction of relationships. So you could argue that managing reputation is actually about managing the risks around the intangible asset of relationships – for it is upon these relationships that the future of the company depends. And if it is all about relationships, we need to spend more time fundamentally understanding those relationships and the drivers of trust within them. That means a great deal more time measuring and monitoring (the Science). With that understanding, we can put more positive emotion into how we relate to people and how we communicate with them (the Art).

Trust is an emotion, and essential to our future economic well-being. Trust is a positive feeling, not the absence of a negative feeling. We won't restore it unless we remember that we need to put more emotionally intelligent thinking into our decision making.

Most importantly, it is about what organizations and leaders do rather than just what they say. It is how people behave, how they treat each other and how well they deliver on promises. And so it is that great leadership is becoming more important in determining the reputation of organizations. Market perceptions of leaders actually move share prices. A report published in 2012 by global accountancy practice Deloitte Touche Tohmatsu, entitled *The Leadership Premium*, reveals that effective leadership can raise company valuations by as much as 16 per cent.

Based on a survey of leading market analysts in the United Kingdom, the United States, China, India, Japan and Brazil, the report found that the quality of senior leadership – including core capabilities as well as personal qualities such as honesty and integrity – has a direct and measurable impact on analysts' assessments whether companies have been successful and will be successful in the future.

According to the report, the quality of leadership could affect analysts' valuations of companies by 16 per cent positively, and by up to 20 per cent negatively. The gap between the value of a company with good leadership and that of a company with weaker leadership could be more than 35 per cent.

Commenting on the report, Deloitte said:

'To succeed in the long term, an organization needs a clear and inspiring vision of where it wants to be and the resources, ability, and drive to get there. It also needs a culture that supports new ideas and that fosters a strong sense of belonging and purpose. These conditions aren't developed accidentally. Effective leaders design them in and analysts recognise that.'

Leaders worth their salt know that whatever kind of organization they lead, no matter how big the team, it is intangible assets that create the platform for success. These intangible assets include: skills and competencies, processes and systems, knowledge, culture and values, relationships, reputation and trust. Whether these assets are fully realized depends on what I believe are the most important intangible assets of all: leadership and communication.

And if it is all about leadership and communication, then I believe that it boils down to this: do you communicate well enough to inspire the people in your key relationships to support you, to commit to your vision and goals, and to go that extra mile to achieve superior results?

The 12 principles of inspiring leadership communication

What did 70 chairs and CEOs of global companies, charities and public sector organizations say were the ingredients of truly inspiring leadership communication? And how do these principles contribute to trust, engagement, relationships and reputation?

How can you improve your performance as an inspiring communicator and make the difference that can change poor performance into exceptional results?

Answer: Study the 12 principles of inspiring leadership communication gleaned from 70 chairs and chief executives of a wide range of global private sector companies, global charities and more than a dozen public sector organizations. I interviewed these people for *The Language of Leaders*, and then discussed my findings with thousands of other leaders and managers around the world.

These 70 bosses had a combined total of more than 2,000 years of leadership experience. Every interview was taped, and the tapes were transcribed. In the transcripts, there are more than 600,000 words. I read those words many times over, trying to understand what was really being said. What could you use to power and inform the way you communicate as a leader?

I believe I made a number of breakthrough findings in those interviews. The most important was that communication is what leaders do before, during and after decisions. It is what they *do* to achieve results. It is how they inspire us.

The purpose of leadership

The dictionary defines language as a system of communication.

What then is the *system* of communication used by leaders?

The leaders I interviewed said that the purpose of leadership communication is to influence and inspire (in order to achieve great results). To do so requires you to deliver 12 key components of inspirational communication.

The 12 principles are shown in Figure 3.1 overleaf.

1 Learn how to be yourself, better, and reveal more of yourself in the way you communicate, in order to build trust.

2 Give voice to a compelling purpose and a powerful set of values, to create a framework that enables empowerment, action and decision making.

3 Combine this with a vivid picture of the future, which you communicate relentlessly to drive behaviours in the present.

4 Keep your people focused on the key relationships that your organization depends on for success; use those insights to drive change, and make building trust in those relationships a priority.

5 Make 'engagement' a strategic goal, and use conversations to engage.

6 Become a fanatic about understanding audiences, before trying to communicate with them.

7 Listen in new and powerful ways, and learn to ask the right questions.

8 Prepare a potent point of view to communicate your messages.

9 Use more stories and anecdotes to inspire the right behaviours.

10 Be aware of the signals you send through your body language and your behaviours, which can overwhelm your words.

11 Prepare properly for public platforms – your reputation is at stake.

12 Learn, rehearse, review, improve – always strive to be a better communicator.

Above all, make the building and maintaining of trust a strategic goal.

FIGURE 3.1   THE 12 PRINCIPLES

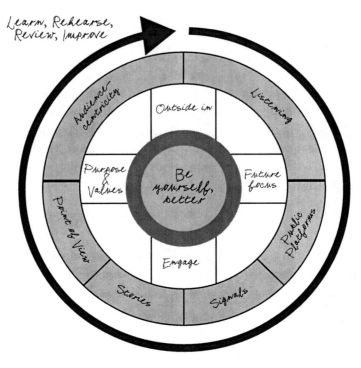

Why are these principles so important? Let's look at them one by one.

Be yourself better

Authenticity as a leader is crucial. Followers will not commit if they do not trust you and believe that you have integrity. So, even if you are a highly introverted individual, you will have to learn to speak with more passion, talk to your values and stand up more often to speak to your beliefs. Followers must *feel* your passion and believe that you believe. When you are clear with yourself about the things you really care about, you cannot help but talk to them with passion.

Most leaders have not spent the time articulating those beliefs, yet the ability to draw on and display that passion and commitment, consistently and predictably, counts for more than skills at oratory and communicates more effectively than even the most perfectly crafted words. You have to be true to yourself, but you also have to learn to 'perform' yourself better.

Purpose and values

Too often, leaders use financial or numbers-based goals to motivate people. They are more comfortable being rational and objective. Too often, followers say they don't get out of bed in the morning to achieve financial or other numbers-based objectives. They come to work and want to be inspired by a sense of doing something important, something that makes a difference.

A strong sense of mission can help shape decisions to be made throughout the organization, and is even more empowering when coupled with a set of values that your people know to be true. In this world of radical transparency, values have assumed far greater importance, for many reasons. Values define how people in the organization behave in pursuit of their objectives, and their actions define a business to the outside world. Those intangible values – often dismissed as 'soft and fluffy' – translate into actions on the ground, which translate into hard numbers in the books. How the mission and values are expressed is crucial.

Future focus

Every leader I spoke to used the future to drive the present. They knew precisely where they wanted to be in a given timescale, even if they did not know exactly how to get there. They were never satisfied with the status quo, and their restlessness was a tangible force. Every question they asked had to do with how people were progressing to the goals, and they kept those goals under constant review.

They painted a vivid picture of success, often describing the future in both rational terms (the numbers) and emotive terms (how it would feel for all concerned). This bringing together of the rational and the emotional was key to inspiring people. Fusing the future vision (what success will look and feel like) to the purpose (what important thing we are here to do) and to the values (how we do it) was what stirred hearts and minds. This future, though, had to be expressed in *benefit* terms for all the people with a vested interest in the performance of the organization – customers, shareholders, local communities, suppliers and partners and, most importantly, employees.

Bring the outside in

Leaders have to live outside their organizations, constantly bringing stories of success and failure in external relationships into the organization to keep everyone fixed on what needs to improve. Successful leaders know that relationships are the engines of success; they keep a close eye on the state of all key relationships, and keep their enterprise focused on those relationships as well. You have to set up 'quivering antennae', as one leader described it – a radar system that keeps you in touch with the outside world.

Too often I heard about the 'reputation gap' – the difference between the promises the business made and the experience customers or stakeholders actually received. Narrowing that gap, or even managing it away, is the goal if you want to be trusted. And you do want to be trusted. Trust is now the most valuable but most hidden asset on your balance sheet. Leaders are increasingly looking to make trust a strategic goal, measured and managed as preciously as any other key asset.

Engage through conversations

More and more leaders are now measuring levels of employee engagement, and using this measurement as a strategic tool to find the ways to keep people motivated and committed to the cause. Study after study has shown that companies with high levels of engagement among employees outperform their competitors by some margin.

Engagement is achieved through conversations – structured, potent conversations that allow employees to fully understand the big objective and work out with their leaders what they have to do to help achieve the goals. It is in these conversations that the rubber hits the road, where the plan gets traction. Too often, these conversations are neglected, and middle managers are neither trained for nor measured on their ability to hold these critical conversations. Worse, top management doesn't check on the quality of those conversations, or seek to get feedback from them in a systematic way.

Audience-centricity

Let us be clear: you have *not* communicated well if people have not heard you, understood you and felt motivated to think differently and act differently as a result of your words. You may have stood up and talked *at* them, but communication has only taken place when your words have had an impact. In any enterprise, leadership communication is all about achieving big goals. It is about changing behaviours. People listen from behind their own filters – filters that may be cultural or emotional, or that may be in place because of their unique perceptions or even misunderstandings.

You have to talk to people about *their* concerns, their issues, before you can be understood on your own. Every leader interviewed for this book, without exception, spoke of the need to be audience-centric in communication, and to recognize that, when it comes to communication, it is all about *them*. You have to set out to achieve change in how they think, feel and act, but that requires you to know how they think, feel and act *now*.

Listening

Quite often, the people I interviewed treated the subject of listening as if it were somehow distinct from communicating. They rated it an essential skill of leadership, possibly the hardest to perfect. Sometimes the simple act of listening, they said, is an act of inspiration in itself. 'You have to give people a damn good listening to.' There is something more fundamental at work here, though, and I call it The Listening Contract – first you have to listen, if you want to be heard.

When you listen *and* then respond with actions that remove barriers, or pick up on good ideas, you create enormous goodwill and demonstrate you are on their side, particularly when you encourage people to open up and create an environment where people can bring you bad news, express their frustrations and voice their concerns, without fear of repercussions. You have to listen beyond the words into the motives and agendas, into the context, into the performance KPIs and the financial numbers and the mood, and you have to show you understand, even if you don't agree. You have to ask great questions and learn to unleash your curiosity and interest in people. It really shows.

Point of view

The best leaders have a potent point of view, and it is always the person with the strong point of view who influences the group, who wins the day. As a leader, you are going to have to stand up and give your point of view, time and time again. You will have to take a position on issues, be courageous and stand up for what you believe to be right. Too few leaders think about developing points of view, yet – when well articulated – they can help you win friends and influence people, and gain a stronger voice in shaping the future.

In a world where people trust the motives, judgement and competence of business leaders less now than just five years ago, shouldn't we be talking to those issues more often, with more transparency, more conviction and, yes, passion? The ideal point of view should therefore bring together your purpose and your values, highlight your behaviours and draw attention to the benefits of doing things your way. And it should call people to action. Powerful stuff.

Stories and metaphor

Getting people to listen to you is tough enough, but getting them to sit up and take notice, and then remember what you have to say, is a supreme challenge. Every leader uses stories, knowing that we are wired to listen, imaginatively, when we are told stories. Good stories get under the cynical radar and touch hearts. Backed up by facts to cover off the mind, stories have the power to *move* people.

The best stories tell us about customer experiences, good and bad, or make heroes out of employees delivering the values of the organization, or show up the frustrations of workers unable to do their best because of the system, or vividly portray the future, or reveal aspects of the leader to the audience. They deliberately avoid the tyranny of PowerPoint, and are the more memorable because of it. Some leaders I spoke with were uncomfortable with the word stories and preferred the word anecdotes, saying this was factual rather than fictional as some stories can be. But they all used them, loved hearing them and re-telling them, over and over.

Signals

Actions speak louder than words. A cliché, you might say, but nevertheless one of the hardest truths for a leader to grasp. Being a leader means looking, acting, walking and talking like a leader. Countless times, leaders forget that they are in a fishbowl and are being watched all the time. A look of frustration here, a preoccupied walk through an office without speaking to anyone, a frown of frustration when someone is talking – all of these send powerful signals that staff take away and dissect for meaning.

Great leaders communicate positivity and optimism, and they often do it through a smile, or by walking with energy, or by standing straight and tall. Equally, there is nothing more corrosive than the conflict between saying one thing and doing another: for example, saying that bullying is offensive, but then doing nothing about a high-earning bullying manager. That says one thing, and one thing only: money matters more than staff welfare. Leaders who clearly love what they are doing, who show it in everything they do, in every expression, are hugely infectious.

Prepare properly for public platforms

Many leaders have had their reputations dented or even shattered because they have not prepared properly for public speaking. Yet, the more senior leaders get, the more likely it is they will have to appear on highly public platforms. Done well, such appearances can do enormous good and drive up sales or the share price, calm nervous investors or unhappy customers, or persuade talented people to the cause. Proper training or coaching is highly recommended, but is not enough by itself. Practice makes perfect, and rehearsal is the best practice. Never get complacent – it is just not worth the risk.

Learn, rehearse, review, improve

If you strive to be an excellent communicator, you will become a better, more effective leader. This is why all the leaders I spoke with focused on continuous improvement, fuelled by full and frank feedback on each and every performance. Brilliant leadership can be the difference between outstanding performance and disappointing failure. Great leaders steer organizations to success, inspire and motivate followers, and provide a moral compass for employees to set direction. They spearhead change, drive innovation and communicate a compelling vision for the future. The ability to motivate and inspire others is the characteristic most commonly cited as important when recruiting senior leaders. Communication is the tool that enables inspiring leadership. The simple truth is that you have to get better at it.

So that's it. Those are the 12 principles. In my book *The Language of Leaders*, I reported on interviews with 70 leaders and told many of the stories they had told me to bring to life the principles. In this book I will show you more about how to think about each of the 12 principles, and provide you with the process to use to improve your own performance.

Figure 3.2 shows where you can find advice on each of these principles.

My goal is to help you become a more *inspiring* communicator, and by so doing help you to become a better leader. It is not my goal to make you a technically perfect orator. You will be all the more effective if you can be both, but my observation is that you don't have to be. Passion, conviction, clarity, character and context – these things matter more, as we will see in the next chapter.

FIGURE 3.2   WHERE TO FIND MORE ON EACH PRINCIPLE

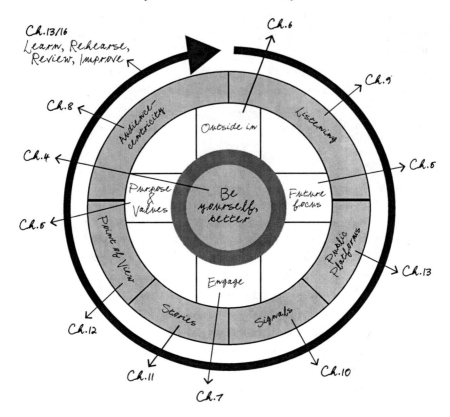

PART II
The leader within

Be yourself better

Why passion and conviction are essential to inspiring leaders

"Authenticity in leadership is crucial. It builds trust. Without trust, you cannot be an inspiring leader. But how do you show more of who you are and what you believe in, in a way that engages and motivates? Follow these 10 steps to help you articulate your personal purpose and values, be more authentic and passionate with your followers, and generate more trust.

On the night before the big conference, my CEO rejected his speech. Not good. Really, really, not good.

My team had spent weeks writing the speech with little input from him, receiving helpful but second-hand guidance from his chief of staff. They had also received advice from an editorial committee drawn together from across the organization. Our CEO had been too busy to give them time. Even with all the help from people who knew him well, the writers had had to intuit what should be in his speech, which was to be delivered at a major conference on customer care. More than 500 people would be in the audience, all of whom had paid to be there, and the event would be filmed for broadcast on the organizer's website and reported on by the media.

As speeches go, it was a pretty good one. It was witty, snappy and well researched. My CEO thought so too. The only problem was, it wasn't 'his'. It wasn't the way he spoke and it didn't say the key things about the organization that he wanted to say, the things he was most passionate about. Because he didn't 'own' it and believe it, he would not be able to deliver it with conviction and would not be authentic, he said.

(It would have been nice if he had at least found the time to look at it the day before and given us 24 hours to respond. The night before was cutting it fine.)

'What to do?' he asked.

'Well, what do you want to say?'

'I want to talk about service recovery and use that to illustrate points about our customer care ethos,' he said. (Now that would have been really nice to know.)

'Okay,' I said, 'then let me teach you the countdown technique. Think of the movie *High Noon* – where vengeful criminals are on the way to town directly from the jail you put them in. They want to kill you at the appointed hour of 12 o'clock. The clock is ticking away the seconds that will lead to this catastrophic moment. Using the countdown method is a sure-fire way to grab the audience's attention.'

'Sounds great, but what story will we tell?'

Just a few months before, the company had been involved in a high-profile service breakdown, due to circumstances way beyond its control. Staff from all over the organization had joined hands to aid customers and ensure they were not inconvenienced for too long. It had been a mammoth effort that drew on the natural desire of our staff to be of good service, our ability to be highly responsive to customers because of our detailed knowledge of them, and an ability to call on suppliers who were wedded to our customer ethos. Things had got back to normal very quickly and had resulted in a flood of grateful letters of praise from hundreds of customers.

My CEO had been intimately involved in the recovery programme, and needed little in the way of speechwriting to recall exactly what had happened. This was it. We had the story and it perfectly illustrated what he wanted to say.

Now we just needed some prompts to enable him to recall the key moments of the episode in the right sequence. We produced a few slides simply showing stages in the countdown to the disaster, describing all the factors that had converged to create the catastrophe. Then one slide to illustrate the big bang moment. And a few more slides filled with customer quotes that enabled him to talk to the key points he wanted to make about service recovery and customer care. He was happy. He could make heroes out of our staff. Better still, he seemed keen to get out there.

I was unable to attend the conference and waited nervously for news of his performance. When, finally, a member of staff called, the news was overwhelmingly positive. Our CEO had been a star! He had paced the stage with passion and conviction and had told the story brilliantly. Questions from the floor had been almost reverent and eventually had to be cut short with many hands still raised.

Instinctively, my CEO had realized a great truth about leadership. If you don't believe what you're saying, you won't convince anyone. If what you're saying doesn't come from your own passions and beliefs, you will be inauthentic and unconvincing. Worse, people may see your lack of conviction, realize the falsity of your words and mistrust your motives. And if you lose people's trust, you cannot lead them. Nor can you influence them.

Instead of taking the easy route and obediently reading what he had been given, my CEO decided not to put his leadership at risk like that. In the end, he had simply told a story he cared about and did not read a perfectly crafted speech. The story he told was the insider's background to a well-publicized service breakdown, so he was revealing the secrets about what had really happened to an audience who already knew all about the incident. He cared passionately about customers and glowed with pride at the customer comments, and naturally spoke highly of how all the staff had pulled together, without much urging, to stage a magnificent recovery. He told the story his way, in his words, from the heart. Although what he said was not perfectly scripted, it was hugely impactful.

Authenticity in leadership is crucial.

At its most simple it's about being true to yourself and true to others. If you're going to get your messages across and influence the way people behave, then there has to be trust in you as an individual and in what you say. When trust in you goes, cynicism takes its place. It is incredibly difficult to influence cynical people or people who are sceptical about your motives.

Followers want someone they can believe in. Followers respond best to leaders who have a strong strategic focus with a clear vision of where they should be going, leaders who speak plainly and truthfully and, when necessary, courageously and with principles. They especially like leaders who stand up for them and defend them to the hilt. Leaders with a strong set of values built on honesty and openness and respect for other people are the most inspirational of all. They are predictable and they are human. Followers want leaders to be accessible, with genuine humility and even, occasionally, vulnerability. They want to be trusted and in turn to trust their leader.

One of the keys to being trusted is visibility. There are so many ways today that you can make yourself more visible, whether you run a small team or a global organization. You can convey your personality on a global webinar as well as you can in face-to-face sessions. People notice whether you're willing to engage on the things that really matter, no matter how difficult. If you don't show up, they won't believe in your courage, and they won't trust that you have the conviction to do the right thing.

When you show up, you're going to have to learn how to be yourself better. People cannot trust you if they don't know who you are and what you believe in. You have to have the confidence to be you and deliver your personal brand with conviction. Whether you like it or not, you will have a brand. People will talk about you when you're not in the room, and what they say about you is your brand. The question is, what will they be saying? How can you influence what they say?

The first thing to remember is that a brand is what a brand does. What you believe will show through. A beautiful piece of writing attributed to Lao Tse, a philosopher of ancient China and the author of the *Tao Te Ching*, says the following:

> 'Watch your thoughts, they become words;
> Watch your words, they become actions;
> Watch your actions, they become habits;
> Watch your habits, they become your character; and
> Watch your character, it becomes your destiny.'

Whether you like it or not, your personal values and the things you believe important will show through in your actions and in the things you focus on. That's what people will see and that's what will communicate your brand. To help you, you need to articulate those values to yourself and take the time to write them out and consider them. Better that you do that and use them deliberately, for they will out, often in ways that you are likely to be completely unaware of.

Recently, I had the privilege of interviewing Ron Dennis, the Executive Chairman of the McLaren group, which encompasses McLaren racing, McLaren Applied Technologies and McLaren Automotive. I saw an example of what I am talking about at work.

Waiting to see him in the reception of the McLaren Technology Centre in Woking in the UK, I was happily observing the Formula One cars on display. A colleague of his, who had received me, asked me if I could tell from the line-up of cars when Ron Dennis had taken over as leader of the McLaren Formula One team.

It transpired that you could see it, because from that moment on the cars were always more aesthetic in their design. Ron, he said, was fixated with aesthetics. I was then regaled with several stories about how Ron paid close attention to detail and often personally oversaw those things that he believed required his eye for aesthetics. The whole organization knew that this was something he cared about deeply, even obsessively, and that he paid careful attention to the tiniest of details.

A little later, during my interview with him, I asked Ron about the values of McLaren. He spoke about innovation, creativity and a commitment to excellence. He said the group had one goal: to win. He never mentioned aesthetics.

Treading carefully, I asked him what a member of staff would have to do to really annoy him. 'Oh,' he said vehemently, 'that's really easy. It would be to do with aesthetics.'

Even though this was not expressed in the corporate values, it was clearly something that was driven into the organization as a powerful value that dictated how his followers behaved. They took their signals from Ron's behaviours and what he focused on.

When you are using your authenticity knowingly and to positive benefit, it brings real business benefits. When leaders are truly authentic, they are able to build strong relationships and trust. If those relationships are about mutual benefit, then you will be able to deal with conflict and difficult situations when the going gets tough. You will be able to build teams that are high-performance collectives, engaged and able to deliver their full potential. You will be in touch with yourself and your people, more in tune with what is happening and therefore able to make better-informed decisions, drawing on the creativity of everyone around you. You will be able to inspire them to great achievements.

If you really want to achieve something, you have to have an emotional connection with what you have set out to do. Don't be afraid of exposing yourself by being more emotional. All communication involves risk, and it is natural to fear that your authentic self will be rejected. The trouble is, being inauthentic is the greater risk. Authenticity is about lowering your guard and being more open about feelings, about uncertainties, about risks and issues. It is only natural to be reserved about projecting your personal beliefs on to others. But, remember this: no passion and no conviction mean no inspiration.

Here are 10 things you need to do to help you better articulate who you are and what you believe in, and enable you to be more authentic and passionate with your followers.

1 Define your purpose.

2 Define your values and your beliefs.

3 Understand your strengths. Play to them but don't trumpet them.

4 Understand, admit to and mitigate your weaknesses.

5 Think about the seminal moments in your career and life and the key learnings that you have carried forward from those. Talk about these.

6 Map your purpose to that of your organization. Create a picture of success. Speak to that more.

7 Map your values to those of your organization. Speak to those more.

8 Show more humanity. Admit mistakes or that you don't know. Always show respect to others.

9 Ask yourself whether you show up for the difficult conversations and are visible in challenging times.

10 Never swallow the truth. Always be optimistic, but never hide the truth.

In short: be visible, be human and be straight.

Here are some pointers on how to achieve each of the above.

1. Define your purpose

This, admittedly, is a tough one. Most leaders go their whole lives without articulating their own purpose statement. They spend endless hours discussing the purpose statement of the organization but no time at all on their own.

What do you want to achieve? Why do you exist? What are you here to do? Why does it matter? How does your purpose draw on the things you believe in and your view of the world? These are the questions you should be asking yourself. When you have, then write it down. The power of a statement like this gives you focus, direction and a sense of accountability to yourself about achieving your goals. It can guide your every action.

Mine? I hear you ask.

'I believe in leadership. I believe that in the modern working environme
leadership has been undervalued, over-criticized and underappreciated.
Yet great leaders can make a huge difference in people's lives. Great
leaders can make great places to work, they can help organizations grow
and prosper, and they can alter the destiny of our lives. Great leaders can
secure the wealth of nations and make a positive difference to many thousands
of people. We need to encourage and liberate the responsible and inspiring
leader in everyone.

Because of this belief, I have made it my mission to make leaders
more effective by making them better, more inspiring communicators.
I do this by one-to-one coaching, by training, by strategic consulting and by
writing books that can help leaders everywhere. By doing this, I hope that
I can make a significant difference to many thousands of people, not just the
leaders I can make more inspiring but also the many more followers of the
leaders I help.

Every person who is or aspires to be a leader has it in them to be a leader.
They simply need to learn about what it means to be inspiring, and abandon
their preconceptions about inspirational leadership.'

Can you put your purpose to words?

2. Define your values

Your values inform your thoughts, feelings and actions, whether you are
conscious of them or not. When you surface your values and give them the
power of clear articulation, they can give you greater consistency, clarity
and focus. They help you to understand what is truly important to you.
They allow you to be more consistent because, by following them, you will
be more consistently you.

I believe that the value of values is enormous. Values are at the centre of
authentic leadership. Taking time to give them clear expression will benefit
every leader. Who you are and what you stand for are just as important as
what you do.

A good way of starting to define your values is to find some quiet time
and think about the things that inspire you. Why do they? What is it about
them that lifts your spirits and makes you want to achieve more? What
are the causes you believe in? Why? What does all this say about the things
you believe important in life?

There are many sites online you can visit to find prompts that will enable
you to identify your values. Just type in 'Defining your values' for example,
and see what Google brings up. These sites will give you lists of words

such as 'accountability', 'growth', 'service', 'respect', 'usefulness' or 'vitality'. You have to look deep inside yourself and write down all the values you believe you live your life by.

Once you've done that, rate them on a scale of 0 to 10 in terms of how important they are to you. Focus on the top 10. Give them powerful expression. Then ask yourself whether they really are important values to you and whether they make you feel good about yourself? Are you proud enough of them to talk about them in public and would you be comfortable sharing them with people you respect and admire? Would you stand up for them even in situations where you found that your values were at odds with the majority in a room?

Once you have identified these values you will be able to use them in any situation to make the best choice, especially when you have no data to help support you. Very often some of the toughest things you have to decide are really about what you value most.

By way of example, four of my 10 most important values are respect, listening, curiosity and storytelling. I believe that everybody deserves my respect. I believe that I should always give people a damn good listening to. I believe that curiosity feeds my soul and prepares my mind for opportunities. I believe that there is a story in everything, that everybody loves a story, and that stories can move people to change.

These values have always stood me in good stead and I would hope that anyone who knows me will recognize that they are part of my character. I hold myself strictly to these beliefs and regularly berate myself when I fall short of delivering against them. If I do not look a waiter in the eye and thank him or her for the service they provided me, I have fallen short of one of my values. If I don't try to understand someone before inflicting my point of view on them, I have sold them and myself short. If I fail to ask the important questions that could uncover truths that matter, I have shirked my responsibility. If I try to present my arguments without using a good story, I am in danger of boring people and not holding their interest. By measuring myself so strictly against my values, I establish a strong connection between them and my behaviours.

These values bring enormous benefits to me in both my personal and professional life. And, as you can see, I have the potential to talk about them for hours.

The most important thing to remember about values is this: true values are simply profound beliefs in action.

What are yours?

3. Understand your strengths

Do you really know what talents make you special? I'll bet you don't. Sometimes people who have incredible talent don't always recognize what they're best at. Long ago I gave up the idea that I am a well-rounded leader. I have huge weaknesses, but I have some great strengths. I know enough about my weaknesses to find people who are truly strong in areas where I am deficient. Together we can make a great team, a well-rounded team. I can be comfortable joking about where I'm weak, and confident when I am playing to my strengths.

All it takes to understand your strengths is to get a well-rounded view from people that you trust. Speak to the people who know you well and ask them to give you their view on your strengths. You will soon see a consistent pattern emerging. You might also be amazed at what they say. One of the reasons this is so important is because very often your strengths are closely linked to your beliefs and can provide clues to your deep-seated values. More importantly, when you focus on trying to mitigate your weaknesses rather than playing to your strengths, people will quickly realize that you are uncomfortable and not being true to yourself. They won't necessarily know why, but it could well lead to them not trusting you and finding you insincere. Your strengths are what make you unique. When you lead from your strengths you are more authentic.

Very often you are happiest when you are in a strength zone and it doesn't feel like you have to make much effort. Others will ask how you manage to do something so well, and you will say: 'Doesn't everyone do it that way?' Watch out! You could well be playing to a strength.

What are the things you naturally do regularly – at work and at home – and why? When are you happiest? What are you doing when you're happiest and who are the people you're with? What else contributes to your happiness?

Let me give you an example of leading from your strengths. Many years ago, while working for British Airways as Director of Communications, I was asked to host a weekend in Dubai for 20 employees and their partners. These employees had been selected as the very best of the best over the previous six months. All of them had gone well beyond the call of duty to deliver excellence in customer service, backroom operations or essential duties that kept the airline running. My role was to be very visible and ensure they enjoyed the weekend and that they recognized that the airline valued what they had done. For the first two days of the weekend, all I had to do was mix and mingle as we were given a fantastic tour of Dubai and its many wonders. On the last night, at a glittering dinner that was the culmination to the weekend, it was my job to make a speech and hand them their cheques and trophies.

I was brand-new in the airline and lacked confidence talking about the operations of the company, and I certainly lacked an understanding of the roles of the various prize winners. I dreaded having to make a speech – especially one that would be so important to all of these people and their partners – and feared that I would fail to make them feel proud.

After a while, I remembered that my strengths included listening, curiosity and storytelling. (Also, as you have just read, these are deeply held values of mine.) I decided that I would lavish them with praise at the event by utilizing all of those strengths. During the two days preceding the gala dinner I spent a lot of time quizzing them about themselves. I wanted to find out all about them, what they had done and why they had gone the extra mile for customers or the airline. I made sure I understood how this had affected their families and partners. On the night of the big event, I decided not to make a speech. Instead, I simply presented each of them with their money-laden envelopes and their trophies after giving them a 'This Is Your Life'-style account of the amazing things they had done.

They loved it. They would. It was all about them, so why wouldn't they? Afterwards, several couples came to me to remark on how well the evening and gone and marvel at how I had managed to turn their deeds into such good and entertaining stories. Some of them were such good employees that they had been to these awards weekends before. They commented that no director had ever attempted to do it the way I had. They had enjoyed this event far more. There was no talk about the airline, no platitudes about the importance of customer service. It was simple, journalistic storytelling about what each and every one of them had done. They felt hugely appreciated and not patronized. I hope they went back to their jobs inspired and prepared to rise to the occasion again if ever the need arose.

For someone who is hugely interested in people, is naturally curious, knows how to ask good questions and listen hard to the answers, and then tell some good stories, this was an act of leadership that really was quite easy and very, very authentic.

4. Understand your weaknesses

Being able to admit that you got something wrong is one of the most disarming things a leader can do. Knowing what your weaknesses are and having the courage to speak about them enables you to bring humility to leadership. (And those closest to you will know the truth of what you say.) You probably know what your weaknesses are already.

If not, find people you trust and trust them to give you honest feedback. Manage your emotions through this uncomfortable feedback and make sure that you encourage them to tell you what impact your failings have on people when you get things wrong. Reflect on these and be alert to when your weaknesses are in play.

Remember also that sometimes your weaknesses, when on display, can you make you seem a pretty unpleasant character. Being authentic is not an excuse for bad behaviour. When you are being yourself you might be overly critical, stubborn, patronizing or sarcastic. You may be being yourself but you are certainly not being yourself better. One of the reasons you need to know what these weaknesses are, and how they impact on others, is so that you can manage them better.

A tactful way to ask about your weaknesses, is to ask trusted colleagues what it is that is difficult about working with you. Again, once you have done this with a few people and feel confident that they have told you the truth, a clear pattern will emerge. You have to take a 360° view of yourself and learn to admit to your weaknesses, before putting the authentic you on display.

5. Learn from your seminal moments

What challenges in your life and career have shaped you as a person?

We've all had those breakthrough moments in our career when we have had to fight and win in extraordinarily difficult circumstances. In those moments we probably learned things that we have carried forward into our careers and used as a template in many other similar circumstances.

Think about the key moments in your career where you experienced either the biggest challenge or the greatest learning. When were those moments? What did you do? What did you learn and what do you keep repeating now? Why?

What were the things that you have achieved that you are most proud of? Why? Who else shared in your pride and what did they say? When have you felt truly fulfilled and how have those moments given your life meaning?

One of mine involved having to rebrand a company in an incredibly short time frame. Having secured funds for the rebrand, and secured the support of the entire management team for the new brand, the challenge now was to implement in just a few weeks. There was no way that I was going to be able to do this with just my small team and some enthusiastic suppliers. Instead, I decided to delegate the task completely to the divisional heads of the business. My job was to ensure they understood the guidelines, set a tight framework within which they could make decisions and trust them to get on with the job as best they could in their own areas. I told them that so long as they stayed within the guidelines, they could implement in the most appropriate way in their areas. They did so magnificently. We achieved the transformation with time to spare. This achievement gave rise to a saying I often use now: 'Universal Prescription, Local Dose.' Having seen it work so well in this circumstance, I now often look to do the same again. That one proud achievement has shaped a belief I have that you can trust others if you give them a clear enough vision and a clear set of guidelines, and the freedom to move as they see fit within them.

6 & 7. Map your purpose and your values to those of your organization

Having now articulated your own sense of purpose and your values, you will be able to bring those more visibly to your leadership. There will always be overlap between your organization's values and your own. Find those spaces of overlap, and speak to them as often as you can. Your values will now work to the benefit of the organization you lead because they will be shared values. When you now speak to these values, your passion and belief will show through and you will be inspiring.

Be prepared to wear your heart on your sleeve. Lead from the heart by having the courage to speak more often to your values. That conviction will give you real strength of character, and this is the source of real influence. Being aligned with your core values and beliefs through what you say and do will win respect, trust and a willingness to listen.

8. Show humanity

Leadership is how you make people feel. Remember this: people won't care how much you know until they know how much you care.

Spend time getting to know others. Believe the saying that the most charming people in life are those who are more interested in you than you are in them. Be charming. Be curious about others and understand their own histories and beliefs, their motivations and interests. Take an interest in their families. Ask them to tell you the story of how they came to be who they are today. Really listen.

Get into the middle of conversations, invite challenge and encourage others to come up with better ideas. Never close your ears to criticism or attack your critics. Never make excuses or refuse to change your mind. (Conversely don't always change your mind too quickly.) Never get sucked into office politics or pass the buck.

9. Be visible

Make sure that you are visible to your people. If you lead a small team you probably have little choice. If you lead a national or global team, it gets a little more challenging. You may have to travel a lot. When you do, make sure you walk about your offices and stop to talk to people. Don't make the mistake of attending only the management meeting you travelled there for.

If you can't get out to the offices as much as you would like, then use videoconferencing, webinars or YouTube and any other way you can show your face. Be approachable. In countless interviews I have done among employees, the one thing they always talk about is whether leaders are visible or invisible. Guess which type garners the most praise from them?

10. Speak the truth, respectfully

How often have you seen people avoid telling the truth at work? They say things to please others or to avoid being different or controversial. Authentic leaders buck this trend. They avoid hurting people with a truth that is stated too bluntly, but they do not shy away from being honest and talking the truth. It takes courage to say things that really matter, especially when people really don't want to hear. Do what is right not what is easy. One of the most important acts of leadership communication, is to provide context – even when that context is unsettling.

Again, you need to be aware of whether people perceive that you are prepared to talk about the 'elephant in the room'. Ask your trusted colleagues whether they think that you always tell the truth, or that you are always prepared to raise truths that need to be addressed. Always make sure that as a leader you are a soothsayer – a bringer of truth.

These 10 exercises will help you to make yourself known to your employees, your customers and other stakeholders upon whom you depend for success. They will help you to be yourself better and form stronger, more supportive relationships. Relationships are the engines of success, and you'll never have strong relationships if you don't let people know who you are as a person.

If your sense of purpose and your values can power your leadership, then it is also true that an inspiring purpose and a strong set of values can power a whole organization. A clear and motivating mission alongside a strong set of values can help shape decisions to be made throughout the organization, by leaders everywhere, as we will see in the next chapter.

The vision thing

How to think about purpose, values and the future

> *Leadership is about achieving great results through others. How do you create a framework that empowers and enables employees to bring their own creativity and commitment to achieving your goals? What makes a good purpose or vision statement, and which ones are rubbish? Here are the seven essential ingredients of a powerful vision framework.*

How do you take the imagination of a writer, and turn it into a movie that delivers box office success? Making a movie is risky and imperfect, and can be hugely expensive. What is the magic element *great* directors bring to moviemaking that enables success? Are there any similarities between the art of directing a movie and leadership in business?

Michael Apted is a prolific British film director, best known for movies such as the James Bond film *The World Is Not Enough*, the fantasy adventure *The Chronicles of Narnia: The voyage of the dawn treader* and the anti-poaching film *Gorillas in the Mist*. He is most proud of his film *Amazing Grace*, the story of English politician William Wilberforce and his battle to end the British transatlantic slave trade.

Michael has been President of the Directors Guild of America, has worked in television and has produced many highly acclaimed documentaries, including *The Official Film* of *the 2006 FIFA World Cup* (football). In a recent interview, I asked him how he managed to inspire a diverse crew of technicians, cameramen, set designers, support staff, money providers, studio bosses, make-up artists and – of course – actors, to create movie magic.

'It's the vision thing,' he said:

> 'It's so important that you have a vision for the film, a vision that you have to fiercely protect, but also use to encourage a collaboration festival where people can build on it.
>
> The most precious thing you have as a director of a film is the commitment, enthusiasm and creativity of all the people involved in your endeavour. You have to encourage their energy by encouraging their participation. You have to say that you know what you want to achieve but you don't know how to do it: can they help you? You have to help them to see what you see, but then let them advise you on how to achieve it. You have to create a great atmosphere that engages people and allows them to contribute to your vision, while never taking your eyes off the prize.'

Michael talked of the paradoxes of leading a film project – the need for both flexibility and firmness, the need to absorb other people's ideas while not compromising your vision, and the need to deal with 1,000 details but one big picture. Sounds familiar!

> 'When you make a movie you are dealing with three different creative arenas. These are the writers, the actors and the editors. They all bring very different skills and talents to the project and all require different handling. As you move through the writing, the filming and the editing, your project is a living thing and it changes all the time, but you just cannot succumb to the movement or get lost in the detail. You have to stay true to your vision and keep it in mind all the time, ensuring that everybody else has the same shared meaning. That's the only way you can bring such a diversity of talent together to create something amazing.'

It's the vision thing that drives you on

As the leader of a project like this, says Michael, you can't ever sit down. You have to provide the energy that keeps everyone going. 'If you do sit down, the film does too. At all times, it's the vision thing that drives you on, compels you to keep trying, to achieve the impossible.'

Does all of this sound familiar? Is it reminiscent of the challenge you face in leading your own team? Have you yet found a way to create a vision that inspires the creativity, commitment and determination of your own team, and keeps you going when times are tough?

Hold this thought for a moment. I want to tell you the story of my interview with Clive Woodward, a former English rugby union player, the head coach of the 2003 Rugby World Cup winning side, and later a director of sport for the British Olympic Association during the 2012 Olympic Games in London.

The 2003 Rugby World Cup was played in Sydney, Australia. England played Australia in the final. Fly-half Jonny Wilkinson kicked a drop goal in extra time to win the game 20–17 for England, who became the first Northern Hemisphere team to win the Webb Ellis Cup and become world champions.

During my interview, I asked Clive whether he had given his World Cup winning team an inspirational speech on the night before the big match. 'No,' he said:

> 'You simply didn't need to at that stage. The focus was on ensuring that every individual did their job. I told them that if every individual did their own job properly, understood what everybody else was doing, trusted them to do it, shared the passion of a common purpose and did their job better than their opponents in the other team, then we would win the match. It was that short and it was that simple.'

So, two stories and two observations: the critical importance of the vision, and the importance of people knowing their job and how it contributes to the vision – and then working as a team to achieve it.

Unreasonable belief drives unbelievable success

One more story, this time about Tiger Woods, arguably one of the most successful professional golfers of all time. Actually, the story is about Chris DiMarco, another professional golfer, who twice lost to Tiger Woods in all-important Majors, including one that has one of golf's most memorable moments at the centre of the story.

The Masters Tournament, also known as the US Masters, is one of the four major championships in professional golf. It is the first of the four Majors to be played each year and is the only one to be held each year at the same location – the Augusta National Golf Club in the city of Augusta, Georgia, in the United States. For many, it is *the* major tournament to win.

In 2005, during the fourth and final round on the Sunday, the tournament came down to a two-man duel between Tiger Woods and Chris DiMarco. On the 16th hole, Tiger Woods made a sensational chip, aiming far to the left of the hole and letting the ball run down a steep slope to it. The moment that followed was captured on television and must have been shown a million times or more around the world, to the delight of golfers everywhere. Tiger's ball, with the Nike logo resplendent, appeared to stop on the lip of the hole, paused, then dropped in for a sensational birdie. DiMarco was two down with two to play. Somehow, Chris managed to claw his way back, win the next two holes and finish the game tied with Woods. It all came down to a dramatic sudden death on the 18th hole, where Tiger buried a birdie putt to win his fourth Masters and his ninth major title.

DiMarco finished at 12 under for the tournament. Afterwards he said:

'I went out and shot 68 around here on Sunday, which is a very good round, and 12 under is usually good enough to win. It was just that I was playing against Tiger Woods.'

Later that year, at the Sun City Golf Classic in South Africa, at the famous Gary Player Country Club, I had the enormous privilege of partnering Chris DiMarco in the pro-am tournament on the Wednesday before the championship. After 12 holes, I felt I knew him well enough to ask the questions that were burning to be asked.

'Where do you go from here? How do you improve in order to beat Tiger?'

Chris looked at me with a scowl, and I feared I had overstepped the mark. He shook his head and said:

'I don't believe that I can make any improvements to my technique. I think my technical skills are as good as they will ever be. The difference is in here,'

he said, tapping his forehead.

'When you play against Tiger, you can just feel his belief. His belief is so strong that it can give him that one shot extra that he needs to beat you. He just sees the end result more clearly. I have to work on that, not on my technique.'

So, my third observation is about the power of clarity, commitment, passion and belief!

How do these three observations combine? First, you have to have a clear and motivating vision. It has to power the passion of all of the individuals in your team and give them a clear sense of shared purpose. The more clear and compelling the vision is, the greater will be the commitment to it. The more clarity around their individual roles and how they contribute to the vision, the more cohesive and competitive your team will be. The stronger their belief in the purpose, your cause, the more likely you will be to achieve your vision.

Rational or emotional?

Too often, however, leaders use the achievement of financial goals as their purpose, because they are more comfortable being rational and objective. Too often, as we noted in Chapter 3, followers say they don't get out of bed in the morning to achieve financial or other numerical objectives. They come to work and want to be inspired by a sense of doing something important, something that makes a difference.

Which one to choose? My answer is that a great vision needs to contain both of these elements, in order to satisfy both constituents. Leaders need to create a framework that enables decision making and empowers front-line staff to succeed without having to go up and down the chain of command. In an age of blinding speed, radical transparency and connected consumers, we do not have the luxury of command and control processes. We need to enable leadership everywhere, and this can only be done by providing a framework for freedom of decision making.

I believe that the 'vision thing' is all about telling a story that is both emotional and rational. The vision of the future needs to describe the commercial goals of the business, but it also needs to describe what success will 'feel' like to all the stakeholders who will benefit from that success – whether this be shareholders, customers, employees, suppliers or even local communities. Feelings and emotions are the driving force of our lives. It is why I put so much emphasis on the word 'feel'.

Great communication has to be about feelings as much as it is about facts. Head and heart. Your vision framework needs to contain elements that are uplifting and inspiring, as well as elements that are about clear goal setting and prioritization.

What elements should such a framework contain if it is to provide employees with a complete picture of the strategic intent of the business? I believe it should have two sides to it.

Purpose and performance

First, it must capture the emotional and inspiring purpose of the organization, the values that drive actions, and the desired standards of behaviours that stem from these values. These are all on the emotional side of the framework and are what employees consistently find most inspiring. This is what I call the PURPOSE side of the framework.

Second, it must capture the desired future, the four or five strategic priorities that must be delivered to achieve the future, and the key objectives that will deliver each of the strategic priorities. This side of the framework is the numerate side – the strategic, highly rational and measurable aspects of the vision story. This is the PERFORMANCE side of the framework.

All six of the elements discussed in more detail below are needed for the framework to work, and provide a full story. It is only when all six are articulated that the story is complete in an employee's mind. Sometimes, I have been able to insert a seventh element in work I have done with clients – something I call their True North. This True North is a never-ending quest, one that they will always be seeking to achieve and, if they have achieved it, always trying to maintain. I will explain this in more detail a little later.

One of the most significant problems I have experienced in this field of work, is that leadership teams always use many different words to describe 'the vision thing'. They use 'vision', 'mission', 'purpose' or 'strategic intent'. The first problem here is that very often people will be using the word 'mission', but everyone around the table will have a different view of what it means. Is it about delivering value to shareholders? Is it about a noble purpose? Is it the top line of our business plan?

When you are working with a team to set a vision framework, it is crucial that everyone agrees the meaning of each of the words you choose to use. So long as everyone has a common understanding of what you mean, you will be more likely to provide clarity.

For the sake of clarity in this book, I define them as follows:

- *Your purpose* is why you exist, what you are here to do for your 'customers' that makes a difference to them.

- *Your values* are your core principles, the qualities you consider desirable, the powerful beliefs which will drive all of your behaviours.

- *Your behaviours* sound obvious, but should clearly link to the achievement of both your purpose and your vision. These are your beliefs in action.

- *Your vision* is your picture of the future, described both in numbers and in terms of the quality of key relationships needed if all of the organization's goals are to be achieved.

- *Your strategic priorities* are the crucial things you have to do if you are to achieve the vision, usually confined to between three and five.

- *Your objectives* are the clearly defined, supporting goals that must be delivered if each of the strategic priorities is to be achieved.

The main reason for setting this framework out so clearly, is to enable line management to communicate and interpret the framework right down to the front line of the organization. The job here is to ensure that all employees on the front line have a clear line of sight from their jobs to the overall vision of the company that employs them. That line of sight is one of the most important tasks of leadership, and is only delivered when leaders work with the teams to interpret the overall framework to local circumstances.

Alignment is the key to success

Front-line managers should be asking their teams the following questions: How does the framework relate to us? What does it mean for our local priorities and goals? What does it mean for our local behaviours? What is our local vision of success? What is our own purpose, and how does it deliver the corporate purpose? Unless leaders help front-line employees to interpret the framework in this way, there can be no alignment and your chances of success will be vastly reduced.

I have often heard it said that success is only 1 per cent vision and 99 per cent alignment and execution. Making the vision accessible, and then ensuring that people are aligned to it through constant communication and conversation, is the work of leadership.

Followers know that it is the job of leaders to decide direction, but they hate having the route mapped out for them step by step. That stifles creativity and limits commitment and effort. Involving them in the discussion about how to achieve the goals is what creates commitment.

Often, I hear leaders talk of setting seemingly impossible goals, stretching the powers and potential of everyone in the organization, of placing 'big bets' on the capability of the people to achieve more than they thought was possible. And, somehow, with that uplifting, ennobling future vivid in everyone's mind, they achieve it.

Really good people need a really good understanding

I interviewed Barbara Cassani, the founding Chief Executive of Go Fly, the low-cost airline spun out of British Airways in the late 1990s and later sold to another low-cost airline, easyJet, in 2002.

Talking of the days when she was building Go Fly, she said:

'Everyone told us what we were trying to do was unachievable. It was a pipe dream. So how did we do it? How did we beat the odds? I believe that this was because we gave really good people a really good understanding of what they needed to do in order to make this crazy idea a success. There was just so much power in that clarity of vision. Everyone – from pilots to receptionists – could see and feel and taste success.

I found it was so important to involve and talk with every single person in the company on the journey. I believed that everyone, whether it was the receptionist or my most senior colleague who ran operations, every single one of us was important to the success of the airline.'

Damon Buffini is one of the best-known figures in the world of private equity. He was chairman of Permira, one of Europe's largest and best known buyout firms, until 2010, when he stepped down to focus on deals. He has years of experience in appointing leadership teams to build Permira's investments into better businesses. He, like Barbara, says that great communication depends on the clarity of your vision framework.

'I often think that poor communication is the result of not being clear about the direction you want to go in, or the goals you are setting. People will forgive poor communication technique if they are able to get a clear understanding of what you're trying to achieve and how they fit into it. You have to explain to your team with crystal clarity where you're going, what they need to do and why it's a good thing for them and the people they serve.

That means you have to be incredibly clear in your own mind as to what it is you want to achieve, over what period of time and what actions are needed to get there. You have to be explicit about what you expect from the people who are going to deliver those actions. You must take the time to articulate your vision and share it widely. Thereafter, leadership is all about being able to inspire people in the different ways they need to be inspired.'

The seven steps to a vision framework

Let's look at each of these seven elements of a complete framework in turn, starting with the 'rational' side of the framework (right-hand side of Figure 5.1) – the PERFORMANCE half (trust me, it's easier). What questions should you be asking yourself in order to fill out these headings?

FIGURE 5.1 PURPOSE AND PERFORMANCE

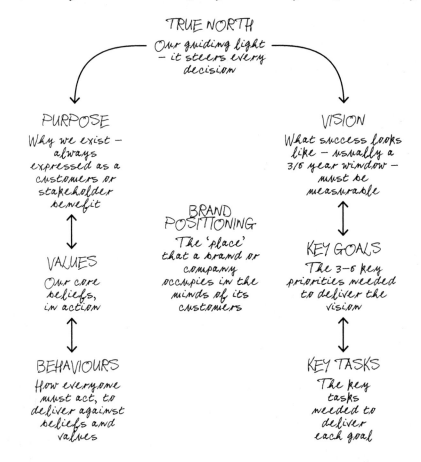

TRUE NORTH
Our guiding light
– it steers every
decision

PURPOSE
Why we exist –
always
expressed as a
customers or
stakeholder
benefit

VALUES
Our core
beliefs,
in action

BEHAVIOURS
How everyone
must act, to
deliver against
beliefs and
values

BRAND POSITIONING
The 'place'
that a brand or
company
occupies in the
minds of its
customers

VISION
What success looks
like – usually a
3/5 year window –
must be
measurable

KEY GOALS
The 3–5 key
priorities needed
to deliver the
vision

KEY TASKS
The key
tasks
needed to
deliver
each goal

Element 1. Vision

Have you got a clear picture of success for your organization or your team over the next three years? Can you paint that picture for others so that they can see that picture as well as you do? Is it memorable and compelling? Have you described it in a way that shows how all the stakeholders who might have an interest in your venture will benefit? Have you got clear financial and or other numerical goals that will be measures of your success at achieving the vision? If you have a three-year vision, can you describe where you will be in Years One and Two? Do you have a shorthand version of this vision, of about 12 to 15 words, that captures the essential meaning?

Do not confuse your vision with your purpose. Your purpose is why you exist. Your vision is your clearly articulated and numerical goal for a near-term future.

Element 2. Strategic priorities

What are the four or five things you absolutely have to get right in order to achieve this vision? These will be goals that will never change. You could decide to say, for example, that to achieve your vision for your new venture, you have to:

- build a stand-out brand;
- build your capabilities and skills;
- build more market-leading services.

For each of the three years of your journey, you would be able to monitor your progress in each of these key areas. Many companies suffer from 'initiative overload'. Much of this is driven by the fact that people can't see how these initiatives are helping to achieve the goals. By having strategic priorities that are constant, you can help people to understand that all the initiatives are helping you to get to your destination.

When describing your key priorities, there can be a significant difference between those things that you have to do to achieve this year's targets and those that you have to do to prepare for the future. Countless times, I have seen employees confused by objectives that they think don't relate to the immediate future and therefore become irrelevant to them. They often talk about 'initiative overload', because they feel that projects are being under-taken that make no sense from their perspective.

I have tried to illustrate this in Figure 5.2. When you prepare to climb a mountain, you can usually see the first peak that you have to scale, and you can see most of the steps along the journey that you're going to have to make to get there. From that same position, you can usually see the top of the mountain, though the first peak may hide the route you will need to take once you have achieved your first goal and head towards the mountain top.

This analogy applies in business as well. You can see what you have to do to achieve this year's budget. You may know what numbers you have to achieve at the end of your five-year plan, but you won't know exactly how you're going to get there. You have to anticipate what you're going to need for that uncharted part of the journey, and are going to have to start getting yourself in a fit state to tackle this unknown territory.

FIGURE 5.2 PREPARING FOR THE UNKNOWN

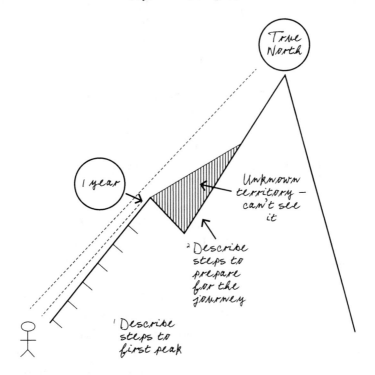

To help make this clearer to employees, you need to distinguish between those actions required to achieve this year's goal, and the things you're doing to get the organization fit for purpose beyond that first peak.

Element 3. Objectives

Now, what are the four or five things you need to do to achieve each of your strategic priorities? Have you defined what it means to build a stand-out brand? Have you set goals for each of the three years of your journey? For example, you could say you want to 'raise awareness of our brand from 20 per cent to 50 per cent of our target market in Year One. Capture more share of voice than our competitors in all of our key trade publications.' And so on.

Does each objective clearly align with the strategic priority? It is in these priorities and objectives that the 'rubber hits the road'. It is here where front-line employees can see how what they do makes a difference to the organization. For this reason, setting out the priorities and the objectives is a key part of the framework. Have you set clear targets to be achieved with each of these objectives? How will people know that they are making good progress to the goals? Have you put in place ways to measure every one of your objectives? As Damon Buffini said, you have to explain to your people with crystal clarity where you're going and what they need to do to help you get there.

That's the right-hand side of the framework completed. Now let's turn to the PURPOSE side of the framework.

Bringing emotion into the mix

While your people may now be able to see and understand and buy the logic of all of these goals and objectives and measures, have they yet been inspired by all of this enough to give their heart and souls to achieving your vision? Perhaps not. For this, we often have to turn to the left half of the framework, and provide an inspiring mission or purpose.

All too often, working in very different businesses, I've seen the difference between the willingness of employees who are inspired by the organization's purpose statement and those who are not. Those who are truly inspired do more, try harder, are more collaborative, more willing to make positive suggestions to improve performance, and are even more likely to recommend your company to friends and colleagues as a good employer. These people will do things for the company even if it is not expected of them: they'll stay later at work, they'll pitch in and help colleagues even when they don't ask for help, and they'll provide you with ideas that could transform your performance. For this reason an inspiring purpose is an incredibly valuable asset.

Element 4. Purpose

This statement should be focused on your customers or consumers. What would be lost if your company or your team ceased to exist? Why is it important that you continue to exist? What do you do that makes a difference to the people you serve? Does this enhance their lives in some way?

I believe that a mission or purpose statement needs to highlight a customer or consumer benefit. After all, it is for them that you exist and it is by them that you are paid. Unless you make your mission statement important to them, why would anyone find it compelling? In the previous chapter I showed how it was customers who are most inspiring to employees. Bring the customer in, let employees experience how delighted customers talk about your products and services, and your levels of engagement and productivity will increase. That's why this purpose statement needs to reflect that customer perspective, even if your customers are colleagues in other departments of your company who depend on you to get their jobs done.

The best mission statements that I have seen are always short, easy to remember and distinctive. Most of the best ones that I have seen are around 15 words long. The very best are around eight words long. They must be easy to understand and credible, and must highlight the key customer benefit that you deliver. While you may change your vision and set higher and even more ambitious goals, while your priorities may change as competitive threats grow, your purpose will always remain constant. A constancy of purpose allows you to change many other elements of the framework and still be consistent.

Is your purpose statement written down? If it isn't written down it cannot be shared consistently across the organization. Is it real? Does it help you to define and optimize all decisions? Is it simple?

Most important of all, does it resonate with every employee in your organization? Do they feel connected to this purpose and agree that it is important?

Let me give you a few examples.

- **Glaxo Smith Kline** (a global pharmaceutical and healthcare company) – *To improve the quality of human life by enabling people to do more, feel better and live longer.* (18 words)

- **Walt Disney Parks and Resorts** (amusement parks) – *To give our guests opportunities to create memories with their friends, families and loved ones that will last forever.* (19 words)

- **Amazon** (online store) – *To be earth's most customer centric company; to build a place where people can come to find and discover anything they might want to buy online.* (26 words)

- **Facebook**'s mission is – *To make the world more open and connected.* (Eight words)

- **Google**'s mission is – *To organize the world's information and make it universally accessible and useful.* (12 words)

- **Nike** (sports clothing) – *To bring inspiration and innovation to every athlete in the world. If you have a body, you are an athlete.* (20 words)

Clients I have worked with have the following purpose statements:

- **HSL** (The Health and Safety Laboratories) – *To enable a better working Britain.* (Six words)

- **Gazprom Marketing and Trading** (an energy trading business) – *The energy to succeed.* (Four words)

- **SAB Miller Europe** (a beer business) – *To brew more great moments.* (Five words)

Here are the purpose statements of some well-known non-profit organizations.

- **Save the children** – *To inspire breakthroughs in the way the world treats children and to achieve immediate and lasting change in their lives.* (20 words)

- **The Red Cross** (a volunteer-led humanitarian organization) – *To help people in crisis, whoever and wherever they are.* (10 words)

- **Oxfam** (an international federation helping people in poverty) – *To help create lasting solutions to the injustice of poverty.* (10 words)

If you struggle to get your purpose statement to less than 15 words, you should consider mimicking some of the world's most memorable slogans – which have the great virtue of being distinctive, short, and highly memorable.

Do you remember any of these?

- When it absolutely positively has to be there overnight – FedEx.
- The Ultimate Driving Machine – BMW.
- All the News That's Fit to Print – *New York Times*.
- Does Exactly What It Says on the Tin – Ronseal.
- We Try Harder – Avis.
- Never Knowingly Undersold – John Lewis.
- The Appliance of Science – Zanussi.

The slogans brilliantly differentiate their companies from competitors while simultaneously summarizing what they stand for. They have catchy phrasing and are easy to remember – and should act as a good prompt for you when making your purpose statement just as effective. They all deliver a powerful customer benefit.

Finally, does your purpose articulate your mission in a way that shows you are a force for good in society?

When I went through hundreds of company mission statements recently, I found a depressing trend for many of them to state that their purpose was 'to maximize shareholder value'. These were companies that were as diverse as you could imagine – from entertainment businesses to mining companies, from motor manufacturers to pharmaceutical companies. They all had the same purpose. How dull.

While this is obviously vital to their continued ability to raise capital, and is the reason their shareholders invest in them, I believe that maximizing shareholder value is a measure of their success in delivering their purpose, *not* their purpose for existing. If they do what they do brilliantly, then they will satisfy their customers, keep their stakeholders happy and supportive, integrate with the communities in which they operate, maintain their licence to operate, and because of all of this, continue to grow and prosper. This is what will provide sustainable shareholder value.

In today's world, you need to have a purpose wider than profit. People expect more of business. Transparency has changed everything and leaders must take more time to explain the benefits of their endeavours and show why they are a force for good.

John Connolly, Chairman of global security company G4S, says:

> 'I believe that we have come to a stage where we have now to imagine a new definition of the purpose of business. What is it for? There has to be more of a focus on long-term sustainable success. It is only if you think long-term that you build more value in your business. You cannot sustain your business in an environment, either social or physical, that does not have a future.'

Ben Verwaayen, former Chief Executive of Alcatel Lucent, a global telecommunications Corporation, says that using 'growing earnings per share' as a purpose statement is irrelevant to the vast majority of employees:

> 'You need to give them something that is inspiring and is relevant throughout the organization. Allied to this is the need to set the tone from the top with all the right values. Together, these two elements will give people enough freedom to add their own intelligence and creativity to what they need to do.'

Element 5. Values

Leaders with a strong set of values built on honesty and openness and respect for other people are often seen as the most inspirational. Shared values enable trust and liberate employees to be leaders; they can then take action within a framework that enables speed, creativity and agility. Values that are truly lived can also create competitive differentiation. The way your people act with the 'customers', whoever they are, says more about you than all the words you ever utter.

Take care to define, and live, the values that you want – delivered in the daily behaviours of your team. These intangible values – often dismissed as 'soft and fluffy' – translate into actions on the ground, which then translate into hard numbers in the books.

For this reason values must be measured for impact; and leaders should ensure that people who don't live up to them should shape up or ship out.

However, defining your values must start with understanding your behaviours. Your behaviours – the ways you do things around here – are your culture. Your culture is driven by your beliefs and values. My suggestion is that you start with behaviours, in order to define the values that you hold important. For example, if people in your team regularly arrive late for work, then you clearly do not value timeliness. Otherwise, you would have made it clear to them that this was unacceptable behaviour. Equally, if all of your staff regularly display behaviours that demonstrate care and consideration for customers, above and beyond normally defined duties, then you clearly have a deep value about delivering best service to customers. If members from different teams often work together on new and different projects, then collaboration is a deep-rooted value.

Most companies I have worked with limit their core values to between four and six. Each of those values, however, may contain four or more desired behaviours. So, start first with the behaviours section of the framework, and capture what those behaviours really mean about your belief system in your values.

Element 6. Behaviours (beliefs in action)

The key questions to ask here are very simple: what things do we do around here that we absolutely must not stop doing, because they are essential to our success? What do we do around here only sometimes that we should be doing a lot more, and why don't we? What do we never do around here that would make a huge difference to our success, and why don't we do it? What do we do really badly around here that we should stop as soon as we can, and why don't we stop it?

If you asked these questions in every part of your organization, you would be doing a behaviours audit, and you'd be uncovering a lot of actionable information about behaviours that either help or hinder your success. If you have a new strategy, then you will most likely need to encourage some new behaviours, while retaining some of the old ones that have underpinned your success. Why? Because a *new* strategy inevitably requires new and different behaviours, and those new behaviours will be driven by new beliefs and values.

Beware of embarking on a new strategy without revisiting your values! The behaviours that are driven by your values will determine whether you achieve your objectives, and ultimately your vision. So it is worth spending time thinking about these behaviours and making sure that you are happy with the ones that prevail at the moment. When you talk with your people about current and desired behaviours, you will usually find that these fit into three camps (see Figure 5.3).

FIGURE 5.3   BEHAVIOURS AUDIT

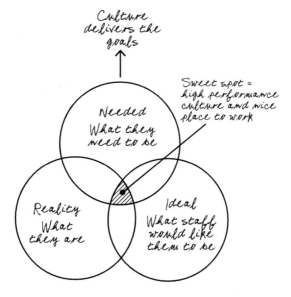

- Ideal – what people would like them to be in an ideal culture.
- Real – those that are exhibited now, good, bad and indifferent.
- Needed – the behaviours you need to instil in order to achieve new objectives.

The sweet spot is where these three circles overlap. This is how you bring together 'a nice place to work' with a 'high-performance culture'. You need to have a mix of all three.

Of course if you are not committed to your values and the behaviours that derive from those values, then you will quickly render your values empty words, alive only on posters on the wall. Very often employees are simply not aware of the values of the organization. Sometimes they are aware of them, but nobody reinforces them or measures them against those values. Most of all, little thought has been given to incentivizing people to the right behaviours. Finally, many values exercises are rendered impotent when staff see hypocrisy at work in the values. The blame here is often laid on senior managers who, staff claim, have one rule for themselves and one rule for others.

Organizational values provide a template for the behaviours of the organization, and leaders should put in place minimal acceptable standards of behaviour. Values must be lived by people at all levels, from the board to the front line. Failure to behave in accordance with the values should always have real consequences. Values stem from your beliefs, and your beliefs drive your actions. Your behaviours are your beliefs in action.

Element 7. True North

This can be one of the most powerful elements of the framework. What do I mean by True North? Some background first.

True North differs from magnetic north, which varies from place to place and over time due to local magnetic anomalies. A magnetic compass almost never shows true north. In fact over millions of years, magnetic north has wandered considerably and occasionally reversed, so that the magnetic north pole has been near the geographic south pole at some periods in the earth's history.

Finding True North is essential for accurate navigation. Hence the metaphor. In life's journey we are often uncertain where we stand, where we are going and what is the right path for us personally. Knowing our True North enables us to follow the right path.

True North is non-negotiable, and it will never change. A route map is of little use in the frequently changing landscape of our times. A good compass, however, always points north no matter where you are. Only if an organization is focused on its own True North, will success follow.

To achieve True North years of effort will usually be required. It should be beyond anything the company can currently do. Almost certainly, you will be uncertain as to whether True North can ever be achieved. Sometimes called 'big hairy audacious goals', these are the statements that really power the vision. Some examples?

- Make $1 billion profits within three years. (When you currently make $100 million.)

- Become the most highly recommended agency in the country by the year 20XX. (When you have only just started.)
- Become the dominant player in the industry and create world-beating products.
- Crush our biggest competitor.
- Be Number One in every market we serve.

Here are some real examples: –

- *Amazon*: Every book, ever printed, in any language, all available in less than 60 seconds.
- *Ford*: Democratize the automobile.
- *Hewlett-Packard*: Be one of the best-managed corporations in the world.
- *Microsoft*: A computer on every desk and in every home.
- *Nokia*: Connect 5 billion people by 2015.
- *VISA Europe*: Be the world's most trusted currency.

Just to be clear, there should be a difference between your True North, your purpose and your vision. Your vision, really, will be an articulation of your three-year business plan. Your purpose will be the reason you exist, stated as a benefit to customers or consumers. Your True North will be a long-term, possibly even unattainable, goal.

All elements of the vision framework must interlink and support each other. For example, all your values should clearly support your vision and your purpose. Your behaviours should be clearly linked to the achievement of your strategic priorities. When you have this degree of coherence in your vision framework, you will be able to create coherence throughout the organization.

When completed, this vision framework becomes a one-page manifesto for change. Although it might be too high level to be specific enough, when teams translate high-level strategic priorities and objectives into specific objectives more relevant to their own areas of work, you create the alignment to your goals through all levels of your organization. Managers must discuss this manifesto with staff and ask the question: What is our version of this manifesto, and how will we help to deliver the corporate goals?

Your vision framework is the fuel for the conversations that can super-charge the pace of change and power the whole organization to success.

Bringing the outside in

When you introduce employees to the people they serve, it unleashes super-performance

We all have customers. Whether we serve people inside our organization or outside, we all have people who benefit from our actions. Connecting employees to how those people feel will turbo-charge performance... more than you can do on your own. Here are eight ways to bring the outside in and boost motivation.

By any measure, Groupon, an online voucher business, was a phenomenal success story. Its name was derived from the words 'group coupon' when the company was founded in 2008. On its website it featured discounted gift certificates usable at local or national companies. In 2008 Groupon had just one market – in Chicago. Within two years it served more than 250 markets in North America, Europe, Asia and South America and had 35 million registered users. It was floated on the NASDAQ in 2011.

The founder and CEO of Groupon was Andrew Mason. He was ousted in 2013 after losses that prompted a huge slide in the company's share price and caused fears that business might be unsustainable. On being sacked he wrote to all of his employees. In a searingly candid memo, he told staff why he had just been fired. He wrote:

'The events of the last year and a half speak for themselves. As CEO, I am accountable. You are doing amazing things at Groupon, and you deserve the outside world to give you a second chance. I'm getting in the way of that. A fresh CEO earns you that chance… it's time to give Groupon a relief valve from the public noise.'

Andrew went on to offer advice to the employees of Groupon. He said:

'If there's one piece of wisdom that this simple pilgrim would like to impart upon you: have the courage to start with the customer. My biggest regrets are the moments that I let a lack of data override my intuition on what's best for our customers. This leadership change gives you some breathing room to break bad habits and deliver sustainable customer happiness – don't waste the opportunity!'

Start with the customer! Break bad habits and deliver sustainable customer happiness! Here was Andrew Mason regretting losing sight of something that had enabled him to found a business on a bold vision and grow it rapidly into a global success story. It is also a salutary lesson to all leaders. Always put your 'customer' first.

But what does it mean to start with the customer? And who, exactly, is your customer? How do you get employees to put the customer at the centre of their thinking? How do you inspire your team to want to deliver excellent service or products?

In all your communication, you need to be providing your followers with meaning. You do this by helping them to connect to activities and things that matter to them. You have to give them a purpose that matters, you have to create an environment in which there is a sense of belonging, and you have to ensure the right rewards and the right work–life balance. All of these things provide meaning and an emotional context for employees. Providing meaningful work makes a big difference to motivation levels.

An old story illustrates what I mean. Three men are found smashing boulders with iron hammers. When asked what they are doing, the first man says, 'Breaking big rocks into little rocks.' The second man says, 'Feeding my family.' The third man says, 'Building a cathedral.'

It is the third man who is the most highly motivated, because he's the one who feels he has a higher purpose – building something where people can come for solace, to dream or to worship. In this way, he was doing something he regarded as hugely important – he was helping others.

No matter where I have worked – in Africa, Europe, the Middle East or the UK, it has always seemed to me that helping others is one of the single most important values in people's lives. People with this sense of meaning in their working lives are not only happier and more committed, they are actually better workers. How you as a leader provide this meaning, through all of your communication, is crucial to their commitment and your success. Putting your success – the achievement of financial goals – ahead of what they think is important, is a fatal error.

I can never forget work I did with British Airways employees when testing a new management mission statement. The new statement expressed the desire to be the Number One in world travel. In discussion groups around the world with British Airways staff from many different disciplines, they kept telling me that this mission statement meant nothing to them at all. What got them out of bed was the idea that they helped people to experience the joy of travel. Many of them talked about the personal joy they experienced when watching passengers greet their relatives at airports. When we produced a movie showing people meeting friends, relatives and business colleagues at airports around the world, and then showed it to staff, there was seldom a dry eye in the house.

Introduce employees to the people they serve

When leaders find ways to introduce employees directly to the people who use their services, and those people tell employees about how they feel when using those products or services, you connect the daily tasks carried out by employees to their deep-rooted need to be of service and help others – and unleash super performance.

Seeing how other people feel changes the way you feel. Whether we work on the front line or in a back office, we all have customers. They may be internal customers, end-users of our products or services, or real customers – but these are the people that we serve. To me, starting with the customer means making sure that you bring the customers into the organization and make how they feel, a driving force of employee behaviours.

Employees are often much more motivated by hearing directly from customers or end-users about how they benefit from their products or services than they are by their managers. Employees are more motivated, satisfied and effective when they work in jobs that clearly have a positive impact on others.

Use external perspectives to shape internal ones

So, why do leaders who connect employees with end-users drive higher performance? One of the reasons is often that employees can be cynical about the messages being delivered by their leaders. In contrast, customers are seen as more credible sources because they provide tangible proof of the impact of their work. Some have called this 'outsourcing inspiration'.

Why does this work? I believe that people are more influenced by truths that trigger emotions than they are by logic and analysis. This is why, as you saw in the previous chapter, it is so important to try to understand how your key audiences feel. You need to convince both the head and the heart in order to succeed, but you have to think hardest about finding ways to help people see problems and solutions in ways that influence emotions. There will always be barriers to change, but these will only be overcome if people have a real desire so to do. By helping staff to see and feel the customer experience, you help to make tangible that which is often intangible.

One of the biggest problems I often see in companies is management putting a lot of time and effort into their purpose or mission statement only to find that staff feel no connection with it whatsoever. This is more than just a trifling problem. That mission statement will be an expression of your leadership strategy, and often will be a promise to customers. If employees feel little or no connection to the purpose statement, then how on earth are you ever going to deliver your plan? This is often even more true for backroom staff than it is for front-line employees. Front-line staff are seeing every day what customers do and how they feel. For backroom staff, it is often true that they're not sure at all how what they do connects to those customer moments. They lack the direct contact one needs to truly empathize with customer needs in a way that is more than intellectual.

When the brand promise is seen as corporate jargon

Having worked in dozens of companies of all types and sizes, I'm afraid to say that, all too frequently, I come across employees who say that they not only don't understand the company's purpose statement or brand promise, but they don't know how it is supposed to guide their daily actions. The brand promise was simply corporate jargon and became irrelevant to them.

Creating alignment between what an employee does and this promise is one of the single most important things a leader can do, because this plays a central role in achieving business goals. However, I'll bet that very few of your employees know how their own performance impacts on your organization's goals.

Intellectually, who could ever argue with the idea that you have to put the customer first? So we can say the words and truly believe it necessary, but still not go the extra mile to ensure that the customer experience is a great one. When you are connected to the customers and can see the emotional benefits they derive from what you do, you are now invested with a will to succeed that it is difficult for managers to inject by themselves.

This is why the really savvy leaders find all sorts of ways to connect customer experiences more closely with employee behaviours. These leaders talk about customers all the time, they bring stories about customer experiences into the meeting rooms and discussion groups, into the corridors and into the groups around the water coolers. They get employees to talk about how they feel when customers express their delight at a service or product. They get colleagues to share stories about how they went the extra mile for a client. They bring research about customer satisfaction into brainstorms and relentlessly focus people on the data. They even bring customers into meetings and get them to provide staff with a deeper understanding of their customer needs, as well as the benefits of the products or services, in their own words. Some leaders even find ways to bring end-users or customers into their teams to work creatively together to find better solutions or products.

By bringing customers or end-users into the team, leaders are communicating without speaking. They're sending powerful signals that it's important. They show that they are prepared to listen and that they care about customers. The communication is powerful even if it is the customer who does the talking for you.

There is no doubt that when customers are connected to employees directly, the motivational impact is greater. But often leaders may lack access to end-users and will have to be more creative in providing the inspiring effect of customer stories.

Pass the baton well to win

Finding creative ways to share those end-users' stories helps to unite employees and encourage teamwork across departments – and that delivers much improved service to customers. I have sometimes facilitated workshops with the heads of different departments in a company and encouraged them to play what I call the 'pass the baton' game. Playing it is simple. Start with the customer, and work your way back through all of the processes that have to work together to deliver the result to the customer. You soon see the workflows that have to operate across silos to succeed. Across the silos, the baton has to be handed on carefully and efficiently for best effect. Very often I have been interested to see how shocked departmental managers are when they recognize how many silo baton passes have to take place to ensure success. Knowing why it's important makes a huge difference.

I've already said that it's always best to get the customer in to talk directly to employees. There is no doubt that this is more effective than any other method. Better still, bring different customers in regularly, and get them to tell different stories about how products and services impact on them in different ways. Use these different stories to illustrate different points about service or product excellence.

If you can, ask your customers to structure their stories on the problem–solution–benefit formula. What was the challenge they had to face? If you are serving a patient, what challenges and difficulties do they have to endure and what would make their lives easier? If it's a customer of a service-based organization, what are the challenges they are facing and how do they feel about them? How does your product or service solve those problems? What features provide the biggest advantages? Finally, how do they benefit from the product or service, both from a productivity or financial basis, and emotionally?

Video customers on a mobile phone

If you can't get the customers in to talk directly, then capture how they feel on video or in a recorded interview. With mobile phones that have cameras on them, this is far easier to do today than ever. We are not talking about videos with high production values here; rather we are talking about videos with high emotional impact. It's the quality of the story not the quality of the picture that will count.

If you can't do any of that, then get employees to interview customers and come back and tell those stories or play the videos themselves. If they have been moved by the customer, they will convey their emotions more convincingly than you.

And if you can't do that, then find other ways to bring the customer in on a regular basis. This could be through feedback, research, or even monitoring online social media sites.

Regular feedback can be a great stimulus for better performance. So, the question is, how do you capture that feedback and how do you use it with your team?

Why not get front-line employees to get that feedback from customers as often as they can? Giving that to backroom staff and then working together to find solutions to problems can have a huge galvanizing effect. Instead of infrequent satisfaction studies, insist on finding ways to get continuous feedback from customers and then use it as a continuous improvement stimulus with your teams.

Think about when you survey customers

Harking back to British Airways, I remember often being bemused by the way customers were in those days being surveyed. Researchers would approach them in the baggage halls – when they couldn't get away because they were trapped at the carousels – and ask them how they had enjoyed their flight. This always seemed rather odd to me. Whenever I wait for my baggage, usually tired and impatient to get home or to meet relatives on the other side of customs, the last thing I want to do is talk about my flight, so my feedback is not likely to be as positive as it could be. I get especially grumpy if it is a long survey. Why, I thought, didn't the air hostess gently probe me on things I did or didn't enjoy about the flight experience while I was still in the air and in my seat? She would be able to judge my mood and whether I was approachable or not. The attendant could then feed this insight back at the end of every single flight and managers could systematically capture that feedback to improve performance. We would get continuous feedback that would enable much greater agility. The same idea can be applied in a thousand different organizations.

Tune in to your customers online

Tuning in to end-users or customers in real time is crucial in a world that moves at such lightning speed. One of the effects of a transparent and digitally connected world is that the tolerance levels of customers have shortened dramatically. They will no longer wait weeks for a response to a complaint. They'll be on Twitter or Facebook complaining to their friends, and if they are creative enough in the way they express the complaint their issue could go viral and global frighteningly quickly.

As an example, the video streaming company Netflix was recently forced into an embarrassing climb-down after user objections became so deafening that they had to kill off an idea before they could launch it. The company had planned to spin off DVD rentals into a stand-alone service called Qwikster. Customers didn't like the idea, and through social media their complaints went viral, causing serious brand damage within just hours.

Netflix spokesman Steve Swayze was forced to admit that the internet was a great equalizer. 'We made mistakes that hurt our brand, and now we're rebuilding step-by-step.'

When one person is able to assemble an army of hundreds of thousands, that person becomes a force to be reckoned with. Thanks to the increasingly savvy use of tools like Facebook and Twitter, the power balance between companies and customers has very much tilted in the latter's favour.

For this reason the best leaders are now monitoring social media on a continuous basis, and using that to provide insights all the time. These insights can be the trigger for improving a single customer's experience, recognizing a negative trend or even spotting an opportunity for a whole new product or service line.

I remember being regaled at a dinner by the marketing director of a chain of women's sex shops about the use of social media for service improvement. Much to my amusement and discomfort, she told me about monitoring the conversations in chat rooms that often caused her to take action the next day. The one incident she spoke of that stuck in my mind was about two women chatting online about a shop attendant who had piercings in her lips, nose and ears. Both women, on the point of buying intimate sex toys, felt there was possibly something unclean about the attendant, and were put off their purchases. The next day the marketing director requested that all shop attendants removed their piercings while on duty in the stores, citing this exchange as the insight behind the action.

Beware of false data

Lou Gerstner was Chairman and CEO of IBM from April 1993 until the end of 2002. He is largely credited for turning around IBM's fortunes. How? By truly bringing the outside in. There is a video available online showing Gerstner talking about what he found when he first arrived at IBM. He asked to see customer research and was amazed to find that it showed customers loved IBM. How was this possible, he asked, when the company's fortunes were nose-diving and customers were deserting in droves? A month later he asked again to see the data, to find it had now improved even as the company's fortunes had worsened! He asked the key question: how was the data gathered? He was told that customer account handlers selected who was to be approached, and if they were too difficult to reach, they filled the questionnaires in themselves, on the basis they really knew what the customer thought. This, said Gerstner, was both funny and tragic.

Sadly, however, this technique is not as rare as you might imagine. I have seen it happening in several organizations where I have worked, including the UK Atomic Energy Authority. At a time when the Authority was preparing itself for flotation on the stock market as a commercial science and engineering consultancy, we were doing a huge amount of work to improve perceptions of the organization. I did a significant amount of research, polling lots of different stakeholders about their attitudes to AEA. The customers we polled gave us some worrying feedback. While they loved the science and technology we were producing, they felt we had a huge amount to learn about being customer-centric and providing a good service.

When I went back into the organization to talk to the scientists and engineers about what I'd heard my report was flatly rejected. They told me they knew their customers and that their customers were very happy. They produced evidence of their own surveys to demonstrate the truth of what they were saying and all of my ideas for change were resisted. Crushed, I went back to the drawing board. This time, I conducted a much wider survey of customers, and asked the researchers to get customers to give specific examples – in their own words – of how they were being disappointed. At the same time I asked for copies of the 'research' that our own consultants

FIGURE 6.1 BRINGING THE OUTSIDE IN

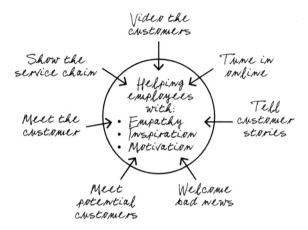

had conducted. Without saying that their research was flawed, I simply compared and contrasted the findings and encouraged debate and discussion to open minds to new ideas. It was only when our staff saw the quotes from customers who were prepared to be named that they started to be shocked enough to move from complacency to action.

Why you should love bad news

As a leader you should always demonstrate that you LOVE to hear customer stories whether they are good, bad or indifferent. If the stories are good you can use them in all sorts of ways to reinforce the right behaviours. Most interestingly, you can use those good stories with other customers to help generate sales. If the stories are bad you can fix the problem. (For this reason, leaders must become bad news junkies. Bad news is a way to fix problems. BUT. Be careful. As soon as you hear bad news and give someone the sharp end of your tongue, you'll turn off the supply of bad news and you'll rob yourself of the essential feedback you need to ensure success.)

How does all of this translate into your action plan? As follows:

- Do you know what stories your employees are telling? Are their stories about customers and service and ways to improve? Or are they about their frustrations, about poor management, about office politics or constraints on their ability to do good work? You really need to know.

- What stories would you rather they were telling? Imagine those stories and describe them. Tell them stories of what it could be like if only you could get it right.

- Are you able to bring customers in to talk to your staff on a regular basis? If you lead an internally focused team, can you bring end-users to your meetings to talk about their issues and perspectives? And are you bringing different kinds of customers to the table? What about bringing in lost customers? Why did they leave? Bring in current customers. What do they like or dislike and what would they prefer to see? What about potential customers? What holds them back from buying your service? These sessions would provide powerful stimulation and would be appropriate in board rooms, executive committee rooms and meeting rooms everywhere in your organization.

- If you are constrained from actually bringing customers into your meetings, can you go out and film them? It's really simple – ask them what they do, how they do it and why they do it. Ask them how what they do benefits from what you do. Simply film them with the camera on a mobile phone if that's all you have available. Many phones have high-definition video capabilities, and believe me that's more than good enough. Simply hook those films up to a laptop or a projector and show them to your staff to stimulate a discussion on how to improve things around here.

- Are you doing regular customer research? Are you asking the simple questions that get to the most important truths on a regular basis – possibly even daily? And are you bringing that feedback back to your team to stimulate the discussions that lead to performance improvement? I am still amazed at how often I see wall charts up in offices measuring progress towards goals. There is a simple reason – they are a visible sign of performance and can be hugely motivational. When you link customer feedback to progress charts in the office you are sending powerful communication to your team that they will see every single day.

- Are you online regularly, checking out how your customers feel and what they're saying about you? And if you're not doing it yourself, do you have someone looking after that for you? Do they feed back to you what's happening on a daily basis? Out there and online, millions of people are talking to each other in a brutally frank way and we have access to a huge and hugely honest focus group. Whether you like it or not, people are talking about you. If you tune in, you can use what they say to develop new services or products, improve the ones you already have or devise new ways to communicate with your customers.

- Never forget that the positive customer stories you dig up and use with your own team, can be hugely motivational when used with potential customers. Encourage your staff to tell those stories themselves, both inside and outside the organization. We all know that word of mouth is a powerful positive force for increasing sales. Why not start with your own team?

- Remember that end-users or customers can provide three kinds of stimulus. The first is empathy, where your team can better understand what customers are facing and therefore provide a more appropriate service or product. This is where inspiration comes from. The second is when customers talk about how they benefited and what a difference it has made in their lives – this provides motivation to work harder. The third is when they simply thank you for what you have done – this can provide the fuel simply to keep doing what you're doing on a consistent basis.

Use the customer as the subject of all your conversations, and the way to engage all your staff in the business.

Engage through powerful conversations

How to use conversations to drive culture, and why culture delivers goals

> *Even in turbulent economic times, organizations with high engagement levels outperform competitors and achieve results far better than the average. Their employees have more positive attitudes and more productive behaviours, and deliver better outcomes. All of these benefits are shaped by the conversations that leaders have with their teams. Here is a guide to more powerful conversations.*

My client looked pleased and puzzled at the same time. He was the CEO of an environmental services business, and he had just returned from a road show that had taken him to his 15 offices around the world.

I had asked him about what revelations had hit him during his travels around the UK, in Europe, the USA and Singapore. (We had a habit, in our coaching sessions, of finding ways for him to reflect on his business and draw out perspectives that would help him with content for his leadership communication.)

He said he had been struck by how absorbed and proud and energized some of his staff had seemed – but only in some of his offices. This both pleased and puzzled him because he recognized how positive the experience was with the energized staff, but wasn't sure why it wasn't the same in all of his offices.

I asked him what he put the pride and energy of some of his employees down to. He thought for a while, and replied that he didn't know. I asked whether those who were more energized performed better. 'Funny you should say that,' he said. 'Where the staff were most enthusiastic and searching and passionate, they were performing much better than the others.'

We agreed he would be more inquisitive about this when he did his next round of visits, two months later.

'Well?' I asked, at our next session.

'I'm not sure,' he mused. 'The only thing I can see is that they seem to know much more about the company, what we're trying to do, how we're doing. They had more ideas and they were more challenging of me. They just seemed more engaged in the business somehow. I think their managers just talked with them more and involved them more in decision making than did the managers in the other offices.'

We decided to work with this insight and find ways to encourage managers everywhere to talk more with their staff about how to improve the business. We ensured this would happen by announcing a survey of staff, where we would be asking whether they had actually had conversations with their boss recently. This would force the managers out of their offices or else the survey would reveal their lack of contact with the front-line staff. Then we gave the managers themes we wanted discussed, with the task of feeding back to us what staff said in response. We would know if they had not done the job, because we would not get the feedback in the time set, which we could correlate with the staff survey.

Guess what? Within weeks we were getting positive signs of more engagement, more ideas, more actionable insights, and within a few months performance started to improve as well. And that was without developing the managers in terms of their ability to lead these team meetings in the right way. It was just about forcing the conversation. We did insist that the managers made decisions where they could, based on those discussions, and refer back up the line decisions that they felt were beyond their remit. Managers above them could then make the decisions that had been delegated upwards, or pass them up again. Often, we discovered that it was only a perception that they could not make decisions, rather than corporate rules that confined them. They also brought to light crunchy issues that did have to be resolved higher up the chain. Everything got faster.

This was a listening process, rather than a briefing process, and it had a remarkable effect.

The power of alignment and engagement

It led me to an inescapable conclusion: the way you talk is the way people experience your leadership. How you encourage them to talk with you, and with each other, will determine whether you create alignment and engagement.

Alignment is crucial if you want the efforts of all of your people to be focused on delivering your strategic goals. And your goals will only be achieved if employees are fully *engaged*.

Engaged, committed employees are the real assets of any business. Yet survey after survey shows that only a third to a half of employees say they are actively engaged at work. The others are simply not delivering their full capability, commitment or potential.

What a waste!

Even in turbulent economic times, organizations with high engagement levels outperform competitors and achieve results that are better than the average. Their employees have more positive attitudes and more productive behaviours, and they deliver better outcomes.

What are the drivers of engagement?

According to David McLeod and Nita Clarke – authors of a report called *Engage for Success* commissioned by the UK government – there are four key enablers that are found in highly engaged organizations:

- visible empowering leadership, providing a strong strategic narrative about the organization;
- engaging managers who focus on their people and give them scope, treat them as individuals, coach and stretch them;
- a strong employee voice throughout the organization, where employees are seen as central to solutions;

- a strong culture where the values on the wall are reflected in day-to-day behaviours, from top to bottom.

How does engagement impact on performance? The evidence is overwhelming. In commercial organizations, engagement delivers higher income growth. For example Marks & Spencer, a major British retailer, found that over a four-year period, stores with improving engagement had on average delivered £62 million more sales to the business every year than stores with declining engagement. Sainsbury's, a national supermarket chain, has found a clear link between higher levels of engagement and sales performance, with the level of employee engagement contributing up to 15 per cent of stores' year-on-year growth.

Engagement delivers higher productivity and performance, greater levels of innovation, less absenteeism and greater well-being, higher staff retention levels, and better health and safety records. Most importantly, high levels of engagement lead to much greater understanding of customer needs, and therefore higher levels of customer satisfaction and retention. In hospitals, for example, patient satisfaction is higher where levels of employee engagement are higher.

What leader wouldn't want all that?

So, the four enablers of engagement – providing strategic direction, giving employees a voice, involving them in solution finding and bringing values to life – become crucial to effective leadership. The way you deliver all four is through conversations.

To communicate, you can use printed materials such as newsletters or posters, you can use intranets or e-mails, you can even use methods such as Twitter, Facebook or SMS messages. By doing this, you will impart information and possibly create more awareness of issues. You may get lucky and even create a better understanding. But to inspire, and inspire consistently, you need conversations.

Conversations drive change – fact

Since publication of *The Language of Leaders*, I have given dozens of talks to thousands of interested leaders. The thing that sparks their imagination the most is the idea that great leaders ensure that the right conversations are taking place right across their businesses. Great leaders understand it is conversations that drive change and ensure progress.

Doesn't that make sense to you? Isn't it through frank and full conversations that you have changed, hopefully for the better, the key relationships in your life? Why would that be any different at work? This is a key part of this book: leaders have to learn how to engage people in and through conversations.

The task of a leader is to inspire others to achieve great results. It sounds simple, but leaders today are operating in an incredibly demanding environment. The difference between competent communication and inspiring communication can be the difference between poor performance and outstanding results.

If you want to be a successful leader, you need to take charge of the conversations in your organization. Whether you like it or not, conversations are taking place every minute of every day among your teams, and many of these conversations are unproductive and aimless.

You need to shape and influence these conversations to ensure that they lead to a clear understanding of the vision, a clear understanding of what individuals are doing to achieve the vision, more engaged employees and more alignment throughout the organization. After that, you need more conversations to enable problem solving, feedback, ideas, innovation, action and continuous improvement.

As I said in the previous chapter, your vision framework must be shared if you want people to deliver it, and simply e-mailing it to them will not do the trick. You have to have conversations to ensure understanding, and you only achieve commitment if people are able to understand and talk about how they contribute to your goals through their local actions.

Effective leaders use conversations and the vision framework described in Chapter 5 to ensure that people truly do understand the True North of the organization, its purpose and values, its goals and strategic priorities, and the actions required to deliver success. These conversations give people the meaning and purpose they seek at work, because they help to create a 'clear line of sight' between the organization's purpose and goals and the actions of the individual. This provides them with context, meaning, a sense of import, and a framework for their own decision making. Because of these conversations, employees can make the right choices and they don't feel victims of change. Their commitment to those choices will make the difference between success and failure.

Is it really just about the pay?

Some people argue that it all comes down to pay. Without money, you can't buy food, pay the rent, pay the school fees or even pay to get to work. Well, yes, but while pay is a big part of a good job, there are many other motivators of high performance.

International investigations of the meaning of work – among workers in the USA, UK, Japan, West Germany, Sweden and Israel – have found that financial reward is held in balance with work interest, belonging, friendship and a chance to do something useful. Asked about 'work goals', people tend to put pay towards the bottom of their priorities, with opportunities to learn new things, interpersonal relationships and promotion at the top of the list. Being empowered, valued and involved in decisions are also key.

Whenever you ask followers what they want of leaders, the reply you'll get is that they want good communication, the ability to motivate and integrity. Research carried out recently by Korn/Ferry Whitehead Mann, the executive search and leadership consultancy, found that being a good communicator is the quality most commonly associated with being an effective leader. The ability to motivate staff is seen as the second most important characteristic and having a good moral compass is seen as the third most crucial 'boss factor'. All three work together and contribute to bosses being seen as 'inspiring'.

Sadly, however, fewer than two in 10 employees see their organization's leaders as inspirational.

Why? Well, let's be honest. Can you inspire all your staff with a single great speech or presentation? Perhaps you can. You might well be an incredibly gifted orator. Most of us are not. But, even if you can, the inspiration from a brilliant speech will at best be transitory. To achieve lasting inspiration, you need much more. You need constant, courageous, powerful conversations. Too often, however, these conversations are neglected, and middle managers are neither trained nor equipped for, nor measured on, their ability to hold these crucial conversations.

Too often also, top management doesn't check on the quality of those conversations, nor seek to get the feedback from these conversations in a systematic way.

Why culture is a secret weapon

And yet, conversations determine culture, and culture is the secret weapon of great organizations. I have heard many leaders say that culture is more important than strategy. Culture is 'the way we do things around here' and it's the only sustainable point of differentiation for many organizations. A strong culture of positive behaviours, driven by powerful values, means that the actions of the organization – at every touch point – will be the right ones. No leader can know about every decision being taken in the name of their organization, but the actions of an individual can land a global company in hot water, and when that happens, all eyes turn to the leader.

We live in a constantly and rapidly changing world. The only solution is a culture of agility. However, such responsiveness will only occur when people are talking to each other all the time and have relationships of trust.

Have *you* experienced a year without change? Unlikely. Much more likely is that you have experienced multiple, organization-wide changes. You might have had a change of leader, a change in the marketplace, redundancies, a merger or acquisition, new computer and IT systems, changes in products and services, moves into new markets and new geographies, or even changes in strategy. Some of you have even had all of the above. Seems incredible, but it is true. I am dealing with one client right now, as I write this, who is experiencing all of the above.

Without the benefit of constant and courageous conversations during periods of rapid change and uncertainty, people can rapidly lose sight of what it is they should be doing, lose connection with the people they depend on to achieve their goals, lose sight of the things they need to know in order to get the job done, and even lose faith in the future. Fear, anxiety and frustration lead to poor performance and failure – the exact opposite of what is needed. Where there is constant change, agility becomes a winning asset. In this sense, agility is both an attitude and an attribute. When people see change as a normal part of doing business, and as an opportunity to develop and grow, their attitudes are more positive. When they have an organizational ability to rapidly converse and make choices, and their attitudes are positive, you have a competitive edge.

Making the impossible possible

What undermines agility? Chiefly, it is an environment where workers think that their bosses are bad leaders and that the majority are arrogant, have poor communication skills and are uncaring. If they feel that the bosses care only about the numbers and not them, that is a recipe for great unhappiness. Conversely, when people are happy and feel good about themselves, they deliver. Work is more enjoyable and more productive. I have often observed that it is the happiest people who seek out the most challenging work. They set themselves harder and harder goals. They stretch themselves all the time. If they can be made to care about the outcome, if they feel what they are doing will be making a difference, they'll make the impossible possible.

It is the job of the leader to set direction. Good leaders will do this after consulting staff, but they'll be using a lot more information besides the views of staff. They'll be looking at market conditions, competitor activity, economic trends and customer insights, among many other things, to decide on strategic direction. Staff know this. They do, however, want their views considered and they wanted to feel that those views are respected by their leaders. Once that's done, the leader must then announce his or her intentions.

It takes a courageous leader to say: 'This is where we are going, and this is our impossible dream. I know we can get there, and we must, but I don't know how. Help me.'

Such a goal will imply considerable change. Having change inflicted on you makes you feel like the victim of change. But when you get to offer up ideas for how to achieve goals and you're involved in making choices that will enable faster change, you feel very much more in control and more committed to the goals. It is why I often advise leaders to stop using the word *change* and instead be much more focused on using the word *choice*.

During my research I came across a great example of this in an experiment involving lottery tickets. Researchers gave half of the participants in the experiment a lottery ticket with the numbers already written on it. They gave the others a blank piece of paper and asked them to choose their own numbers. They then offered to draw the winning number, but paused for a moment to offer to buy back the lottery tickets. They wondered if there would be a difference in how much they would have to pay those who were given a number versus those who chose their own number. As a lottery is so random, there ought to have been little variation in price. The answer to this question, in experiment after experiment, in location after different location, was always the same: the researchers had to pay five times more to those who had chosen their own number.

Choice over change, any day of the week

When we choose for ourselves we are more committed to the outcome. So, work conversations have to be structured in a way that allows employees to make choices for themselves. For most leaders, I know, this is extremely difficult. They may enter into conversation with colleagues, listen for a while, and then run out of patience and say: 'Right, this is what we're going to do.' Usually they know what the answer is, and they've come to a view long ago about what is necessary. They impose their decision, rather than lead their team to the right choices. Doing it this way, however, ignores the choice equation. Giving people time to come to the right conclusions and make the right choices is far more inspiring and gains far more commitment than telling them what to do. Think of the task of leadership not as telling people what to do, but rather as getting your team to want what you want them to want.

In another, different, experiment (one that I personally witnessed), I took part in some team games being carried out by a client. The games were designed to illustrate what was happening in the marketplace, and by playing the game employees would come to a better understanding of the changes that were necessary in their working lives. In one particular session, the facilitators asked a team of eight of us to solve a problem – without speaking. We were able only to nod, shake our heads, gesticulate, wave our hands, point, shrug or roll our eyes. It was remarkable, but somehow we managed to get to a solution. It demonstrated how powerful body language is as part of our system of communication, and made us all much more aware of the impact of body language during conversations – a subject we shall return to later.

There's only one potential pitfall in all of this. What if you have massively engaged people who then keep running into organizational barriers because they're not empowered to make decisions nor enabled to carry out their jobs? Result? Lack of performance and, even worse, frustration and resentment.

The moral? Any process of engagement must also deliver empowerment. The one without the other will be frustrating in the extreme for all parties involved.

Too often, leaders think of communication not as a process of conversations, but as a process of broadcasting messages through corporate channels of communication. They use newsletters, e-mails, corporate videos, intranet sites and other means of 'push' communication. Some even spend considerable time doing this. And then they wonder why nobody seems to have heard, why nobody understands, and why nobody has changed the way they behave.

The reason is simple. Face-to-face communication is always best. Using the phone or videoconferencing is next best, but effectiveness is more limited the more people that are involved. The least effective tool in driving change is e-mail or text-based messaging. Why? Because, at best, written communications will inform or instruct but cannot guarantee understanding, support, commitment and new behaviours.

The engagement ladder

Let's examine the engagement ladder in Figure 7.1 for a moment before we move to the subject of conversations. I have always used this as a way of thinking about culture change, which really is about encouraging employees to make the choices that change one set of behaviours to the ones needed for performance improvement.

The first stage of any change process is that of coming to the realization that change is needed. Developing a strategy is beyond my purview for this book, so let's move quickly to Stage 2 (Figure 7.1). This is where you have decided on your plan, which now needs to be communicated. Through

FIGURE 7.1 THE ENGAGEMENT LADDER

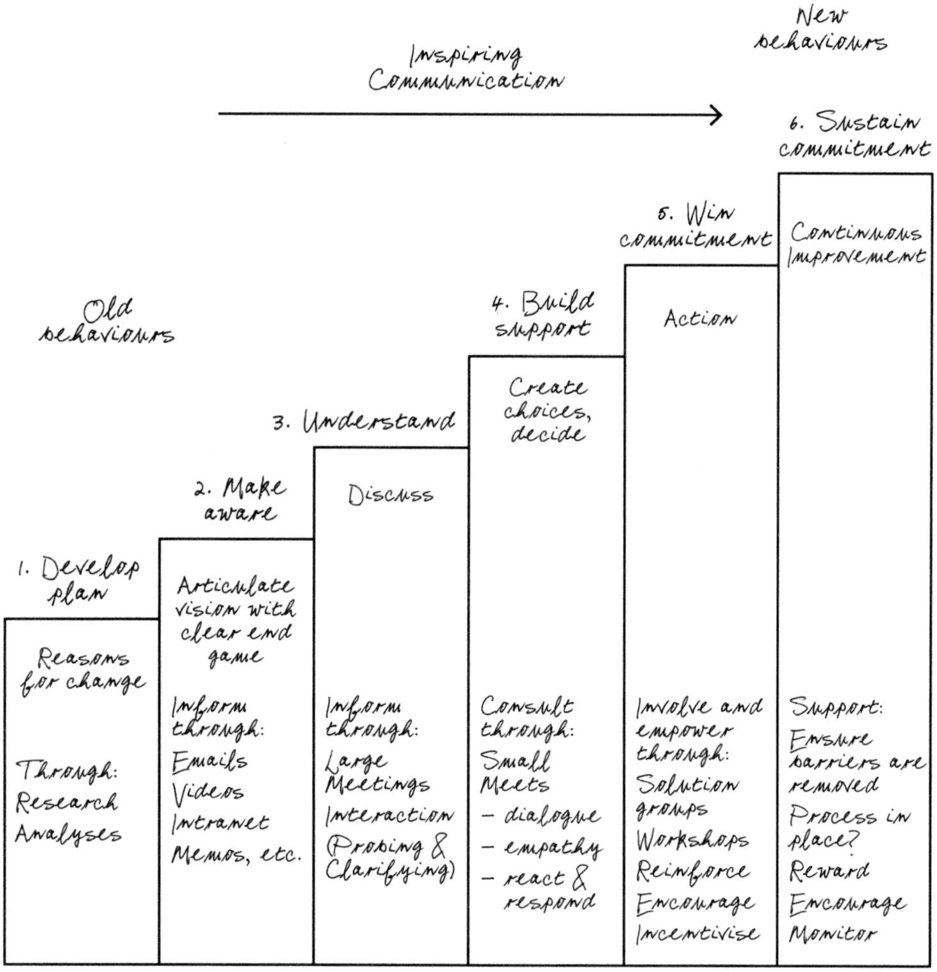

1. Develop plan	2. Make aware	3. Understand	4. Build support	5. Win commitment	6. Sustain commitment
					Continuous Improvement
			Create choices, decide	Action	
		Discuss			
Articulate vision with clear end game					
Reasons for change	Inform through: Emails Videos Intranet Memos, etc.	Inform through: Large Meetings Interaction (Probing & Clarifying)	Consult through: Small Meets – dialogue – empathy – react & respond	Involve and empower through: Solution groups Workshops Reinforce Encourage Incentivise	Support: Ensure barriers are removed Process in place? Reward Encourage Monitor
Through: Research Analyses					

Old behaviours — New behaviours

Inspiring Communication

publications, memos, videos and e-mails, you can create awareness of the need for change and the fact of change. Through written means, this is *all* you will achieve. You will not have got close to the buy-in you need to deliver new behaviours. The third step is to ensure people truly understand what has to happen and why, and get them to participate in deciding what to do. But for people to truly understand what is necessary and what is coming, you need to stand in front of people and allow them to question and probe. People don't always hear what you're saying. They listen through a filter of their own views, prejudices, fears and perspectives, and their take-out may be very different from your message. Unless you have checked what they are hearing, given them a chance to clarify, then you cannot be sure that you have communicated.

To build support for the change programme, you move to Stage 4 – where smaller meetings are needed in which people can talk about how they feel about the changes, often simply to vent, but from here you can start talking with people about the new behaviours and what they mean. This is the stage where you finally persuade people of the need for change and focus them on what is needed. You have to make it understood. Do people know about the problem? Do they know about their own behaviours? Do they understand what's necessary? Do they believe change is necessary or relevant to them? Encourage acceptance.

In order to win their commitment and change their behaviours, you have to move to Stage 5, and have the powerful conversations that allow them to offer up their ideas, and make the choices to which they commit themselves, and empower them to get on with things. This is where conversations are most powerful and most needed.

However, sustaining commitment to the new behaviours means that you have to be constantly removing barriers to change, responding to suggestions, making sure that the support structures are in place and that the teams have the resources and skills they need, as you can see in Stage 6. You have to reward the right behaviours, offer constant encouragement and recognition, make heroes of those who display exemplary behaviours, measure outcomes and feed that back to people to stimulate continuous improvement.

I call this approach FIDAR – find and define, align and refine. When planning your own communications, think about how you phase the communications along these lines. Most leaders I talk to, at this stage, balk at the length of time this process looks like it's going to take. They wanted to simply tell people and get on with things. This impatience is a killer. Successful leaders know that they have to take the time to have these powerful conversations, because this is the only way of ensuring a speedy and successful change programme.

Successful change comes from a real understanding of people, their habits and their motivations (see Chapter 8.) First you have to look at barriers: what are the things that stop people from adopting a new behaviour? Then you need to consider the triggers. How can you get people to start a new behaviour? Finally you have to consider the motivators – the ways to help people stick with new behaviours.

Using this method will greatly increase the likelihood of delivering successful behaviour change. Simply broadcasting at people, instructing, imploring and exhorting, is very unlikely to deliver the changes required – yet this is most often the preferred methodology of many leaders.

The three parts to powerful conversations

Great workplace conversations are about three things – Process, Themes and Skills (Figure 7.2):

FIGURE 7.2 THE THREE PARTS TO POWERFUL CONVERSATIONS

Process — Have you got a systematic empowering process?

Themes — Are you discussing the right themes?

Skills — Do people understand how to conduct a powerful conversation?

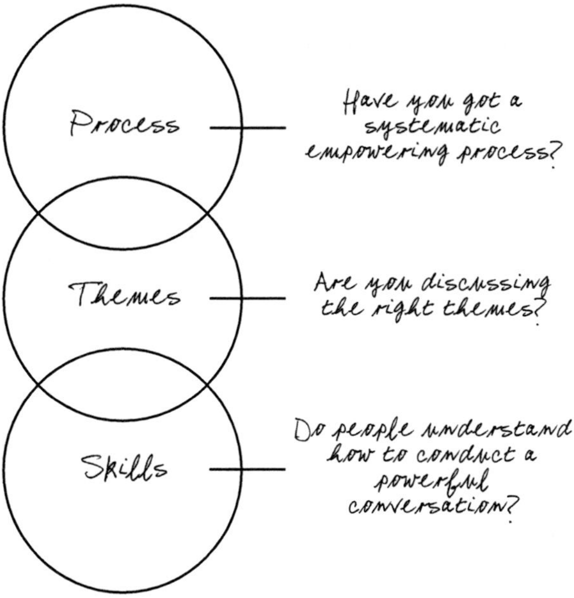

1 *Process*: Does the conversational process deliver empowerment at the front line? Does it enable greater agility? Does it provide for rapid feedback when problems need solving higher up? Is it carried out systematically and consistently throughout your organization?

2 *Themes*: When your people get together, are they focused on the right issues? Are the conversations framed in the right way and informed by the right content?

3 *Skills*: When your leaders do get people together to have the necessary conversations, do they have the right skills to hold quality conversations? What skills do you need when people do sit down to talk?

The right process

Most organizations have a form of team briefing process that ensures information is passed down the line from the senior team to front-line staff. This is usually in addition to the internal 'push' channels such as e-mail, internal newsletter, intranet or video. The team briefing is usually supplemented with materials to help managers communicate to their own teams, and this material is provided from the centre in some shape or form.

This sort of process has some significant weaknesses (see Figure 7.3).

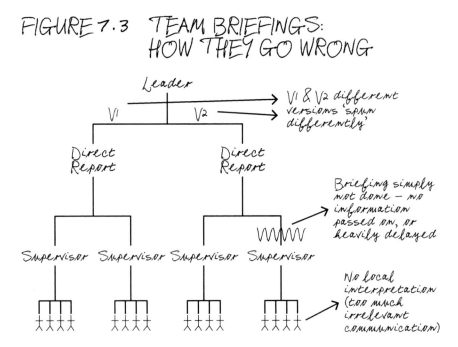

FIGURE 7.3 TEAM BRIEFINGS: HOW THEY GO WRONG

Sometimes (more often than is recognized) different managers interpret the information in different ways and employees sometimes get very different messages from the top. Alignment is impossible because the messages are fragmented. By the time the message has got to the frontline, it can be significantly different from what was intended. The result is a lack of alignment to the corporate goals, a lack of cohesiveness and a lack of trust in the senior leadership team. All of which can be damaging to performance, and the opposite of inspiring.

Sometimes the messages are passed on with little or no local interpretation, causing a 'so what?' reaction that undermines the messages. 'How is this in the least bit relevant to me?' Employees lose interest and feel disconnected from senior leadership. Worse still, often the information being delivered actually is of little use or value to them, and they feel swamped with irrelevant communication.

Managers often take too long to hold the briefing sessions, and weeks can pass before employees are told of important developments, if at all. It amazes me how often leaders are surprised that staff say they have not heard important news. They feel they have communicated, and that it has been up on company notice boards and in e-mails, and that managers have been informed higher up and so should have communicated already – ('how can you not know this?') They feel angered that the communication has not taken place, but neglect to castigate themselves for not having any checking and quality measures in place to ensure it does!

How do you ensure that information is speedy, relevant, interpreted properly for local action, and empowering?

You have to think differently about the process, and differently about the job of line managers in the cascade process. When I have investigated these failures in different companies, one of the frequent issues that arises is the discomfort people have standing up and presenting to their teams, especially when they themselves have not yet bought in to changes from on high. Everybody, however, can ask questions without too much training. If key messages have been delivered directly to employees (thus dealing with the speed issue), then the manager's job should be to ensure people understand the relevance of those 'corporate' messages, and to encourage dialogue about what this means for the team.

Discuss, decide or delegate up (see Figure 7.4)

The real purpose of the conversation is to discuss the implications of the new information, decide on the actions required and implement them as fast

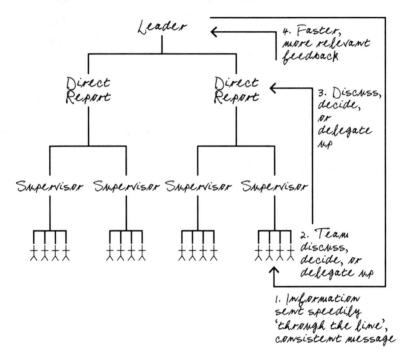

FIGURE 7.4   TEAM LISTENING PROCESS

as possible. Teams are encouraged to discuss what this means for them, debate choices to be made and decide on how to implement. Problems or barriers that prevent implementation locally should be fed back up the line as rapidly as possible. At each higher level of management, decisions should be taken to enable action, barriers removed, and decisions fed back down again quickly. Where issues really are tricky, the sooner they are brought to the top team for a decision, the sooner problems can be resolved. If decisions are passed back up that could have been decided at a local level, senior managers should ask why people felt they could not make the decision, and correct false assumptions and perceptions about levels of improvement. This is the process that truly embeds empowerment in the organization, and enables the agility that most organizations now need.

What are the benefits of this process over classic team briefing methods? First, it ensures consistent messaging and more alignment throughout the organization. Second, it delivers speedier communication. Third, it enables the all-important local interpretation, decision making, empowerment and action. Fourth, it enables faster feedback and greater responsiveness by senior management – one of the essential ingredients of being inspiring. And fifth, it enables leaders to feel reassured that communication has taken place (no feedback = no communication).

Having put the right process in place, how do leaders ensure the process is dealing with the right issues?

The right themes

Basically, powerful conversations are about one of five themes: informing, aligning, solving, implementing or improving. Sometimes they will be isolated to just one of these areas, and at other times they will deal with all five. Always, the conversation will have the True North framework as its reference point. It will be about staying true to the purpose and values, or about achieving goals that enable progress to the vision, or about the strategic priorities or key objectives.

- *Informing*: You need to be clear about the intent of the conversation you want to set in motion. Is it about ensuring employees have, and understand, the information they need to do their jobs correctly? In such a conversation the main purpose will be to ensure that they are apprised of any changes, developments or new processes that might affect their jobs. Do they understand what is now required? Can they interpret this in new behaviours that are now required in their daily work? How do these contribute to True North?

- *Aligning*: This is the most important conversation of all. Have your people seen the organization's purpose and values, do they know what the overall targets are for this year and do they know what the strategic priorities are? Can they directly translate these into their jobs? Can they talk about how what they do delivers the corporate purpose? Can they translate the values of the organization into their daily behaviours? If you have produced the vision framework discussed in the previous chapter, does each team in the organization have its own version of this framework? This conversation – how to contribute to the corporate purpose, values and goals – is what creates organizational alignment. It is why the leaders I have spoken to say they spend 80 per cent of their time communicating purpose and values. With a clear understanding of this framework, everybody in the organization has enough information to make decisions without having to keep going back up the line – creating agility, responsiveness and empowered employees.

One of my favourite stories is about when President John F Kennedy went to visit NASA, after having committed the USA in 1961 to achieving the goal, before the decade was out, of 'landing a man on the moon and returning him safely to Earth'. (His vision set the nation on an incredible and epic journey. Eight years of focused and aligned effort by thousands of Americans came to fruition on 20 July 1969, when Apollo 11's commander Neil Armstrong stepped out of the lunar module and took 'one small step' in the Sea of Tranquillity, calling it 'a giant leap for mankind'.) Many of the leaders I speak to remember this legendary anecdote about JFK. He was apparently visiting NASA headquarters and stopped to talk to a man who was holding a mop. 'And what do you do?' He asked. The man, a janitor, replied: 'I'm helping to put a man on the moon, Sir.'

The leaders who quote this story love the fact that the janitor seemed connected to the mission of the organization that employed him. Few of them have heard the story about what happened next. If they had, they'd be even more pleased. JFK, curious about the janitor's reply, apparently asked how, exactly, the janitor was helping to put a man on the moon? The cleaner, so legend goes, was very clear: his job was to keep the restrooms clean and to make sure the astronauts were well tended with towels, hand-cloths, hot water, soap and sparkling tiles and taps whenever they visited. 'I want to make sure they know I care about them and am doing everything to keep up their morale. By doing that I'm helping to land a man on the moon.'

Whether or not the story is true, it serves to illustrate the importance of a clear 'line of sight' between a person's job and the mission of the organization. Knowing exactly how what you do makes a difference, makes a huge difference to performance. This is the purpose of alignment conversations.

- *Solving*: Productive conversations are about finding solutions to problems. They should be held to find ways to remove barriers or do things differently in order to achieve different and better outcomes. They are not debates in which one side wins and another loses, a platform for a heated exchange of points of view without resolving any of the issues on the table.

- *Implementing*: This conversation is about what we are doing to make sure that everything that needs to happen is being seen to. Who is doing what, and what are the performance criteria we're using to set standards by? By when do things need to be done? Who else do we need to involve? Very often, this conversation is also about...

- *Improving*: How are we doing? Have we hit our deadlines and our targets? Have we delivered to the required quality? Are our customers happy? What feedback are we getting to help us improve our performance? What help do we need from management in order to be able to do our jobs better? What barriers get in the way of us performing, and what decisions do we need from above in order to perform better?

The right skills

The process and the themes, however, are of no use whatsoever if people are not having the right quality of conversation… so let us examine the six crucial elements of powerful business conversations, which are: –

- What's your *intent*? What are you gathering to achieve?
- Who needs to be *included*? Who can help achieve the outcome?
- What *information* do they need, before the conversation?
- When all are gathered, are all being fully *involved* in the conversation? Is it powerful and productive?
- Once decisions have been made, who now needs to be *informed*?
- Have we agreed measures of success, so we will know what *impact* our decisions are having?

The most important of these is step four, which we will address at some length. Here are each of the six elements in more detail. (see Figure 8.5)

1 *Intent*. Are you clear on which conversation you want to have? Is there a specific issue that needs to be addressed? What exactly are you trying to achieve? Clarity about the subject of the conversation leads to much better-quality conversations, which you are more easily able to keep focused and productive. Are you regularly returning to the vision framework and discussing strategic priorities, your values and whether you are making progress towards your purpose?

2 *Include*. To achieve these goals, who do you need around the table? Unless you have thought carefully about the participants, you could spoil the quality of the conversation. Who has insight that needs to be delivered to the team? Who is involved in implementing the actions to be agreed? Which partners from other teams need to participate? Can you get an internal or external 'customer' involved?

3 *Information*. Are you able to give the people involved in the conversation some information before you meet? If not, you will have to recognize that some part of the conversation will be devoted

FIGURE 7.5 HOW TO CONDUCT POWERFUL CONVERSATIONS

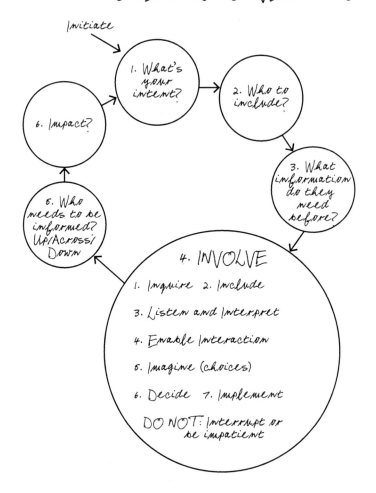

to bringing people up to speed. Would you prefer that they give it some thought before coming to the meeting, so as to generate more, and more productive, ideas? Is the information sufficient to give them a complete picture? Will some part of the meeting have to be dedicated to the missing pieces of information that will enable a fuller understanding of the challenges that now require action? Remember, the quality of the provocation for the conversation will often determine the quality of the conversation and results!

4 *Involvement.* Employees want their ideas to be heard. They want to feel respected and they want to be involved in making decisions that directly impact on their working lives. Unless you, as a leader, can get people to talk up and participate in a productive discussion, you will not be inspiring to employees. For those of you who think it is all about making brilliant speeches, this is the moment where you can fall flat on your face. This is where you have to give people 'a damn good listening to'. It is not all about you, is all about them. Mostly, these conversations will not be about telling. They will be about listening.

During these conversations, you have to exhibit the skills of appreciative inquiry if you are to encourage everyone to participate. That means appreciating them as individuals, and appreciating their views and ideas. It also means being genuinely inquisitive and interested. If you keep pulling rank, all you will do is encourage them to shut up. Most importantly, it means you have to make it a safe environment for people to tell you bad news, and you have to be extraordinarily careful not to send negative signals when you receive the bad news. Bad news is essential to good leadership – it enables better informed decisions and, if you are responsive, much greater agility. During those conversations, you need to encourage everybody in the room to voice their opinions, and guarantee them a no-blame culture.

Inquiring in a way that encourages people to talk up means asking lots of open-ended questions and inviting people to give their views, and then being interested in their responses. It means asking them to inform you about how they feel and give real voice to their emotions, ideas and dreams. Interrupting and being impatient are deadly sins. Holding eye contact with them, showing them that you are listening and that you understand, by interpreting what they have to say, is key. When people give insights into the challenge, recognition will encourage them to do it again and build their confidence.

Try to include everyone in the conversation. Watch for body signals or silence. Encourage involvement.

Listen well, and interpret what people are saying, so everyone understands what is being said.

Encourage people to interact and talk to and with each other.

If you can encourage people to talk about what is working well and what could be done to make things even better, if you can encourage them to imagine new possibilities, if you can get them to interact and improvise, you can generate positive ideas and a wide variety of choices that can be made to achieve the objectives that you own.

As I have said before, employees love choice and hate change. A choice they make for themselves is one they are far more committed to. As we saw in the 'lottery experiment', you are likely to get people five times more committed to the choices they make than the changes that are imposed on them by others.

Having encouraged them to make these choices, and having secured their commitment to them, you now have to discuss ways to implement to best effect. Agreeing who owns actions, agreeing performance measures, agreeing deadlines and agreeing quality standards are all crucial parts of the conversation. Having done that, you obviously need to make this item Number One on your next meeting's agenda – how are we doing against our measures?

Your people will be watching you in these meetings, so it is imperative that you watch your own behaviours. This is where they will see your values in action, through the stories you tell, the way you ask questions, the way you listen, decisions you make or help them to make together, things you act on or don't act on, your body language and the interest you show in them. Your energy levels will have a direct impact on the energy in the room, so my advice is that you learn to listen with *vigour*.

Most important is to recognize the huge difference between a debate and genuine dialogue. Debate is where people each have their view, from which they are unlikely to move, and use it to beat down other people's views in order to win the argument. Often, people with authority use their positional power to win the argument, leaving subordinates frustrated and uncommitted.

Dialogue, however, involves genuinely trying to access different perspectives to uncover new meaning and new solutions. If you want to facilitate a positive dialogue, you have to listen deeply, ensure you are suspending your assumptions and judgements, and look for win–win solutions.

- *Inform.* Once you have finished the conversation and decided on the actions, you now have to agree who else needs to know about the outcomes of your discussion. Have you uncovered barriers that need to be resolved higher up? How will these be resolved? Are you taking actions that will involve other parts of the organization and do they now need to be informed? Think through the implications of your decisions and make sure that you do not fail simply because you have forgotten to communicate with everyone who needs to know.

- *Impact.* Having set measures of success, it is now crucial to ensure that you are checking on the impact of your new behaviours. Have you put the right measurement processes in place? Are the measures being reported regularly enough? And are you using them to inform the conversation the next time you get the team together? Can you bring your customers into the next conversation to give direct feedback? A team that looks at measures together grows together.

Figure 7.6 at the end of this chapter shows how the three parts fit together:

- an empowering *process* in place that makes sure information flows up and down the line quickly, that discussions are made at the front line, and that feedback is passed up the line as quickly as possible;
- consistency of *themes*, so that all-important alignment is created, and that people always understand the context of their work, how they are progressing to goals, and how they contribute to achieving the organization's vision;
- the right conversation *skills*, to ensure people are engaged and committed, high performing, and continuously improving; and that effective communication takes place up, down and across the organization to ensure coherent action.

Not having the right conversations will have a corrosive effect on your team and your chances of success. Sometimes, you'll have to have courageous conversations, where you tackle issues you'd rather avoid. Sometimes, you'll have to be brilliant at leading a conversation that transforms performance. To do this, you'll have to bring your authentic self to the conversation, live your values throughout and always stay fixed on your goals.

What is the ultimate measure of successful conversations?

At the beginning of this chapter, we looked at the drivers of engagement and made the link between engagement and conversations. The way you engage employees is through the conversations you either lead yourself or ensure are happening throughout the organization in a structured and positive way. Ultimately, the quality of those conversations will determine the level of engagement in the organization.

Are you measuring engagement? Most leaders I spoke to have ensured that engagement is a strategic priority. They have set up measures to ensure that levels of engagement are being improved, because of the direct link to improved performance. This isn't only about improving employee happiness and satisfaction. It links directly with your ability to achieve your goals.

We are living in the age of conversations. Conversations are not only necessary inside the organization but outside too, with all stakeholders. They are the lifeblood of all relationships, a fact that is heavily influencing the entire communications industry today. Long gone are the days when broadcast messages could suffice when building a brand. Leadership is about relationships, and good relationships are about dialogue.

Why? Because great leaders inspire others to achieve great results. They influence how other people feel and by so doing they influence their behaviours. This simple thought has been the fundamental goal of all of my communication advice to leaders over the past 30 years: in order to communicate well you have to know the people in your audience, you have to know how they act and feel, and most important of all, you have to know what you want them to feel and do instead.

In that time, I have used a simple but devastatingly effective communication planning process to ensure that leaders are focused on the right things when communicating.

FIGURE 7.6 THE THREE PARTS TO POWERFUL CONVERSATION: HOW IT ALL FITS TOGETHER

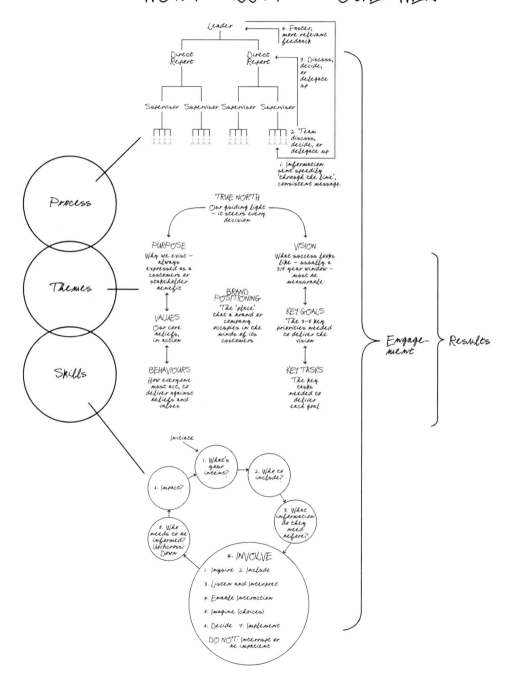

PART III
Connecting to the emotions that drive behaviours

It's all about them

How to become more effective by being more focused on people and behaviours

> *If you really want to connect and persuade, and turn ideas into action, you have to understand how people think and feel now, and how that drives their behaviours, and then pay close attention to why they should do what you need them to do in the future. Here are 10 steps to a better communication plan.*

It was the nightmare that all leaders fear. A much-dreaded overhaul of the company's IT infrastructure went live and immediately fell over. For a national furniture retail company, selling hundreds of thousands of items every day, this was a catastrophe.

The company not only sold and delivered furniture, but it also manufactured and then assembled furniture on site for its customers.

Customers were purchasing items for every room in their homes, handing over their cash, and expecting in good faith that the furniture would be delivered and fitted within a short space of time. However, as soon as the

IT fell over, the company started losing track of stock. Within days it was in chaos and soon that chaos was spreading to customers who were becoming increasingly anxious, and often hugely inconvenienced, by the fact that they were not receiving what they had bought. The company had a massive shortfall in delivering items to customers and it was growing by the day.

Of course, the leadership team rapidly assembled a crisis team, which not only included the IT advisers who had got them into difficulty but now other IT advisers as well. It also included key personnel from across sales, warehousing, distribution, manufacturing, marketing and human resources. The team was working 24 hours a day to find solutions to the problem and to shore up the processes that needed to be carried out if sales were to continue.

I was asked to help the company communicate the problem externally. Immediately, I was ringing alarm bells. When I asked what they were trying to achieve, exactly, the answer was: 'To inform customers about our problem and minimize reputational damage.'

We assembled a team and we began looking at the various audiences they needed to communicate with. This included customers, employees, MPs, consumer watchdogs, the media, shareholders and other groups. Yes, but which customers? We needed more closely to segment the audience. This broke down into existing, potential and former customers. Existing customers were the ones who had placed orders and were now becoming more and more agitated. Former customers were important as the company needed to retain their loyalty and ensure return visits to the stores. But the key to the problem lay with potential customers. Their actions now could turn their crisis into a disaster from which there would be no return. Can you spot yet what had been bothering me about making an external announcement?

With no more than 16 people in the room we began to look at each of the key groups in turn and examine their situations and attitudes in more detail. Who were we talking about? How did they feel about what was happening? What were they likely to do as a result of how they felt? What would we rather they do? And what would we have to do to provide sufficient incentive to encourage them to supportive behaviours?

For example, we looked at young mothers, who formed a high proportion of the company's customers. How would a young mother feel, with a baby on her hip, her kitchen ripped out in preparation for a new one, but no replacement kitchen in sight? The answers were obvious to everyone – she would be frustrated, increasingly angry and massively inconvenienced at a stressful time in her life. What would she do? Obviously she would complain directly to the salesman, and from there to the manager, to family and friends, and perhaps even to MPs and the media. She'd tell a lot of people if she remained angry. She would likely also cancel her order.

How would the salespeople in the store feel when this young mother came in for a second or even third time, with still no solution to her problem? What would they do? Again the answer was obvious – they would run and hide, especially as they had no solution to offer. Their job was to earn commission by selling furniture, and every moment they spent trying to deal with an inconsolable customer was not only unpleasant and uncomfortable but also hitting them in their pockets.

And so we went round each of the audiences in turn, looking at every stakeholder and thinking about how they felt and what they were likely to do. We came to potential customers. What would happen if they were to learn that, should they buy something at the store, they would likely not receive their items for months? Again, the answer was obvious. They would go to a competitor instead. This chain of stores received more than 700,000 potential customers every day and was crucially dependent on footfall. The more people who passed through their doors, the more sales they made. Were they now to do or say something to dissuade people from even coming into the store, they would suffer a cash-flow blow from which they would never recover.

Now we had to ask the question – what would we rather they did? In the case of potential customers, the answer was once again very obvious – we wanted them to keep coming into the stores. Once there, of course, should they not be able to take home with them from the store an item that they had purchased, we would need to be entirely honest about the situation and offer discounts or other incentives to persuade them to endure the inconvenience. However, it was crucial that we did not allow the communications to run out of control so that this audience was negatively affected in ways that would damage the business for ever. This meant continuing to advertise, controlling fallout from the IT chaos, and stepping into overdrive on direct face-to-face communication with every audience the company had.

For example, with the salespeople, we obviously wanted them to continue to sell to clients. Should the disgruntled customer come in again, how should the sales staff handle her? The answer was to provide a customer liaison in every store who could deal directly with every unhappy customer returning to complain. A special process would need to be set up so that those customers could be taken away from the sales areas, comforted with a cup of tea and some biscuits, while the liaison officer did their best to sort out their problems.

Call-centre staff who were receiving the telephone complaints needed to be briefed on how to handle these complaints and how to keep disgruntled customers from cancelling their orders and going somewhere else. This involved giving them special scripts that allowed them to offer discounts or free items from the store to keep customers from leaving while they were sorting out the mess.

Every single stakeholder was addressed, and a huge and complex communication plan was put in place. Gradually, the crisis team was able to get on top of the IT chaos, and orders were fulfilled, discounts taken and free offers accepted. This crisis was dealt with without becoming national news, and without putting off new customers. The organization's leaders were able to inspire their staff to the right behaviours in very challenging circumstances and overcome a crisis.

The lesson here was that the original communications objective would have been catastrophic. Communicating their problems widely would simply have dissuaded potential customers from coming to the stores. The new objective became: ensure that we can keep customers coming into our stores to buy furniture while we sort out the crisis. As you can see, by framing it this way, the leaders of the company were much more likely to ensure success through its communications programme.

Most importantly, however, the leadership team was able to provide much better leadership. They were able to provide context, they were able to show that they understood the problem as well as how all stakeholders felt and what they needed, and they were able to provide clear direction to everyone in the company about what they needed to do and how they could work together to solve the problem.

They succeeded because of a simple planning process that forced them to be more audience-centric before attempting to communicate.

How to be audience-centric

One of the 12 principles I outlined in the previous chapter is that of audience centricity. This is the art of thoroughly understanding your audience before attempting to communicate. Without this basic understanding of the people you are talking with, the danger is that you simply talk *at* them and fail to have any impact. Leadership communication is what you do to achieve big goals. It is all about changing behaviours. So failing to have any impact is not an option (if you want to be an effective leader).

When it comes to communication, it *starts* with the people you lead. You have to set out to achieve a change in how they think, feel and act, but that starts with you first knowing how they think, feel and act *now*.

No doubt, as a leader, you have a plan that you are trying to deliver. No doubt, also, that plan has daunting numbers in it. You need to achieve higher revenues, higher margins, lower costs, and a greater percentage market share, to win more clients, generate more donations, achieve faster innovation or an uplift in customer satisfaction. No matter what the numbers you have to deliver, whether you are in the private sector, a charity or the public sector, those improved numbers can only be achieved by changing behaviours.

That starts with defining the goals *as well as* the behaviours needed to achieve the goals. Which behaviours do you want to keep, or stop or start. Which do you want more people doing?

If you take the time to develop a better understanding of the people you are relying on for success, your change plan will be rooted in this better understanding and be focused on delivering the new and supportive behaviours you need from your stakeholders. Successful change can only come from understanding people's habits and motivations. If you do that, you will be able to communicate in ways that are better targeted, more relevant and more compelling.

Monitoring how well you communicate, and how well people are responding to what you say, will provide a continuous improvement process that will improve the odds on achieving your objectives. The end result will be a better organizational performance aided by more supportive stakeholders.

Only if you think about how to inspire the right behaviours will you succeed.

The more senior you get in any organization, the more help and support you are likely to receive with your communications. But even then, the help may be focused on crafting your messages and creating channels of communication, and completely miss the point. That help may make what you want to say more articulate, but it may miss the audience completely because it doesn't go to the heart of what they need to hear. Without thinking about this, you might even communicate exactly the wrong thing. As I demonstrated with the story that opened this chapter, I have sometimes had to prevent leaders from communicating what they instinctively would like to have done, on the basis that doing so would have had catastrophic results. It was only by using a simple process that I developed more than 20 years ago that we got to the right communication plan and therefore to the right result.

The process I use is simple but devastatingly effective.

I developed it while working as Corporate Affairs Director of the United Kingdom Atomic Energy Authority in the early 1990s. In an organization that had more PhD scientists and engineers than almost any other in the world, I was charged with leading our change programme. The leadership team, of which I was a member, had to split up the organization in preparation for floating a part of it on the stock market as a science and engineering consultancy. The organization employed many brilliant minds, people who were at the forefront of technology developments because of its nuclear research and development heritage. Most of these brilliant minds, it seemed to me, opposed the idea of privatization. Whenever I went to talk to them about our communication needs and our reputation, I was argued in circles by clever people who felt they knew more about communication and reputation management than I did.

One day, in one of the many UKAEA laboratories, talking with a group of scientists who once again were arguing with what I felt they had to do, I noticed that every wall was plastered with process charts. It dawned on me that these process charts, adorned with scientific equations, were simply a representation of a series of actions or steps needed to achieve an end. Wherever I went from then on I saw these process charts everywhere. One day it dawned on me. Why didn't I simply design my own communication process chart to better explain what it was we were trying to do and what we had to achieve? The result was the chart I share with you now. I have used this process on countless occasions since, helping clients to avert crises, generate more sales, achieve change or even influence national debates. The beauty of the process is that it works as effectively for a one-off speech, as it does for a complex communications campaign.

In AEA Technology, using this new process chart, I was able to have much more constructive conversations, and it enabled people to co-create communication plans with me, rather than see me force my plans on unwilling, uninspired resistors. (AEA Technology was successfully floated on the stock market in 1996.)

It is a 10-step process illustrated in Figure 8.1.

1 What, exactly, are you trying to achieve?

2 Who do you most need to influence in order to achieve this objective?

3 What do you want them to do, exactly?

4 What's in it for them to do what you would like them to do?

5 Do you need to behave differently to provide sufficient motivation?

FIGURE 8.1 COMMUNICATIONS/BEHAVIOUR PLANNING PROCESS

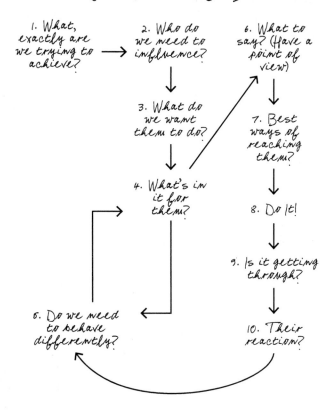

6 What do you need to tell them? (And do you have a compelling point of view?)

7 What are the best ways of reaching them?

8 COMMUNICATE!

9 Is it getting through to them?

10 How are they reacting?

(11.   If the results are not as you would like, analyse why, change what you are doing or saying, and start again.)

From here you are in a continuous improvement loop that is all about listening, responding, and the continuous dialogue that enables change.

Behind several of these steps are more tools to use to think about how to maximize communication effectiveness.

Let me take you through each step in more detail to enable you to use this process yourself.

1. What, exactly, are you trying to achieve?

Can you paint an accurate picture of success? Can you describe what will be happening and how people will be feeling? Can you answer that question very specifically?

For example, it could be something like: 'Communicate our new vision statement to all staff.' In which case, I don't believe it would be good enough. To satisfy me, it would have to be something like: 'By September, communicate our vision to all staff and ensure that they understand it, can remember it, and are able to explain how what they do contributes to the vision.'

Very often, I find myself working with a leader or a team who are actually not crystal clear on what they are trying to achieve. They may have a very broad sense of purpose, but they cannot articulate with precise detail what it is they need to do. As illogical as this might sound, it is nevertheless true. They will come to me because they're in the middle of a crisis, or because they face a significant challenge and need to respond. When I run into this situation, I often leave this first step to one side, or allow (for the time being) a vague objective. The second step will make objective setting much clearer, simply because it involves the task of thinking about the people you need to influence and the behaviours required to deliver a solution to your problem. It is the second stage that often helps to clarify the question at the first stage.

One of the management books that I most value is *The Seven Habits of Highly Effective People* by Stephen R Covey. It is probably one of the best selling business books ever published with more than 25 million copies sold in 38 languages worldwide. One of the seven habits that Covey advocates is: 'Begin with the end in mind.'

To me this means being really clear about what it is you need to achieve, and why.

Defining the problem is really what this first step is all about.

If you define the problem in the right way, it will help you to determine the nature of the communication required. Sometimes I have seen clients achieve breakthrough solutions by spending quality time on defining the problem. Why is our current situation not satisfactory? Why do we need to change? From there you can move to a more future-based vision. What will be happening if we manage successfully to change? How will everyone be interacting? How will everybody be feeling? What will they be doing and how will this contribute to our goals and enable us to achieve our numbers?

Sadly, I have seen many more occasions when people have not been sufficiently rigorous in defining the problem they're attempting to solve or even articulating why the problem is important. As a result, they answer the first question in vague terms and then wind up chasing programmes that are not aligned with their goals. I have a profound belief that leaders need to become better at asking these questions so as to ensure that they tackle the right problems.

You may be fooled into thinking that, as a new leader of a team, you aren't solving a problem but creating a new vision of success. If that's the case, then what was wrong with the old one? If there was no need for change there would be no need for you as a leader. There is a problem or you wouldn't be trying to galvanize people into action.

The rigour with which this stage is tackled is one of the most important factors in finding the best solution. As a leader, you're going to have to explain the need for the solution, so what is the need? Who will benefit from a solution? Why will you and your organization benefit from the solution, and how is it aligned with your plans and strategy?

Sometimes, you also have to pay careful attention to how you phrase the objective. For example, I have learned to my cost how talking about productivity gains can be a real switch off to staff. Even though they intellectually agree the necessity, in their hearts it just feels like they're going to have to work harder and harder. If, instead, you talked about how to make their jobs easier to do and more fun, you would likely get a vastly different reaction. It is always worth getting multiple perspectives on how you phrase the challenge, which is why Stage 2 is so necessary...

2. Who do you most need to influence in order to achieve your objective?

Think about the people who are going to be crucial to your success. Who are they? Where are they? Why are they important to you? How important are they to your success? Do you need their absolute commitment and active support? Or, do they only need to know what's happening but you do not need them to do anything?

Mapping this out is a crucial stage of the exercise and really needs some thought. It's no good saying 'all employees'. That's too vague. Are we really talking about everybody? Or do you really only need to target the senior leadership team? If it really is all employees, then you will need to segment that audience to be able to do Stage 3. For example, do you need to think about line management, as well as sales staff, distribution staff, warehouse staff, the marketing team, secretaries and receptionists (see Figure 8.2).

FIGURE 8.2 SEGMENT (EMPLOYEES)

I call this your Court of Public Opinion (COPO), because you're going to have to influence these people's opinions in order to change their attitudes and change their behaviours. It is a 'court' because their opinions will determine your fate, just as a jury does in a law court. I have seen clients go through this process of considering their audiences forensically and as a result move from an urge to communicate with the broad public through the national media to a campaign focused on getting a message to a single person.

FIGURE 8.3 WHO ARE THE PEOPLE WE DEPEND ON FOR SUCCESS?

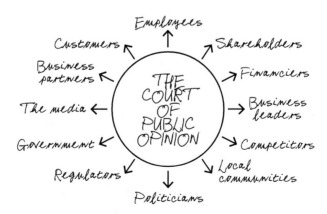

However, if you have a communications campaign to consider that does involve a broad range of people that you might have to interact with, I offer Figure 8.3 as a prompt to help you think about how to map out all your potential key audiences. Each of these groupings is, however, still too broad. To be successful, you must segment as far as you possibly can. For example, if you are talking about customers, do you need to segment by age group? By gender? By existing, potential or lost customers? By region, life stage or lifestyle? (See Figure 8.4.)

FIGURE 8.4 SEGMENT (CUSTOMERS)

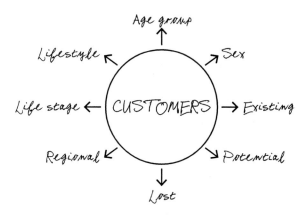

The more closely you segment these audiences, the more easily you will be able to understand who they are and what communication will be most needed to influence them.

3. What do you want them to do, exactly?

Now it becomes easier to think about what you want each of these audiences to do if you are to succeed in your quest. But first, it is useful to try to understand how they are behaving now, and why. What do they think, feel, believe and do? How do we know this? Why do they feel this way and how is that impacting on their behaviour? (It is essential to answer the question about how people are feeling. How we feel determines how we behave.)

Try, for example, phrasing the problem in the language that they would use. How would a secretary think about this? How would a receptionist put it? How would customers see it? These multiple viewpoints can often throw up fantastic insights into the nature of the challenge that you're actually facing.

Once you have done this you can now start mapping out what you would rather they were doing. Obviously you would love to have your key stakeholders change instantly to the ideal behaviours, but you need to be realistic here. What would ideal behaviours be? What would satisfactory behaviours be? What would the worst possible result be? What will be the cost or revenue benefits of the changed behaviours? If you can answer the last two questions, you'll have a business case for change and the ability to measure Return on Investment.

4. What's in it for them to do what you would like them to do?

The advertising industry has a wonderful phrase called WIFOM. It means: What's in It for Me? It's a great question because it forces you to define the benefit of a changed behaviour, but this has to be what the people in your audience would perceive as a benefit, not the benefit to you of changed behaviours. It is in these benefit statements that the key messages lie for any communication campaign. (Sometimes, it might be the awful consequences of not changing behaviour that you have to communicate.)

Take care to articulate the real benefit, not simply a feature or an advantage of your plan. Take buying a new car as an example of Feature/Advantage/Benefit: a *feature* would be that the car has a fifth gear. The *advantage* is that this enables less fuel to be burned at high revs. The *benefit* is cheaper running costs or a greater range from a tank of fuel.

Why should people change? What are their motivators? Do they prefer cheaper costs or greater range? How do we know this? Do the different audiences that you have to address actually have different motivators from you and each other? Does that mean different messages for the different audiences?

Often, at this stage, you might begin to realize that the original objectives that you set yourself are actually too vague, unrealistic or even unachievable. It is worth checking back on your answers to Question 1 to make sure that you really have defined the task well enough. The results to all of these questions will certainly raise some issues that will be covered by the next question.

5. Do we need to behave differently to provide sufficient motivation?

If you examine the answers to the questions about whether you are providing sufficient motivation to people and find your answers lacking, it could well be that you have to think differently about your own actions. Do you need to do something different in order to provide sufficient motivation for change? Do you have to change your policies, or your incentive programmes, or your processes? Or is it that people simply don't understand the need for change well enough? Do they know what consequences will follow if they do not change their behaviours? Does that mean you have to change the way you are communicating or what you are communicating?

6. What do you need to tell them? (Do you have a compelling point of view?)

By now there should be a great deal more clarity about what you need to say and how you need to tailor the message for each of the key audience groups. Do you have a powerful point of view about the need for change? Can you describe how you see the world and how you envisage success? Can you describe not only what the financial benefits will be, but how people will feel and how they will be behaving with each other when your changes have been achieved? Can you describe exactly what each group needs to do and why and how they will be interacting with other groups? Do you have the right stories to help them understand the context or spirit of your intent?

7. What are the best ways of reaching them?

Now that we know more about who we want to reach, and what we need to say, we can pay attention to how best to reach and influence them. Will it be through an e-mail? Would it be best to bring the groups together for a seminar? Do you need to do a webinar or a pod cast? Is it through a line management cascade process? Do you need to do a road show? Do you need to use a combination of all of the above? How are you going to ensure that the right conversations are being had with the right people at the right time in the right way to ensure everyone understands the issues, feels you understand their interests, knows what to do and what success looks like? Have you built in feedback loops?

8. Communicate!

A simple word, but this is a huge and never ending task. In other words, execute the plan and communicate, communicate, communicate.

9. Is it getting through to them?

Communication has not taken place if people have not heard you, have not understood you and have not changed their behaviours as a result. You must find ways of checking whether people have heard you and whether they've understood. This is the chance to engage in more and more effective communication if it becomes obvious that what you've said is simply not getting through. Understand why not. Remove the barriers.

Remember that, although you communicate in a way that seems clear to you, people listening to you will filter what you say through a complicated set of preconceptions that will often distort the messages you are trying to send. Listeners receive messages selectively. They hear and process some of what you say, but block other things. While you may feel you've explained the whole picture, it will be almost certain that the whole picture wasn't received. And, even if it was, they may be incorrectly interpreting your words.

The *only* way you can ensure that people understand you is by asking what they have heard and what their reactions are to what you've said. Without this check, you can only be sure that you have communicated *at* people, not whether you have communicated successfully.

10. How are they reacting?

Are people now behaving in ways that will help you to deliver your goals? The only thing that matters here is the outcome. If people are not changing their behaviours, why not? Is it because they are simply not sufficiently motivated? Is it because they don't understand? Is it because there are barriers you have not seen? What, now, is the problem? Once clarified, return to Step 5 and repeat the process. You will now be in a continuous improvement loop – a virtuous circle that vastly improves your chances of success.

Now you need a good measurement framework to ensure the success of your communication. For a quality programme, you need to be measuring quality in several different places (see Figure 8.5).

As we have already discussed, any good plan will have an assessment of where you are now and a clear vision of where you want to be. By following my process you will have a plan for how to get there.

FIGURE 8.5 MEASUREMENT FRAMEWORK

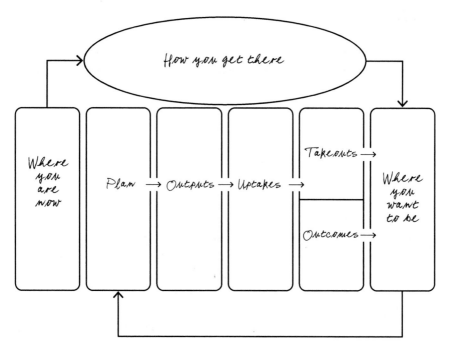

The plan will have a variety of outputs. These can be various communiqués, events, webinars, e-mails, videos, team briefing packs – any communication that leaves your office. Was it a quality communication? Was it well written, clear and easy to understand? Was it delivered to time, cost and quality?

Any communication will result in what I call 'uptakes'. Here I am talking about how many people have taken up the communication? How many people attended the webinar or seminar? How many people visited the website? How many people actually read the e-mail? Do you know the answer to these questions and have you put in place mechanics to measure them?

What are people taking out of the communication? What are they hearing and what do they understand? How does that make them feel? Again, have you got systems in place to check?

Finally, and crucially, is your communication having an impact on their behaviours? Are you achieving better outcomes as a result of your communication? Are these new attitudes and behaviours moving you to your objectives on time and to cost, with sufficiently high-quality results? If not, return to your plan, in order to change the plan.

The importance of tackling the right problem

Let me close this chapter by giving you an example of defining a problem in a way that can improve the chances of achieving a much more effective solution. Some years ago, before the big recession, I was in conversation with some army officers over a growing problem they were facing. The number of new recruits applying to join the Army was declining, and this was exacerbated by the fact that more people than usual were leaving. The annual spend of many millions of pounds worth of recruitment advertising was having a decreasing effect and, no matter how they tweaked the message, numbers were still declining. They were clear that doing the same thing was no longer an option.

We started by trying to articulate exactly what they were trying to achieve. Their answer was obvious: 'Drive up the number of recruits!'

It was said with such vehemence that I decided to move onto the next stage, even though I was unhappy with the broadness of the statement at this stage. We started examining who it was the Army most needed to influence in order to achieve this goal. Obviously, they needed to reach young men and women who could be potential recruits into the Army. They needed to reach the general public, so that such a move would be seen as an acceptable career option for youngsters. They needed to ensure the Army was seen as a good thing, supported by the general public.

As we probed harder, this court of public opinion began to widen. When thinking about the people who most influenced potential recruits, we then looked at parents (and mothers in particular), teachers, mentors, career guidance centres, family and friends, and even former soldiers now in the community and unrestricted about what they could tell people about life in the Army.

When I asked what they were most proud of in terms of the recent communications, they talked about a very popular TV show called *Ross Kemp in Afghanistan*. They said that research among potential recruits had shown that this show was effective in attracting youngsters into the Army. Why? The reality of active duty actually appealed to many of them was the answer.

But what effect did that TV show have on the key people who most influenced potential recruits? What effect would such a show have, for example, on mothers? The answer was, they didn't know. My assertion was that this would have a far from favourable effect, as mothers, friends and relatives would be made even more acutely aware of the danger of their son or brother or friend dying while on active service. If this different perspective was true, and these people were now more actively dissuading youngsters from going into the Army, then a very different communications approach would be needed.

What possible benefits would those people see in advising youngsters to pursue a career in the army? What could possibly mitigate the risk of dying on active duty? We needed to know much more about how these people were feeling before we could design an appropriate communications programme. We simply didn't know enough to define the real problem. This led to a programme of research among these stakeholders, which verified the conclusions we had come to as we answered Questions 2 to 4 of the process. In order to persuade these people to consider a career in the Army, it was going to be necessary to do a great deal more about talking up the merits of training and career-enhancing skills that youngsters might receive in the Army. Mothers did worry about the Army as an option, and needed strong mitigating reasons to support such a choice. This was, indeed, going to have to be a very different communications campaign. We had to redefine the objective. It now became: to persuade the key influencers of potential recruits of the benefits of a career in the Army.

While the Ross Kemp programme was still suitable for potential recruits themselves, something very different was required for the influencers. A much more targeted, sophisticated and persuasive campaign would be required to overcome the inherent fear any mother would have about encouraging her child to take up a career that involved the very real risk of dying on the battlefield. Without such a campaign, it was likely that parents and relatives would continue to dissuade recruits and the Army's leaders would continue to see dwindling numbers.

However, before we were able to start working with the Army to help write a communications plan, an entirely new circumstance arose. The recession. In a market where jobs were suddenly and dramatically being terminated and job security in industry became a thing of the past, young eyes turned more readily to a career in the Army. For the next six or seven years, the Army's recruitment problem went away.

If as a leader you truly want to inspire behaviours that will help you achieve your goals, then be clear about this: you have not successfully communicated if people have not understood you, or felt motivated to think differently and act differently as a result of your words.

That means that you need to be crystal clear about the nature of your problem, the solution you need to put in place, the benefits this will bring to all parties involved, and how to communicate with them in a compelling and resonating way.

It is by influencing how other people feel that you influence their behaviours. You have to know the people in your audience, you have to know how they act and feel, and most important of all, you have to know what you want them to feel and do instead.

At the heart of good relationships, is good listening. The way you listen during conversations, the way you listen to your direct reports in one-on-one meetings, the way you listen to the outside world and all of your external stakeholders, will be one of the key determinants of whether you are seen as an inspiring leader. Sometimes, giving people a damn good listening to can be the most inspiring communication of all.

Let us examine how to be a brilliant listener in the next chapter...

The listening leader
Why you need to listen louder

> *Leaders who are great listeners are the ones who are most likely to be perceived as effective leaders. Employees will not care about how much you know until they know how much you care. Those who know you care will work harder and try to exceed your expectations. Here are seven techniques to be a better listener.*

Some of the most inspiring leaders I have met are also the most skilled listeners I know.

They look me in the eye. They make me feel like I am the only person that matters to them. They concentrate on my every word. They resist distractions around the room. They make notes and send the signal that what I am saying is noteworthy. They wait for me to finish, and never interrupt unless it is to clarify. They ask powerful questions and dig deep for my ideas and views. They empathize with my views, even if they don't agree. They make me feel understood. They disagree where appropriate, with respect, to stand up for what they believe. They take action based on our conversation, or they explain why they will not act. Either way, they make me feel that they care about me, and that makes me care about meeting or exceeding their expectations.

It is no coincidence that leaders who are great listeners are the ones who are most likely to be perceived as effective. Incredibly, some leaders I have worked with believed that listening is a soft and unnecessary skill, and a sign of weakness. (Perhaps that is exactly why I was brought in to work with them?) Ironically, though, I have found that listening leaders have even more power. They don't seem to give in as much as others on deadlines, standards, projects or goals – precisely because they make employees feel as if they understand them. When people feel heard and understood, they also feel important, valued, respected and cared about. When they feel that way, there is a much greater bond between leader and follower, and much more alignment with the goals and objectives of the leader.

Being a great listener gives you enormous presence. I often say that the most charming people in life are those who are more interested in me than I am in them. 'Go and be charming,' I exhort my staff.

I have heard time and again how President Bill Clinton was mesmerizingly focused on people. Many who only ever met him once say that they were captivated by him because he gave them his complete attention, his eyes fixed on theirs, and they felt for that brief moment that there was no one in the world more important to him. It had a stunning effect on them.

Whenever I have asked employees what behavioural skills distinguish great leaders from merely competent ones, they always say that the ability to listen empathetically is the most important skill of leadership.

Not listening actually turns people off

In the same employee research, when I ask about whether they feel that their own bosses really do listen to them, a worrying gap emerges. While they feel that the best leaders are those who listen well, they say their own bosses don't listen to them very much at all. As a result, their motivation levels and sense of engagement drop dramatically, as does their performance. They start doing what is necessary or what they are contractually obliged to do, rather than giving of their all. In the gap between doing only what they have to do and going the extra mile lies the difference between acceptable and exceptional performance. Not listening demotivates by reducing feelings of responsibility, control and importance.

The benefits of listening

Genuine listening generates respect, rapport and trust. Productivity is improved and problems solved more rapidly. Miscommunication and conflict are uncovered quickly. People's true motives, values and feelings are surfaced. Ideas and solutions are generated. Most importantly, genuine listening generates shared purpose, values, meaning and alignment – all key to effective teamwork and to high performance.

As we have seen, the purpose of leadership communication is not simply to message; it is to engage. To engage, you have to listen. If you want to be truly inspiring, if you want to win hearts and minds, you have to learn to listen with *great* skill. No matter how senior you are, the chances are that you are not as good at listening as you should be.

I was lucky enough to work for Dr Peter Watson when he became CEO of AEA Technology. Peter was tasked with moving AEAT from a Civil Service culture to a consultancy-based business capable of thriving in a commercial world. Many employees were extremely angry at what they perceived to be unnecessary changes enforced top down. It must have been tempting for Peter to surround himself with a layer of management and hide behind his authority. Instead, he did the opposite: he took away the barriers, went out on the road and had conversations with people everywhere.

Peter chose meetings small enough for his audience to feel personally engaged and for him to hear individual opinions. He listened to everyone's point of view and answered everyone's questions. If he did not know the answer, he promised to find out and respond individually. He always did so. This resonated; people felt they had been heard. Anger began to dissipate, the organization was able to evolve.

Peter understood what every leader needs to understand: the power of the 'listening contract'. This says: 'I'll listen to you and hear what you say and think. Therefore you owe me the same.' The contract is simple, but requires leaders to escape the trap of handing down messages to the troops. Peter faced a largely hostile workforce. Instead of lecturing, he listened. This gained him credit: as he had listened, so people listened to him. His authenticity won them over; they came to believe that Peter himself believed in what he was doing.

Secondly, after meetings were over, Peter acted on the things people said, not only by finding answers to questions but in the way he built and communicated his plans for the organization's future. He capitalized on the benefits to be derived from listening 'beyond the words' by hearing not only the concerns but the positive ideas that lay behind them.

Peter's story demonstrates how listening is one of the most valued attributes of leaders, how it can open up audiences, influence and refocus them on more positive and profitable objectives. It changes behaviours and achieves results.

How good are you as a listener?

Do you recognize any of the following traits?

- You tend to speak more than others.

- You interrupt, and believe this is a natural part of conversation.

- You come to conclusions quickly and form opinions before the speaker is finished.

- You get impatient and can't wait to talk.

- You find yourself thinking about what you want to say instead of concentrating on what the speaker is saying.

- You are easily distracted.

- You make judgements about the speaker.

- You get angry when you hear things you don't like and you show your displeasure, especially at bad news.

FIGURE 9.1 WHERE DO YOU FIT?

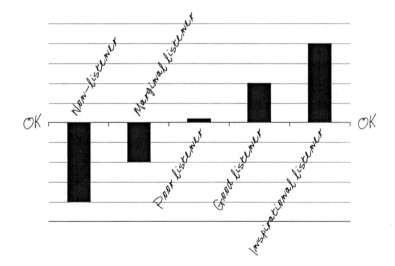

If some – or even all – of these points ring true, then you are a non-listener, or at best a superficial listener. Beware! Not only are you likely to be a poor leader, you might even be disliked.

What about these traits?

- You want to get to the bottom line quickly.
- You want facts rather than ideas.
- You're not interested in how people feel, you just want to know what they've done.
- You often forget what people told you.
- You listen selectively, dipping in and out of attentiveness.

Beware! You may now be a marginal listener. You will be missing a lot of the content and exposing yourself to huge misunderstandings. Worse still, the speaker may leave the room believing that he or she has been listened to and understood, while nothing could be further from the truth.

And what about these traits?

- You actively try to hear what the speaker is saying, but you don't always try to understand the intent behind the words.
- You are more interested in content than feelings.
- You don't try to observe body language and facial expressions, and you stare into space while listening.
- You tend to listen without facial expression, remaining silent.
- You propose solutions as soon as the person is finished speaking.

Beware! You may fall into the trap of believing that you are a good listener, and that you understand the speaker's message. The problem is that you may have missed important clues to what the speaker was really saying and will be puzzled as to why there appears to be little progress because of the conversation. The speaker could leave the room feeling that you had heard but not understood, and remain frustrated. Worse, if you have 'taken over' by giving people solutions to problems when all they wanted was some coaching, they may now feel disempowered and demotivated.

Poor listening is a common trait, and the most dangerous consequence is that leaders are cut off from the information that could prevent a crisis or enable a breakthrough. In today's world, it is essential that leaders create an environment in which people can bring them bad news very quickly. The faster bad news gets to you, the faster you can take action. However, when you display your displeasure at bad news, people will soon stop bringing it to you, and you will be cut off from the very things you need to know to do your job. Indeed, without getting this constant stream of bad news quickly, you may soon be out of a job.

You have to make sure that you don't only listen to those who agree with you. You have to actively seek out those whose opinions and thoughts are different to yours. You have to listen to those who will challenge you, stretch you and even confront you. It is often in this discomfort zone that you will make the biggest progress. And, sometimes, you simply have to listen in order to let people vent.

A seminal moment to do with my own listening

I want to tell you about a moment in my own career, a moment that was seminal for me on the subject of listening. It made me realize that, sometimes, simply listening is the most inspiring thing a leader can do.

The Atomic Energy Research Establishment was formed and based at Harwell, near Oxford in the United Kingdom, in the 1940s. It was the main centre for atomic energy research and development in the UK from then to the 1990s. Pressures on government spending resulted in the Atomic Energy Authority UK having to redirect its research efforts to the solving of scientific problems for industry by providing paid consultancy and services. After several years, the UKAEA was divided into two parts – the first retained ownership of all land and nuclear infrastructure, and remained in government control. The remainder, made up of the scientists and engineers providing consulting services to business, was privatized as AEA Technology and floated on the London stock exchange in 1996.

In 1992, in the run up to privatization, I was appointed as director of corporate affairs for AEA. My job was to lead the communications and change programme that would enable successful privatization of AEA Technology. My CEO, Dr Peter Watson, himself a foremost engineer, appointed me as site director of Harwell.

The irony did not escape me that I had never done particularly well at science at school, nor done any science since leaving school – and now I was director of one of the foremost scientific facilities in the world. I was to act as 'point man' for all AEA Technology employees on the site, and ensure our best interests were met by our landlords.

Harwell was a vast and sprawling site. To me, the site had the feel of a university campus, complete with offices, laboratories, nuclear testing facilities, lecture halls and playing fields. On those playing fields, employees enjoyed lunch-time sports activities from rugby to rounders.

I discovered that rounders (a game like baseball for those who don't know it) was really big at AEA. The employees had a league championship. The Harwell site newsletter reported regularly on the progress of the different teams. In one edition, the newsletter gave offence to the captain of one of the teams, by apparently insinuating that there had been an element of 'gamesmanship' during one of the matches. This so upset the captain that she made representations first to the editor, then her line manager, then the head of communications, and went as high as the then head of the Harwell site (before I took up the position).

No one was able to satisfy her, in spite of a retraction in the newsletter, and she continued to express her dissatisfaction to senior management for some time. This was such an issue that she featured in the briefing note to me when taking up my new role. It became such an intractable problem that even the most senior managers began to fear having to meet with her.

One of my first duties as director of the site was to attend that year's rounders final, when it fell to me to present the trophies to the winning team. I stood watching the match from the table that contained the gleaming silver cups. Chatting with some of my colleagues, I did not notice the approach of the 'infamous' aggrieved rounders captain. My first inkling came when I realized that I was suddenly standing alone at the trophy table, wondering where my colleagues had gone.

She confronted me and asked if I knew who she was. I said yes and asked what I could do for her. She asked whether I knew about her grievance. I said I'd heard about it but did not know the detail. Would she please tell me?

Part of me feared that I would meet with the same failure that had befallen every manager before me. Another part of me empathized hugely with her plight. She had, in her view, been maligned in the newsletter and felt that her reputation had suffered as a consequence. My empathy showed, as I related to her pain, and I kept asking her about what happened next and how she felt about each stage of the process.

Out on the field, I could see the final was drawing to a dramatic close, and that I would soon be required to hand out the trophies. After much questioning, and a lot of tears (from her) I said that I understood what she had been through and asked what I could do to make her feel better. She thought for a while, consulted her husband (who also worked on the Harwell site and who also attended many of the grievance meetings with her) and then surprised me with her response.

She said: 'You're the first person who's really listened to me. Others before you have cut me short, or suggested things before I'd finished, or defended the status quo. I don't know if there's anything you can do but I feel better because you listened. I'll let you know if I can think of something.' With that she turned and left, in time for me to do my official duty.

Months later, when I had still not heard from her, it finally dawned on me that I had managed to resolve the problem no one else had managed to fix. By listening to her with empathy and respect, not defending and not trying to provide solutions, I had at last made her feel understood. I had been concerned about her feelings, and not just the facts. That was all she wanted.

Give people a damn good listening to

The experience taught me that sometimes, as a leader, you simply have to give people a damn good listening to. Only then can they move on. You have to recognize their emotions. By recognizing those emotions, you validate them and show that you understand. By asking questions to clarify, you show that you are interested. By resisting the urge to propose solutions, by simply listening to them and showing that you care, you give them one of the most precious commodities that you as a leader have – your time. That shows them respect, and generates respect from them.

I have spoken about the 'listening contract'. This simply means that you have to listen first in order to earn the right to be heard. When you listen first, you can come to a better understanding of the other person's point of view, where they stand on issues, how they feel about matters, and you can better tune your own communication to their view of the world. Also, when people feel they have been heard, they are much more likely to be receptive to what you have to say.

To be a good listener, leaders have to have a rare mix of humility and confidence and curiosity. They must have the humility to admit that they do not have all the answers, that they do not know everything and that they are prepared to learn from others. To show that level of vulnerability requires confidence, and to be interested in people requires curiosity.

I have said before that great leaders are prepared to take big bets and set stretching goals, even though they are not sure how they are going to attain them. They need only to be sure about and trust their team to be able to find solutions. They need to respect the team's ability to come up with the ideas that will enable success. When people contribute their own ideas to solving big problems or achieving big challenges, they are much more committed to what has to be done. Probably, as a leader, you would already have seen what needs to be done, but allowing other people to get there by giving them a good listening to and nudging them to the solution that they 'discover' for themselves, means that their level of commitment will be higher than you could ever otherwise achieve.

I have heard it said that 85 per cent of what we know we have learned through listening. In a typical business day, we spend 45 per cent of our time listening, 30 per cent of our time talking, 16 per cent reading and 9 per cent writing. Listening is critical and yet less than 2 per cent of the leaders I have interviewed said that they had had any formal learning to understand and improve listening skills and techniques.

The seven essential techniques of great listeners

Great listening is about:

1. active attention;
2. empathy;
3. clarifying and interpreting;
4. questioning;
5. reflecting;
6. summarizing;
7. action.

Let's look at each of these in turn.

1. Pay attention, actively

When you listen, the first thing to remember is that it's not about you. You need to focus on the other person, what's being said, and stop worrying about what you're going to say. Don't listen to have your ego stroked. Look at the speaker directly and put aside distracting thoughts. Avoid also being distracted by things around you. Try to put the speaker at ease by looking and acting interested. Smile and help that person to feel free to talk. This requires others to believe that you really want to listen. They must feel that if they tell you something, it will be received in the proper spirit.

Do your very best to avoid judging. Leaders who are judging are not listening. If you ask questions that have a judgemental tone to them, you will very quickly shut people up. People will also shut up if you keep interrupting them. How do you feel when you are rudely interrupted? If your train of thought is disturbed and you can't thereafter return to your point, it becomes frustrating. Sadly, interruption is a common occurrence and shows huge disrespect. The more people are interrupted, the less they feel like persisting with their point and the result is disengagement.

Conversely, employees respect those leaders that do listen, because they know how difficult listening can be. Leaders earn respect from their peers and their followers by being patient listeners. You have to learn to stay in the moment. Concentrate, or take notes to signal that you are paying attention. Try to clear your mind and give the speaker your undivided attention. If something comes into your mind that needs your attention, make a note so that you can return to it later and remove it from your radar now. Some leaders I know talk of notebooks filled with notes taken during meetings that they never refer to again, because by taking notes they are both retaining the information and sending a signal that what the speaker is saying is noteworthy.

You need to show that you're listening. Nod occasionally, smile and use other facial expressions, and encourage the speaker with small verbal comments like yes and uh huh. Watch the speaker for non-verbal clues – body language, facial expressions and eyes. People can say as much with their own non-verbal signals as they can with their words. Very often, when people are not giving voice to their opposition or disagreement, you will be able to pick up clear messages of negativity if you pay close attention to their body language. The tapping foot, a furrowed brow, clenching fists, bitten nails. These all reveal the feelings behind the words.

Watch out for your own body language – crossed arms or hands folded behind your head are negative signals. Lean forward, nod often, smile – recognize that your own facial signals will be conveying messages back to the speaker.

There are physiological reasons to explain why concentrating so hard is so necessary. People can listen about 5 to 10 times as fast as others speak. In the time it takes the speaker to say 100 words, the listener has the capacity to hear 500 to 1,000 words. It is easy to drift away and find other thoughts entering your head with that difference in speed. Having that much capacity allows you quickly to turn to worrying about the next meeting, planning your presentation, or even thinking about what you're going to have for dinner tonight. One of the keys to effective listening is to use this capacity to analyse what is being said, instead of letting your mind wander.

2. Empathize

Demonstrate that you are aware of how the other person is feeling. They may not express their emotion, but the clues will be there. Name the emotions that you see. If you say something like 'I can see you are angry about this', they can either disagree and tell you how they are really feeling, or they will appreciate that you have recognized their state of mind. Better still, say 'I can see you are angry about this, because you think that...' This will allow speakers to know that you understand how they feel, and why they feel that way. They could just say, simply, that you understand. Or you might say: 'I know how you feel, I've often felt that way myself.'

Don't tell people that they shouldn't feel the way they do. By doing that you are invalidating their feelings. If you try to solve their problems immediately they feel underestimated and disempowered, pressured or even controlled. Most often, what people really want is support, trust and encouragement.

To be able to identify the underlying cause of the other person's perspective, you have to be listening for all the clues as to why they think and feel the way they do. Don't just cynically name the emotions – you need to show that you empathize with how they feel. There is no harm in saying that you too might feel that way in the same circumstances. It will not weaken your stature or your authority as a leader. But it is a powerful way of encouraging them to open up further.

If, however, you allow your own emotions to interfere with your listening efficiency, you will rapidly close down the conversation. You have to listen objectively and keep a tight rein on your temper. If you allow your emotions to run high, you will tune out the speaker, become defensive or even attack the other person. Don't argue with them – even if you win the argument, you lose.

3. Clarify and interpret

Use open-ended questions as often as you can. 'What happened next?', 'How did you feel when that happened?', 'Why do you think they did that?' Use clarifying questions such as: 'Let me see if I am clear – I think you mean this...', 'I'm not sure what you mean, could you repeat that a different way?' I often use the phrase: 'You haven't used these words, but it seems that you are saying...', or 'So you really felt undermined, is that it?'

Beware of too often using: 'Why?' It can be seen as quite an aggressive question, one that forces people to justify themselves. Soften it by saying something like: 'Tell me more about why you chose that option?'

4. Question

Questions are the breath of life for powerful conversations. Learning to ask questions in a non-aggressive way is crucial to good listening. Your questions should be filled with interest and even curiosity. People are naturally inclined to answer questions that are posed to them. If the questions are honest and sensitive we usually answer them. We all respond to questions in a much more positive way than to pointed advice.

When people feel trusted and listened to, they will be much more open to the power of questions. What is the right question? That's hard to say; it might very well be a closed question seeking a firm conclusion, or it might be an open question continuing to explore. The trick is to create an atmosphere in which searching questions can be asked. Try not to clutter your question with your own preconceptions, and especially avoid make a question sound like a lecture. The good leader asks incisive questions, but avoids making people feel beaten up.

Most of the leaders I have spoken with talk about the power of one particular question. That question is: 'How did you feel about that?' The reason it is such a powerful question is that it invites people to share their emotions with you. It is a powerful way to get to the bottom of issues very quickly, especially if people trust you enough to answer honestly. It is a valuable shortcut to getting to the real issues quickly. Until people have given expression to their emotions, it can be difficult to have a constructive discussion about how to solve a problem. Leaders have to give people the licence to be emotional.

You have to listen for what is not said and ask the questions that will surface the things that have not been expressed. Listen for opportunities in between the words. True wisdom doesn't see opposition, it sees only opportunity. Where are the opportunities in what you are hearing?

5. Be reflective

A key listening technique is to rephrase what has been said. Reflect what the other person is saying to you, but make sure it is not in their words. It requires immense concentration, but when you reflect things back to people in different words, it can often help to crystallize or clarify an issue. By repeating things back in your own words, you also allow people to correct you if you have come to inaccurate views about what they are saying. Remember, your goal is to understand, and reflective listening is the most important technique to use to ensure understanding.

Do not simply parrot what they say, and avoid using reflective listening to develop data that you then use to move in with solutions, evaluation, judgement or even punishment. Use reflection with discretion, making sure that it aids progress and is not interruptive. Never assume that you understand the other person. The biggest challenge of communication is believing that it has actually taken place. Until you have checked the meaning with people, you are in danger of wrongly interpreting what they've said. Learn to listen beyond the words, and listen with your heart and your eyes and your ears.

6. Summarize and thank

Either at the end of a conversation, or periodically through the conversation, it is powerful to summarize what you have heard. Use the phrase 'What I hear you saying is...', or 'What I have heard so far is...' You could even ask the other person to summarize. This is the moment to make absolutely sure that you understand each other, in order to move on. If you now want to make some of your own points, the other person will feel much more able to listen to you now that you have demonstrated that you understand their point of view.

Never forget to thank people for sharing their thoughts with you, especially when they open up and reveal their innermost feelings, or contribute ideas. Even if you really don't think that they delivered you any value, thank them for their time and input anyway. Remember that your job as a leader is to build relationships and trust. If you even go so far as to praise them for the way they express themselves, you will see people blossom before your very eyes.

7. Commit to action

Leaders must have a bias to action. Listening is all about action – it is about drawing people out so as to take action based on what they say. It is about getting people to focus on what good things they do that should be done more often, encourage them to try new actions that could generate better results, or stop doing things that are not productive.

When we listen, we are listening to learn, listening to share or listening to act. For example, we listen to our market or to our people in order to know what they think about us, our services and products. We listen to staff because they know about things going on every day that we don't. We listen to all this data, to all these ideas and we learn. When leaders listen this way, they are likely to make much better-informed decisions. Sometimes, we listen in order to start or join conversations. This is listening to share.

Listening to act is the secret key to leadership. It enables change. When we listen to act we are positively seeking out things to do, barriers to remove, ideas to implement, people to bring together – anything that enables us to get closer to achieving our goals.

Always end a listening session by summarizing and then suggesting key next actions. Make a note of them and follow up. When you take actions but don't tell people, you are missing a huge opportunity to further build the relationship. People will be far more committed and engaged when they believe you will act on what they've said.

There are, of course, times when you have to take control of the conversation and steer it in a different direction. This is more palatable when you first demonstrate that you've heard the speaker, and then state that you have a different perspective. You may also decide not to act on suggestions. All of this is in your remit as a leader. However, it is often cowardly not to explain why you are not going to take action. Explaining can further understanding and builds respect. At very least, it can further the relationship. Leaders are respected and trusted when they explain their decisions, even if people don't agree with the course of action to be taken. If they feel their views have been heard and their point of view has been respected, it will be much easier for them to go along with the decisions and commit to the actions.

Listen up, down and all around

Great leaders listen up, down and all around their organizations. They listen to individuals. They ensure that they meet with people in small groups, and have informal listening sessions with them over breakfast meetings or in the evenings. They hold town hall meetings with larger groups of employees, and encourage open debate and challenging questions.

(Most of the leaders I know, are always better and more convincing as speakers during the question and answer sessions of town halls. They may have delivered a brilliant opening talk, but it is when they answer questions that people see the real leader. They see the person who has strong views and can respond to questions with passion and knowledge. Or, they see the leader who is humble and says 'I don't know' when asked a question for which they do not have the answer. They can see the leader committing to finding out or committing to sorting out a problem, and they are more inspired during these sessions than by any formal speech.)

Even if they can't attend them themselves, leaders often systematically organize focus groups in order to hear employee ideas. They listen to employee surveys and pay close attention to what people are saying about the organization. They worry about poor engagement levels and are constantly tuning in to the mood of employees in order to make sure their organization is working optimally. Many even use the systematic listening techniques I outlined in the previous chapter, making listening routine in their organizations, checking that feedback is moving rapidly from the front line to wherever decisions need to be made.

These leaders do not only listen to people inside the organization. They listen to all of their stakeholders – customers, commentators, competitors and communities of interest. They bring what they learn back into the organization to encourage the conversations that improve performance.

Wherever they are, whoever they are listening to, great leaders use big, powerful, evocative questions. The five most powerful questions I know are:

- What do we do around here that we should keep on doing?

- What should we stop doing, and why don't we?

- What should we do better or do more, and why don't we?

- What should we start doing, and why haven't we?

These '4 x Do' questions are incredibly valuable, because they enable leaders to find out about strengths, weaknesses, opportunities and threats without sounding like a management consultant. The questions are straightforward and extremely productive. However you phrase them, they are easy to ask and get people engaged in talking about the key behaviours that impact on your business. When you ask the questions consistently at all levels of the organization and in different parts of the organization, you can quickly build a view of key actions you need to take. They work because they reveal unknown barriers and stimulate inspiring ideas. (These questions are also closely linked to the engagement ladder explained in Chapter 7, as well as the communications planning process explained in Chapter 8. Both of these are about the communications necessary to change behaviours and improve results.)

The fifth powerful question to consider is: 'What would you do if you were in my shoes?' I have often seen leaders use this question, and it provokes some very thoughtful responses, often surfacing ideas for action that might not otherwise have been considered. It forces the speaker to put themselves in the shoes of the leader and give a very considered response.

One of my favourite quotes is from Doug Larson, a United States newspaper columnist. He is widely quoted on the internet, but this one is a gem: 'Wisdom is the reward you get for a lifetime of listening when you'd have preferred to talk.'

How people react to poor listening

Recently, one of my managing directors came to see me – at my request – at the end of a brutally long day. I had asked him for an update on a big project he was leading on my behalf. I was tired and anxious to get on with some reading I had to do for a meeting early the next morning, with one of our most important clients. Worse, I had forgotten what the meeting with him was about, and told him so. Every signal I was sending told him that I was in no mood to listen.

He made a valiant attempt to bring me up to speed, but ran out of steam when he saw how distracted and impatient I was. I didn't bother to ask any questions, and at the end of his report I simply offered a weak thank you and a half-hearted congratulations on the progress he had made. He left the room and I could see from his body language how dispirited he was.

All that night I was bothered and feeling guilty about how badly I had treated him. The next day I visited him in his office and frankly admitted to how badly I had performed the night before. I apologized and said that I had not given him a good listening to and would he mind telling me again where he had got to?

This time I listened more attentively and with much greater enthusiasm, asking more questions and showing a lot more interest. His own body language and enthusiasm was dramatically different, and I could tell that my apology and second attempt to listen to him had gone a long way to repairing the damage I had inflicted the night before.

I had not offered solutions or suggestions during either session. The only difference was how enthusiastically I had listened. The outcomes could not have been more different. At the end of the first session he went away disillusioned and demotivated. By the end of the second session, his enthusiasm and motivation were back again.

As I have already said, listening is one of the most important behaviours of good leaders. It is the one that employees most desire, but it is most often the one they feel is least delivered. Employees watch leaders for their behaviours and scrutinize their actions for the signals that tell them what their bosses think is really important. If they pick up the signal that their bosses don't think listening is a good thing, then you can be assured they will, in turn, not bother to listen to their own followers, peers and other colleagues.

Talking of sending signals, leaders are often unaware of how their behaviours impact on their followers, and are shocked and dismayed when they learn how what they do is disrupting the organization – very often in ways that are the polar opposite of what they are trying to achieve, as we will see now...

Sending signals
How you inspire – or demotivate – without saying a word

The gap between your actions and your words is potentially one of the most toxic to your leadership effectiveness. When leaders make sure that there is no gap between their deeds and their words, their inspiration quotient rises dramatically. This chapter gives you a guide to sending more positive signals.

This is one of the shortest chapters in the book, but possibly the most important, because it will almost certainly be the one subject about which you are least aware.

As a leader, everything you do is an example to others, and you are being watched closely all the time. Your body language and your behaviours are being assessed by your followers every moment of every day. Your followers will come to their own conclusions about the right way to behave... from the way you behave. They will see patterns in your behaviour and they will take their cues from those patterns, not the words you utter.

The gap between your actions and your words is potentially one of the most toxic to your leadership effectiveness. It is one of the main reasons that people mark down their leaders. When leaders make sure that there is no gap between their deeds and their words, their inspiration quotient rises dramatically.

It is as simple as this: if you don't understand the behaviours of your team, you almost certainly should be taking a look at your own. If everything you do is an example, and you are being watched closely all the time, then your actions are also being assessed by people who will be coming to their own conclusions about the right way to behave, the acceptable ways of getting things done around here or what really matters to you, and they will shape their behaviours accordingly.

I have seen this time and again in companies – more times than I can remember. I have stopped being surprised at how surprised leadership teams are when they get that feedback.

> 'It is your own behaviours that are negatively affecting the organization, and not that your staff are simply trying to be obstructive.'
>
> 'What?!! What do mean my behaviours – I could not be more clear about what I tell them.'
>
> 'Yes, but what you tell them is conveyed not only through your words, but also through your actions. And what they see you doing is confusing/ upsetting/demotivating them.'
>
> Silence.

Over the past year, I have worked with four different leadership teams in four very different companies. They are businesses you would recognize immediately, and their brands have definitely touched your life in very different ways. The work I was doing was to help them to articulate a compelling purpose and a clear set of values, and involved interviewing each of the members of the executive management teams, as well as many of the next level of senior managers. (Most executive committees in companies have between 8 and 10 members, including the CEO, and each executive committee member has between 10 and 15 direct reports, which gives a substantial number of interviews.)

In every case, these leadership teams were guilty of behaving in ways that created dissonance in their organizations. Their followers were very clear – their leadership behaviours sent powerful signals into the organization that people recognized, spoke about and acted on. As a result, what was happening in the organization was the exact opposite of what the leadership team was trying to achieve.

We have all been there. The conflict – when it exists – between what we are told and what we see with our own eyes has a dramatic effect on our attitudes. At best we will lose faith in our leaders and try to achieve our goals in spite

FIGURE 10.1   THE SIGNALS YOU SEND

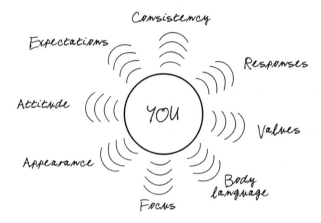

of what they do, not because of what they do. At worst, we can become confused and demotivated, and our performance drops off dramatically.

It is in your behaviours and what you focus on

Let me give you an example. In one of the companies I worked in, the leadership team was trying to create much greater collaboration across the divisions of the business. It was imperative if they were to improve customer satisfaction ratings, which had plateaued and were threatening to start waning. The leadership team could not understand why they could not improve co-operation between the departments. They were exhorting their teams to do so daily. However, our research showed that staff felt the leadership team was divided and its members were actively speaking out against each other, pursuing individual and competing agendas. The CEO was shocked, as were all of the executive directors. The CEO encouraged robust debate at his weekly executive meetings, in the belief that this was the only way to achieve robust solutions. The only problem was that the robust debate did not stop when the executives left the CEO's meeting room. They continued to argue with each other in e-mail exchanges that were copied to their subordinates for example, thinking that the signal they were sending was that they were open and challenging with each other, which is what they wanted from their staff. Wrong. The signal wasn't taken that way. Far from encouraging collaboration, it encouraged staff to see collaboration as dangerous to their own careers.

As their bosses were so outspoken about the silly ideas of their peers, there was no way that they would take steps to work with people in other departments when they knew their own director was openly opposed to the suggestions of his opposite number. It took considerable effort to convince staff otherwise and repair the damage.

In another case, as a reward to his executive management team for six solid weeks of 18-hour days, my CEO client treated his directors and their wives to a special dinner at a fashionable restaurant in London. His team had been working on a cost-cutting programme, essential to improving margins when revenues had temporarily stopped growing. He failed to see the irony in his action, but his staff did not. As one employee noted: 'It is a curious signal you send when you take your top team out to a lavish and expensive dinner, and then come back to the office and tell us to cut costs in every possible way.'

In this case, the leadership team was horrified. What had been a gesture of thanks was being interpreted as hypocrisy. They had not thought the issue through, and I'm sure that if they had they would have been much more mindful and found another way to recognize the efforts of the top team.

Everything you do is an example, and everything communicates. Decisions you make, policies you put in place, things you do or don't do, issues you fail to act on – all of these communicate more clearly than your words. If you say that sales are the most important thing to achieve but then you focus on cutting costs, guess where everybody's attention will be! If you constantly bang on about the need to achieve great results but then give just one poorly performing person a break, you will confuse everyone around you. As uncomfortable as that is, leaders have to recognize that they send signals beyond the words they use. A truly adept leader uses this to his or her advantage.

It is in your consistency

How often have you heard people talking about how unpredictable their boss is? One day, the boss will serenely ignore failure and calmly discuss ways to solve the problem. The next day, he or she will explode into a rage and it will be days before you can talk to him/her again. A classic case of Jekyll & Hyde. I am afraid that this is all too common, in the modern workplace. Acting consistently with people – whether it's big new client wins, client losses or simple mistakes – will be key to creating a positive working environment for all your staff.

Ask people whether you send consistent signals into the organization through your behaviour. Remember that your signals are dangerous when they are ambiguous, because different people will interpret them in different ways. That's why there is power in consistency.

For this reason, articulating minimum standards of behaviour, and then consistently reinforcing those standards, is one of the most important things a leader can communicate. Even if people don't like what you require of them, at least they will know where they stand and know that you will be even-handed in the way you deal with people.

It is in whether you live the values yourself

Mostly, you have to model the behaviours you want and you cannot demand things of people that you aren't prepared to do yourself. If you are the leader of a business or team, it means that you have to be an exemplar of everything that business stands for. You can't do things that seem hypocritical when compared with the things you say. That's very dangerous.

The biggest danger is saying that you want one thing but inadvertently sending a message that says you really don't. This is a communication phenomenon called meta-messaging. A meta-message is an unspoken, implied message that we unknowingly deliver when we are communicating. The meaning of the meta-message is so strong that it overwhelms your message and leads to people interpreting what you say very differently. Meta-messages can kill trust and openness in the workplace. The very worst of these other meta-messages are those around company values. If you put the values up on a poster on the wall but all of your behaviours are inconsistent with the values, then people will treat the organizational values with the contempt they deserve.

Why go to the bother of putting values up if you have no intention in following them? It would be far better not to bother, because you would then at least not be creating dissonance – the ultimate thief of credibility.

I often advise leadership teams to be very specific about defining the behaviours that they need to deliver as a team in order to exemplify the values of the organization. This requires thinking about the behaviours that will send powerful signals into the organization, agreeing to abide by them, and holding each other to account when you don't deliver on them.

It is in your responses

How you treat individuals when they are undergoing a personal crisis will be noticed. How you set your organization to respond to bigger crises, perhaps facing colleagues in other parts of the world, will be noticed even more. Whether you recognize birthdays, marriages or personal successes will say a lot about you.

I was once walking with a very stressed CEO from a boardroom to his office, when a secretary walking in front of him slipped and fell on a wooden floor. The CEO stopped and watched as another PA rendered assistance. He said nothing, and then resumed his journey to his office. I thought little of it at the time, because I know that he did stop to check that the secretary was being attended to. His head was filled with other things and he needed to make some crucial phone calls as his business was facing a major crisis.

The next day, I kept being told about how the CEO had simply ignored a member of staff in distress, and had cold-heartedly walked past her even though she was hurt and embarrassed. How he responded to the situation was misinterpreted, but widely transmitted the next day. His credibility as a leader took a severe dent.

Many of the leaders I have dealt with say one of the hardest signals they have to send is that of standing up to be visible, even during very difficult times. When things are at their most uncertain, and when there is honestly nothing to say because there is no news that will help anybody, simply showing up to listen to people and hear their concerns is an act of courage that wins enormous kudos from staff.

Being visible and available is a powerful signal of integrity.

It is in your body language

Consider the negative messages that leaders can send to followers when they are not conscious of their facial and body language:

- a sense of lack of confidence or trust in an employee;
- the degree to which the leader accepts the feelings of employees;
- implicit acceptance of inappropriate behaviours;
- his or her own negative feelings about an issue;
- their own lack of commitment to a course of action.

These are powerful messages that no leader would want consciously to fire into an organization. Without knowing it, we react to people every day on the basis of what we see when we look at them and observe their facial expressions and their body language.

Leaders must always remember everything that is expected of them, including that they should always be positive in their appearance and in the way they behave towards people. How we are feeling is reflected in how we stand and walk. Non-verbal communication reveals to the world how we feel inside, so it is critical to achieve emotional mastery if we are to prevent our body from sending signals that may be at odds with the messages we wish to communicate. How you hold your head, where you put your hands, whether you fold your arms – all of these send signals.

Negative body language is leaning away from someone, crossing your arms or legs, looking away to the side, rubbing your eyes or the back of your neck, or (my personal favourite) folding your hands behind your head. Positive body language includes moving or leaning in towards people, having relaxed uncrossed limbs, long periods of eye contact and genuine smiles.

It is in your expectations

When you expect the best of people, it's amazing how often they deliver. If you expect the best, you unconsciously send the best signals. By expecting the best, your approach and your body language towards your team changes. You look forward to interactions with them, you like to hear about their progress and you delight in their high achievement. When you don't expect much of someone, even if you say nothing, that will show as well and they will not surprise you.

Go and search 'The Pygmalion Effect' online. It is a classic and controversial piece of research that showed that the greater the expectation teachers placed on students in an experiment, the higher the performance. It was named after *Pygmalion*, a play by George Bernard Shaw. Apparently, the opposite is called the Golem effect, in which low expectations lead to a decrease in performance.

In the experiment, teachers were given a list of students who had been identified as 'high achievers'. The teachers were told that these students would deliver remarkable results. At the end of the year those students did deliver great results – even though they were, in reality, not high achievers and had been chosen at random from the pool of pupils. It turned out that it was the teachers' belief in their potential that was enabling their exceptional results, a belief that was never communicated directly to them, but was constantly communicated through non-verbal clues. The teachers unconsciously conveyed empathy, likeability and approachability. When dealing with the pupils, they did not use any 'power' behaviour and would give more positive feedback, would display encouraging body language whenever they dealt with them, and regularly gave many other signals that showed approval and encouragement.

It sounds absolutely too good to be true, but university researchers have found the Pygmalion effect to have positive outcomes with all sorts of work groups. Simply by holding a positive expectation, this is communicated and has an influence on whether the team delivers outstanding results. It is how you inspire without words.

On the other hand, when you send signals of status, power and supreme confidence, by standing tall, keeping your head straight, minimizing facial expressions and speaking in a forceful tone of voice, you are very unlikely to engage people. There are occasions when such signals are needed, but you need to be conscious of how you are using them.

It is in your attitude

As a leader, you have to take responsibility for the fact that it is you, more than anyone else in the team, who impacts on how people feel in the office. How you make them feel determines their engagement, and their engagement determines results, for which you are ultimately responsible. As the boss you have a disproportionate power to make people feel important or unimportant depending on the signals you send. Everything you say or do is hugely amplified by the position you hold, and even the mildest telling off can create feelings of unimportance.

Ask yourself how you feel about feeling important. This ties directly to your sense of self-esteem, and the link between self-esteem and performance is straightforward. Like President Bill Clinton, if you treat every employee as if she or he is the most important person in the company, you will have a dazzling effect on them.

I have often said that if you tell people exactly what to do, you are far less likely to achieve great results than if you encourage them to come to the answers themselves. To do this you have to listen to them, ask the right questions and lead them to the solutions. They will feel important because you've given them your time, you've taken an interest, and they were able to propose a solution that you agreed with – and now they'll not only be committed to the action, but determined to deliver a great result.

The work environment is crucial to people's levels of enthusiasm and engagement. It isn't only about desks and seating and paintings on the wall; it is mostly about the atmosphere – and that's determined by you.

It is in your appearance

When I first started out in sales, my boss decided that I was to take up golf. His view was that, in sunny South Africa, being a golfer would enable me to network and lead to relationships that would result in more sales. He was right. He was also clear from the outset that I had to look like a golfer, so he personally accompanied me to a golf professional store one day to oversee the clothes, shoes, bag and kit that I chose. He was the ideal boss, because he also got me membership of a golf club and instructed me to attend the club every Wednesday – the only rule was that I had to make sure that I was there with a client or potential client.

Although I had dabbled in golf up till that point, I had never really felt like a golfer. And the first time I stepped out onto the course in my matching golf outfit and kit – to my surprise – I really did feel like a golfer, and I carried myself with much more confidence simply because I looked the part.

There is a lot of truth in the need to look the part. People do judge you on your appearance, which is the first filter through which you communicate. Looking like a leader is the first step to becoming one. If you want to portray executive presence, you must have a degree of gravitas and excellent communication skills as well as a polished appearance. Personal grooming matters a great deal. Many of the leaders I interviewed specifically told me that they looked at personal grooming and were swayed enough to decide against candidates very quickly if they did not come up to standard. This does not mean having to wear a suit if the company culture is for casual clothing, but it does mean making sure that you don't have unkempt attire – wrinkled, dirty or too tight clothing. Clean nails, shiny shoes, manicured nails and a good haircut all send signals. Be aware and take more care.

Send signals to yourself

How we hold ourselves can change our minds, and what's in our head changes our behaviour, and our behaviour determines results.

Being a leader means looking, acting, walking and talking like a leader. Leaders who clearly love what they are doing, who show it in everything they do, in every expression, are hugely infectious, not least to themselves. Great leaders communicate positivity and optimism, and they often do it through a smile, or by walking with energy, or by standing straight and tall. People definitely notice.

I read recently about Charles Garfield, the author of *Peak Performance*, who told about how facial expressions had an effect on the performance of the Russian Olympic weightlifting team. Apparently Garfield noticed that when weightlifters were lifting to the point of exhaustion, they would grimace at the painful effort. He encouraged them to smile when they got to that point of exhaustion, and this enabled them to add more weight and further improve their performance.

They were sending signals to themselves. Grimace says this is a difficult job, and your brain actually sends stress chemicals into your blood. The more stressed you are, the more difficult things become. On the other hand, when you smile, the signal you send yourself is a positive one. You most definitely can do this.

Never forget to recognize, encourage and thank

Bosses are always challenging. That's how they got to where they are – by always demanding more, seeing opportunities, never accepting second-best. They have a powerful vision and drive people to success. As a leader, you would have no purpose if there wasn't a reason to try to improve performance.

However, if this is a relentless and joyless pursuit that is not counter-balanced by a number of other softer qualities, the danger is that you are simply going to be seen as a hard and relentless task master. You will be seen as constantly critical and disapproving.

One of the most important signals of all to send is that of gratitude, by recognizing great performance when you see it. It amazes me how poor most leaders are in this area. I frequently ask the direct reports of the leaders I work with about how they see their leaders, and the area that is consistently marked lower than others, is that of recognizing contributions from others. Saying thank you and recognizing good work is so easy and so powerful that I am at a loss to understand why more leaders don't spend more time doing exactly this.

Holding little celebrations when people achieve landmarks, sending thank you notes, telling stories about people on your team who have done well, singing their praises in the newsletter – all of these things send the most powerful signal of all: that performance matters and people who perform are important. Celebrating achievements is a way of making high perform-ance more visible to everybody in the organization, and sends them strong signals about the behaviours and standards that are required. It is win–win signalling that I simply cannot commend highly enough.

Conduct signal audits

For all of these reasons, I now advocate the idea of doing signals audits in your business – to make sure you understand what signals you are really sending. Ask employees what behaviours they see from their leaders, and what they do as a result. I bet you'd be surprised at the findings.

Purposeful, persuasive stories

11

How you can use stories to drive action and shape culture

> *Stories have an emotional power to persuade that gives them the edge over pure logic. As leaders, we are all about persuasion, so we have no choice but to master the art of storytelling. Not only are stories the superglue of messages, but they also help to animate us and supercharge our passion. Here are the six steps to more persuasive stories.*

You'd think I would want to start a chapter on storytelling with a story, but I don't. Instead, I want to talk about the way we listen to stories.

Why? Because stories engage the brain differently from logic, and this is the main reason stories are so important to leaders.

When we listen to a story, we use different parts of the brain from those we normally activate in discussions and talks. During a formal presentation, we use only one part of the brain – the language-processing part in our left brain. Listening to a presentation, our inner cynic also engages to challenge what we hear, to filter it through our own perceptions and experiences. By tomorrow, we most likely will have forgotten most of what we heard.

When we listen to a story, however, we engage not only the language-processing side, but also the other parts of the brain that we use when 'experiencing' the events of the story. If the storyteller describes the smell of coffee, say, our sensory cortex kicks in; if he describes a roller coaster ride, our motion cortex fires up. When we listen to a story, we start to co-create the story, imagining the scenes, engaging our senses, and – most importantly – suspending our critical faculties. In this way, messages get through. Our right brain is engaged alongside our left brain – painting mental pictures, making connections and finding the emotional side of the story. A story transcends intellectual argument because it puts our whole brain to work, not just one part of it. Because of this, stories are more memorable.

We are far more likely to consider very different viewpoints with a story, because it puts us into a more receptive state of mind. We are more open, and we set aside our limiting beliefs and values and opinions. We become so engaged with a good story that we turn it into our own experience. How often have you heard a friend or colleague telling your story again, as if it were their own? They might not remember it was you who first told them the story, but they remember the story!

Head, heart and soul listening

That is one of the main benefits of a good story, well told. Unlike a dull slide presentation, by tomorrow, if the story is well told, we will still remember it. We listen to stories with our heads, our hearts and our souls. And, because we are emotionally engaged and moved by the story, we are motivated to behave differently.

One of the earliest coaching habits I learned was to stop trying to tell my clients what to do, and instead tell them a story. First, I would try to get them to realize the action they needed to take by asking them a lot of searching questions. If that didn't work, I would tell them a story – something from my own experience that was similar to the problem they were experiencing. The effect has nearly always been dramatic. Even though my clients might not reach exactly the same conclusion I had in mind, they used the story to relate to their own world and create their own idea for action from the story.

And that is the point: a story enables you to package your message so that it is understood – uniquely – by every listener.

Why do we respond to stories this way? Because we are wired to think in stories all the time. Whether we like the idea of storytelling or not, we tell them all the time. Most of the day, every day, we are gossiping about colleagues, friends and relatives in story form. We are born experts in both story listening and storytelling.

As children, we naturally love stories and are excited by them. That excitement for a story never leaves us, but gradually, through school and university and our early careers, we learn to think that logical argument is better. We are taught to present our key messages in PowerPoint slides, and we come to believe that this is the way to persuade.

In their heads, the listeners are arguing

Because of this attachment to logic, many leaders struggle to communicate successfully, let alone inspire people. They get lost in company jargon and their messages are met with cynicism. A leader's job is to motivate people to achieve objectives. To do that the leader has to engage the emotions of followers. However, leaders tend to construct logical arguments that discuss challenges and actions, building the argument with statistics and facts and quotes. In their heads, the listeners are arguing. They have their own statistics and facts and quotes. Even if the arguments are powerful, even undeniable, they may not have reached the heart, the seat of action.

London Business School's Emeritus Professor of Organizational Behaviour, John Hunt, produced a study on 'Introversion among CEOs'. It revealed that:

> the majority of people who moved to top jobs are not all the smiling,
> hearty, extroverted types espousing vision, values and emotional stimulation
> described in popular reviews. In fact, whether in the private or public sector,
> CEOs are more likely to be introverted, task oriented and private individuals
> who do not find the drama expected of leaders comes easily.

Professor Hunt found that 70 per cent of the 105 CEOs he surveyed were trapped in logic and analysis, and uncomfortable about displaying any vulnerability. On the other hand, research by Cognosis Consulting of 1,600 managers in the UK discovered that the success or failure of any business strategy depends significantly on the 'emotional engagement' of employees and front-line managers. Leaders, said the research, need to go beyond 'reason' and conceive strategies that are not only intellectually astute but that also have real 'emotional edge'. Here, then, is the vital gap. While most leaders are introverted, task oriented and logical, employees and other stakeholders want emotion. Again and again, I have found that stories can move people and fill this vital emotional gap.

Leadership is persuasion

Stories have an emotional power to persuade that gives them the edge over pure logic. And as leaders, we are *all* about persuasion.

Persuasion is at the heart of leadership. We persuade employees to believe in our cause, to work smarter, and faster and more efficiently. We persuade our financiers to give us more money; we persuade customers to buy our product. Persuasion is what good leadership communication is all about, and stories are the most persuasive tool in the armoury.

There are other reasons stories have the edge. We live in an age of information overload. Stories cut through. Stories are sticky. They create those 'Eureka' moments by enabling us to share great 'truths' without being abrasive and confrontational. They allow us to deal with issues and problems and challenges without having to instruct or preach. Stories can kick start the difficult conversations you need to have to improve performance. With stories, you can challenge, enable, inspire and encourage the behaviours your organization needs from all of your people.

Stories have emotional power in ways even the best-crafted presentation can never match. Logic may get to the brain, but stories get to the heart. I learned this painful lesson when working in the 1980s for the CIA. (No, really, I did!)

Obviously, you are thinking of the Central Intelligence Agency. I mean the Chemical Industries Association. At the time, I was employed by Bayer, the chemicals and pharmaceuticals company. I was based in Newbury, Berkshire, in the UK. The CIA (the Chemical Industries Association) was running what it called a national 'Speak out and Listen' campaign. This required people from member companies of the chemicals industry to go out and talk to local communities all over the country, at Woman's Institute meetings, at Round Table meetings, at town hall meetings and in schools. The idea was to show that people were at the heart of the chemical industry, and to try to explain more about what the industry did that was positive in people's lives. The CIA prepared a brilliant PowerPoint presentation, gave me my speaking notes and I was all set for my first encounter with the public.

I had rehearsed and rehearsed the presentation and felt I was pretty good at it. My first presentation was in the local town hall, and I went along eager to do my talk. There, I showed an audience of more than 100 people slides of chemical plants, great photographs of the products of the chemical industry – from the steering wheels in cars, to bricks and medicines. I walked people through the history of the company and I talked about how much of a contribution we made to the UK, and to Newbury in particular. I used all the charts and graphs and statistics the CIA had given me. It was a fantastic data dump.

Unbeknown to me the organizers had also invited a speaker from Greenpeace. After a scattering of polite applause for my presentation, the next speaker stood up and told some terrible stories about the chemical industry. They weren't factual, they were not even necessarily true, but they were powerful and they were emotional. The crowd turned against me. I feared for my life. As soon as a lot of hostile questions were over, I slunk from the town hall, now eager to end one of the most embarrassing and difficult evenings of my life. The next day I promptly wrote to the CIA and told them that I would no longer do 'speak out and listen' events.

Some months later, we held an exhibition in our foyer at Bayer for our neighbours. Our offices were set beside a residential area and we literally did have neighbours. The exhibition showed how chemicals went into furniture materials, into running shoes, into car steering wheels and hubcaps and dashboards. It showed how our pigments coloured the bricks our neighbours built their houses with. It put on display drugs such as aspirin that Bayer had invented, tennis rackets and other sports equipment – none of which could exist but for chemicals and plastics from Bayer. I stood and watched as our local neighbours studied the exhibition, examining each and every exhibit, amazed that they were enthralled by what they saw. The next day I phoned the CIA and said they should put me back on the 'speak out and listen' roster, but from now on I would do the talks my way. For the next couple of years I became a sought-after speaker, as I arrived at various events with my 'box of toxic chemicals' – all the exhibits that had so enthralled our neighbours when they came to our exhibition. I would start by telling people to stand back from my box of toxic chemicals, much to their bemusement. All they could see was a box of everyday household items – which was exactly my point.

Then I would tell people the story of how Bayer workers at a dye factory were responsible for inventing aspirin. I told them about how our synthetic pigments enabled them to have colourful bricks in their homes, without which every house would simply be a dull grey colour. I told stories of science, of problems solved and great innovations. They loved them. Once I had told them all these stories and handed out the exhibits for them to study, I would then open the floor for questions. Never again did I encounter a hostile audience, and every time we had a robust, healthy and mutually respectful debate. The lesson was clear – people love stories and people love props. Not only did those stories deliver messages, but they created relationships and built trust. Never again did I use a PowerPoint presentation.

Stories, metaphor and props: the ideal mix

In my office I have a 10-inch-high wooden elephant. It was given to me by a colleague returning from a visit to South Africa. He thought it would make me feel more at home. Or perhaps he thought it might encourage me to go home? Either way, I have kept that elephant for years, simply as office decoration. Lately, however, I have been putting it to different use. When I have to have a difficult conversation with a member of staff, I put the elephant on the table and say: 'In this office, we always talk to the elephant in the room.'

The prop serves as an ideal metaphor that enables me to raise a difficult matter, one that everyone is aware of but does not address. It also does so with a dash of humour that lightens the moment. People laugh, but now we can get on with discussing the difficult issue.

A good metaphor, allied to a good prop, is a powerful way to communicate.

We use metaphor all the time. For example, we talk about 'planting seeds' or 'being stabbed in the back' or 'missing a piece of the puzzle'. Everyone knows that we are not really planting seeds, nor really putting together a jigsaw puzzle, and, hopefully, not really sticking a knife in someone, but our audience understands exactly what we mean. Metaphor is an easy and visual analogy that can simplify the complex and provide a shortcut to understanding. Good communicators consciously use metaphor to engage the audience. However, they are highly aware of the danger of using metaphors that are so clichéd that they have lost meaning.

Metaphors such as 'run out of steam', 'draw a line in the sand', 'level the playing field' are in danger of being overused. Research shows that overused words and metaphors are simply ignored by the listener and lose their effectiveness.

To avoid this trap, all you have to do is put a twist on an old metaphor in order to use the familiarity that comes with it so as to engage the audience in a different way. Take the metaphor 'kick things off', for example. Sigh. Tired, isn't it? You could provide a fresh twist to this by saying: 'Let's kick things off the right way… [pause…] and by right way I mean right off the edge of a cliff. We have to start again.'

Or how about 'Finding a needle in a haystack... is easy when you're holding the end of the thread to which it is attached'? It doesn't take much to give a new twist to an old metaphor.

You could, if you want, use the metaphor of a football team – to get your point over. Let me give you an example. A recent poll of 23,000 employees from a number of companies and industries found that:

- Only 37 per cent said they had a clear understanding of what their organization was trying to achieve.
- Only one in five was enthusiastic about the organization's goals.
- Only 15 per cent felt that their organization fully enabled them to execute.
- Only 20 per cent trusted their colleagues and were prepared to collaborate with them.

If this was a football team, it would mean seven of the 11 players didn't know what they were on the field to do. Eight didn't really want to be there. Only two felt they were able to do anything about winning, and only two were prepared to work with their team mates to achieve the goals. I ask you: How much of a chance does this team have of winning?

When you combine metaphor with prop and with good story you have a potent ability to engage.

Purposeful stories

Given the power of storytelling, it strikes me as really odd that some of the leaders I have spoken to simply don't like the idea of telling 'stories'. Perhaps they feel that stories are for children only and that they do not have a place in business? Instead of the word 'stories', they are often more comfortable with using the word 'anecdotes'.

From my many interviews with leaders, I have collected hundreds of business stories. Whether these leaders described them as anecdotes or stories, made little difference to what they really were. These were what I now call 'purposeful stories'.

And it was clear that these leaders really loved telling their stories because it was striking how, when they told them, their whole demeanour changed. They became more animated and expressive, they used their hands more, they leaned into me, and they became more authentic and persuasive. They became much more human when they resorted to stories, often being self-deprecating – talking to their personal quirks and failings. They used stories to tell me more about themselves. They spent even more time making heroes out of their staff in the stories they told.

I can remember every single one of these stories. When I studied them, I made three important discoveries. First, every story had a point, a provocation designed to stimulate thinking and action. Second, all the stories all had similar structures. Third, there were six places to look for stories.

Let's look first at the concept of purposeful stories.

What is a purposeful story?

Leadership stories are designed to change the way you think and to stimulate action. That means that stories are carefully chosen to achieve objectives. This means knowing exactly what you are trying to achieve with the stories you tell. To achieve a purpose, you have to think about what people will take from the story. And that means that you have to know the audience, and use your story to connect and resonate. A purposeful story has a strong core – and will have substance, sincerity and a great truth at its heart. It will be entertaining and thought-provoking, and usually have a call to action.

Selecting the right story starts with selecting the takeaway first. You have to know what you want the listener to believe, understand or do when you've completed the anecdote. The key principle, as always, must be to change behaviours and achieve results.

A story to illustrate how stories work

I'd like to illustrate my point by repeating a story that I told in my book *The Language of Leaders*. The story was about my encounter with the safety director of a home construction company. His name was 'Steve' and I was called in because he was being ineffective in his communication and adversarial in his style. The HR director who brought me in said that although Steve was passionate about his role as head of health and safety, he was actually angry and controlling all the time and was having an adverse effect on staff morale.

People had no sense of what drove him or why he pushed so furiously for every last detail to be checked. Steve fumed that his people 'weren't paying attention', hated that they merely responded to crises and never sought active ways to tackle problems or bolt the fine points down.

We dug into his beliefs and values to find what really drove him. Steve told me how, at a previous company, a boy had strayed onto one of his sites. He had managed to get through a gap in the fence after everyone had gone home, fallen into a deep pit excavated for foundations and had been severely injured. In pain, bleeding profusely, he died alone in the night.

Steve took on the agonizing responsibility of telling the boy's mother himself. It was his duty, but it was the most harrowing experience of his life.

It was made all the more bitter when he learned the gap in the fence had not been secured by one person in his crew. The pit too had not been protected properly by a different member of his crew; by themselves, minor omissions, but a confluence of details that proved fatal.

Steve's credo became that no detail was too small when it came to health and safety. No one could have mistaken the strength of his feeling when he told me, 'I never want to have to tell another mother that her child has been in an accident on one of our sites.'

I advised Steve to go and tell that story everywhere in the organization. Every chance he got, he was to tell that story without making any other points. 'Just tell that story and then get out,' I told him. His story, when told, had a profound and positive impact on his business.

Steve's entire workforce saw why attending to such details of health and safety practice was important, and responded wholeheartedly. His story moved them in a way that rules and regulations never could. Authentic, based on his strong point of view and entirely appropriate to his organization, it changed behaviours and raised the benchmark for safety. His people did what was right whether he was there or not, and were happier doing it.

Initially, Steve had acted rationally in pursuing a strategy of active health and safety for his company, but this alone left him frustrated and his people cold. His story channelled his passion and produced a win–win for all the stakeholders – especially Steve, who now knew what his integrity could achieve.

This story has six essential elements, the crucial components that go to make up a powerful and purposeful story. In a few pages I will deconstruct the story for you, and show you how you can construct your own compelling stories that will help to drive change in your own organization.

Time for a new story

First, however, I want to tell you the different story, one that contains the same six essential elements. Both these stories are very different. In the first, the subject of my story used his story to change the culture of a whole organization. It was a one-to-many story. This next one is an example of a story I used in one-on-one coaching.

Recently I was coaching one of my senior consultants. He had been exhibiting a tendency to rush into action without properly thinking things through. Sometimes he was lucky and quick action delivered rapid results. Often, however, he took hurried action that had unintended consequences, creating more work – unnecessary work – and costly complications. I wanted him to think about the need to pause and reflect before rushing into things. I wanted him to understand that sometimes doing nothing was a better option.

I told him this story of a recent journey home:

'Every day I commute by train from London to my home in Oxfordshire on a 40-minute journey. Last Friday, at the end of a long week, I could think of nothing but getting home to a glass of wine, putting my feet up and enjoying a late sunset with my wife. I really, really wanted to get home quickly. When I finally boarded the train, I began to relax and anticipate the weekend. Opposite me was a friendly businesswoman. We started a conversation. Just then an announcement warned us that there would be a delay because of a death on the line a few stations beyond mine at Didcot. Those of us wanting to stop at Didcot should leave this train (currently on Platform 1) and get on board the train now waiting to leave on Platform 10. Difficult choice. Stay comfortable and wait for hours? Or make the sprint across the station to ensure I got home early? I reluctantly excused myself and dashed across the station.

Aboard the train on Platform 10, I soon learned that this too was delayed. A fresh announcement said that those of us travelling to Didcot should now hurry to Platform 5 instead, as that train would leave 'in five minutes'. In a panic, I hurried from the train on Platform 10, but bashed my arm on a protrusion on the train door as I left. Great pain. Checking to see that my suit was not torn, I suddenly remembered that I had left my raincoat on the train on Platform 1. I ran from Platform 10 to Platform 1, clattered aboard the train and greeted the businesswoman with whom I had been chatting. By now, I was sweating profusely. She looked startled as I grabbed my raincoat and excused myself again, running back to Platform 5, where I managed to get aboard with seconds to spare.

I sat down, looked at my watch, and realized with horror that blood was pouring from my sleeve and dripping from my fingers. On investigation, I discovered that whatever I had bashed my arm on had gouged a chunk of skin from my arm, which was now bleeding profusely. Luckily it had not yet soaked through the sleeve of my suit jacket, which I took off to save it from ruin. Using my pristine white handkerchief, I bandaged my arm in order to stem the bleeding. Quickly, the handkerchief soaked with blood.

Using my smart phone, I discovered that the train I was on was not going all the way to Didcot. I was going to have to change trains again. I looked up online how I could connect to Didcot from Reading Station where this train would drop me. I saw that I could connect to my train, but I would have to hurry because I had just three minutes to cross four platforms. Running all the way, carrying my briefcase, my raincoat and my jacket, I made it just in time.

By now, I was a sight to behold. My collar was open, my tie undone. I was sweaty, dirty and bleeding. There was one spare seat that I could see, so I made my way over and literally fell into it, panting. Can you guess who was sat opposite me? It was the businesswoman from the train on Platform 1! She looked at me with a mixture of horror and amusement... and we began to laugh. We had both made exactly the same progress, only I was much the worse for wear. "Sometimes it pays to just sit tight," she said.'

Upon hearing the end of this tale, my senior consultant also broke into laughter, but I could tell that he had got the point. I did not have to say any more. He understood everything I was telling him about his own tendencies, the consequences of rushing about without thinking things through, and the need to stay calm in the face of urgent distractions and sometimes just do nothing.

A few times since then he has urged me to repeat my story, simply for the amusement of others, but in the meantime, his decision-making performance has improved.

The structure of a good story

Any good story must have heroes and villains and insurmountable odds if it is to be entertaining. But it must also follow a basic structure (see Figure 11.1).

1 *The lifeblood of any story is a great desire, an overwhelming need, a challenge or significant problem.* A keen desire or need drives our behaviours and motivations. Your hero must have a goal. In the case of my train story, the desire was all about wanting desperately to get home early. This is a pretty banal, if perfectly understandable, goal. In business stories you will usually seek to bring to life much bigger goals and aspirations. In the story about 'Steve', the safety director, the challenge for me was being brought in to deal with an ineffectual but passionate leader.

2 *A protagonist to care about.* In my train story this was me, tired at the end of a long week, keen to get home to my loving wife. Could

FIGURE 11.1 THE ESSENTIAL INGREDIENTS OF A COMPELLING STORY

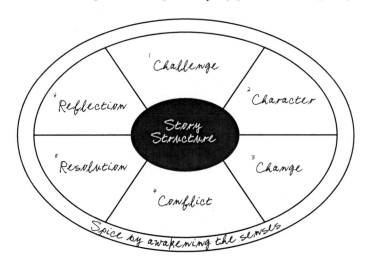

you see me with my feet up sipping at a cold glass of Chardonnay? It could just as well be a young man struggling to pay his way through university, a scientist devoting her life to finding a cure for the disease that killed her father, or a mad inventor obsessed with the idea of making a wind-up engine to power generators in areas without electricity. In the case of the story about 'Steve', it was him – someone powerfully motivated by a tragic past.

3 *The status quo – about to be interrupted.* Every movie or TV show you see will involve people going about their normal lives when, suddenly, fate intervenes to disrupt the status quo. What happens next is all about change. Whether people respond well to the change or fail to meet the challenges it throws up becomes the point of the story. In my case it was the death on the line that was about to cause interminable delays. In the case of the business story, it could be about the arrival of an innovative competitor or a disruptive technology that changes everything. In the case of Steve, the interruption to the status quo was me arriving to give him a good listening to.

4 *A conflict to resolve, followed by trials and tribulations.* Will s/he succeed or will s/he fail? Every memorable story is made by the severity of the obstacles or the insurmountable odds our hero has to overcome. In the case of my railway story, this was me rushing

about the station, bashing my arm, forgetting my raincoat, using technology to find my way, but staying resolute in my determination to find the train that would get me home. Going back to the scientist seeking a cure for the disease that killed her father, it could be about her struggle to find funding, and several blind alleys with research that turns up nothing new. For Steve, it was his struggle to deal with his haunted past, which turned him into an aggressive boss.

5 *A turning point leading to a resolution.* This was me arriving on the final train to find the businesswoman I'd befriended in the seat opposite me, with us both dissolving into laughter at the irony. For the scientist, however, it could be the discovery of the compound that leads to a new medicine that can now save millions of lives. For Steve, it was the realization he could channel his anger and past into a story that could help him achieve his goals.

6 *Reflection.* Help the audience to understand what they are supposed to get from the story, but don't be blatant. In my railway story, this was about me and my serene lady friend realizing we had both experienced very different journeys to get to exactly the same point. Whose journey had been the more pleasant? In the case of our scientist, it would be that perseverance and a tireless belief in a cure led to ultimate success. For Steve, it was that even the most personal of experiences could be turned into a story that could change the culture of a whole business.

See? Every story you ever read or hear will have this basic structure.

Flavour the dish to appeal to the senses

Now, you need to flavour this dish so that you awaken the senses. Notice how I become increasingly *hot* and *agitated*, *sweaty* and *bloody* on my train journey? Notice how I clattered on to the train and *collapsed, panting*, in my seat? Could you see the bright red blood on my *pristine white* handkerchief? The more vivid I make the images, the more your brain engages in co-creation, imagining the scenes and 'seeing' the story. Notice also how I keep the punchline to the very end and tried also to keep you from predicting the end?

I stress again that most business stories will be more dramatic than the one I have just used, especially if they are designed to move not just one person, but a whole organization.

If you boil it down to essentials, most stories are about a *problem*, the *solution* and the *benefits* of the solution.

- *Problem?* A hungry wolf wants to eat the three little pigs.
- *Solution?* Build a safe house. The first two pigs try and fail, but the third succeeds with a robust brick house.
- *Benefit?* The pigs take safe refuge in the house, while the wolf self-destructs by falling down the chimney into a pot of boiling water.

The best stories either deliver a powerful lesson or highlight a great and resonating truth. Through these stories, people identify with the issues, and the leaders who tell them become truth tellers to their followers.

Where to look for stories

Great stories are everywhere in your organization, and in your past experience. I often get asked about where to find stories, and I am equally often told that an organization does not have enough stories to tell. Poppycock. Perhaps it was my journalistic training, but I have never, ever been short of good stories. I find them all over the place whenever I go into organizations. Fascinating stories that tell you about the organization's culture, beliefs and behaviours. Stories that tell of breakthrough discoveries and delighted customers, heroic staff and supportive suppliers. The real issue is about being able to tune in to good stories. You have to learn to be alert to those that you can retell, or be alive to incidents in your own experience that can be turned into a story.

Once you have found them, keeping a note of them is crucial.

I often give my clients Moleskin notebooks to use as story databanks. I tell them to keep them in their jacket pockets or handbags. Every time they hear a good story, they should write it down. If you do this, you will soon fill it up! Simply pay more attention when you hear something interesting. Let part of your mind be recording incidents as they happen to you, because every experience can be turned into a story. There are various places to look for stories (see Figure 11.2):

- *Stakeholder needs stories*
  Listen out for stories about customer needs, or experiences of your organization both good and bad. Do the same with suppliers,

FIGURE 11.2 WHERE TO LOOK FOR STORIES

shareholders and other stakeholders whose views are relevant to your own business. This will help you to build a rich picture of external views of the organization, and enable you to talk to the needs they all have of your organization. These stories can be the most compelling. A need is a problem unsolved.

- *Strategy stories*
  Try to bring your strategy alive by telling a story about a day in the future. What will be happening and why? How will you be measuring success? Why will this be important to people? Who will be benefiting most? When you tell a story about the future as if it already exists, it becomes a powerful motivator. Demonstrate your purpose at work, or how a member of staff has moved you closer to a strategic goal.

- *Values and behaviours stories*
  Watch employees and find examples of them living your values, or not, as the case may be. By doing this you make heroes out of

your employees at the same time as reinforcing the values you really want to see everyone else living. Every day your employees are making choices, deciding to go the extra mile and do something extraordinary for clients or customers or their colleagues or even their local communities. These are the heroes you need to talk about – much more often.

- *Quality stories*
  Find stories that demonstrate the extraordinary lengths people in your organization go to when producing your products, or how much research has gone into developing a service.

- *Stakeholder benefit stories*
  Use the customer's voice to describe the benefits of your products – or how one product benefits lots of customers in lots of ways. This will be one of the richest areas of all to explore. As a leader, you should have dozens of these stories. (See Chapter 6 for much more detail.)

- *The 'who you are' story*
  Think of the seminal experiences you have had in your career, the ones that have shaped what you believe and how you make decisions today. Craft those into stories that you can tell. Not only will the stories say something about you, but you will also be able to share knowledge and your own values through them. The more you can find ways to tell the stories in a self-deprecating way, the more people will relate to you.

The transformational story

Nearly every leader I know has had the experience of what I call the transformational story. This is the story they used to transform the culture of an organization. This was 'Steve's story'. It is the story that sets the organization off on a new quest or transforms behaviours in the organization because people suddenly understand the impact of what they're doing.

It could come from any one of the six sources above, but this will always be a story that is often repeated, and that is used in a consistent way to drive home the point everywhere in the organization. The difference with this story is simply that the leader will tell the same story everywhere over and over again in order to ensure consistency and ubiquity.

How to tell them well

First of all, it helps to really love the story you're telling. When you do, you will naturally get your audience involved in your story by using your voice, hand gestures and facial expressions. The more animated you are, the funnier or livelier your story will be. When telling the story about my search for a train to get home, I mimic the action of bandaging my bloody forearm, or wiping my sweating brow, or carrying an invisible but heavy briefcase.

It's important to use descriptive terms that appeal to the senses – sights, sounds, smells all enrich the story.

Make eye contact with the audience and show that you care that they are getting your story. It will also make them more attentive.

Use pauses for dramatic effect. This takes practice but adds hugely to the quality of the story, especially to funny punchlines.

Don't rush the punchline. Milk the story, but don't make it too long. Remember, also, that suspense is key to holding people's attention all the way to the end – can you tell the story in such a way that the ending is *not* predictable?

Never start a story by telling the listener how he or she should feel. I hate it when people start by saying: 'You're going to love this story!' What if I don't? Now I'm under pressure and I can't relax because you have an expectation of me that I might not be able to deliver. This is a distraction I don't need.

Beware of tiresome phrases and over-emphasizing. If you emphasize every-thing, nothing will have emphasis. If you use tired phrases, your listener will bore quickly.

Always, always, always perform your story many times before taking to the stage. When I am coaching leaders on storytelling, I insist that they tell me a story at least three or four times. Together we will refine the story until they tell it with as much brevity, clarity and character as they can muster. Then, I insist that they tell their stories in front of a mirror to ensure that they use facial expressions and animate their stories. Only after at least 20 tellings will I unleash them on the stage. The same applies when you are telling a story to groups of people across the business. The more you practise the better you get. When you hear people responding to parts of the story, you will learn to polish those parts and even – sometimes – embellish the story to get the best reaction. Never manipulate stories to tell untruths, but a little garnish in the form of embellishment here and there can give you the spice you need.

When to refrain

Sometimes, you just know the audience doesn't want a story. When my CEO has asked for a forecast for the remainder of the year, he wants a factually based prediction, not a story that is likely simply to annoy him. I might choose the right moment to tell the story of how a new contract was won in order to gain his approval for investment in more people with the same skills as those who won this contract, but I absolutely have to judge the moment.

The worst mistake is to tell a story before you or the story are ready. There is nothing worse than launching into a story and then stumbling, losing momentum and losing your audience. Even when you know that a story that springs to mind may be singularly appropriate, if you haven't practised, my advice is to refrain. I have sometimes told a story many times, just testing it on people, before taking it into a public forum. I like to know how people respond to the story before I use it in earnest.

I may have made you think that I'm against logical argument, but I'm not. There are many times when charts and statistics and flow diagrams are far more appropriate. It all comes down to knowing the audience, knowing the need and knowing the best way to achieve your objective.

Narrative or story?

There is, I believe, a difference between a story and a narrative. A narrative brings together a series of stories in a timeline to create context and meaning. It is an account of connected events and enables you to tell a bigger, more strategic story.

The narrative needs to explain the business background, your vision, your purpose and strategic objectives, in order to provide the wider context necessary to make individual stories more meaningful (see Figure 11.3).

In this way, the story relates to a single incident that is deep with meaning, especially when seen within the context of the overall narrative.

Vitaly Vasiliev is the CEO of Gazprom Marketing and Trading (GM&T), a wholly owned subsidiary of the world's largest gas producer, the Russian energy business OAO Gazprom. GM&T's principal activity is the marketing and trading of energy products, including natural gas, electricity, LNG, LPG, oil and carbon emission allowances in the UK, continental Europe, the United States, Asia and other world energy markets. It also engages in

FIGURE 11.3 NARRATIVE VS STORY

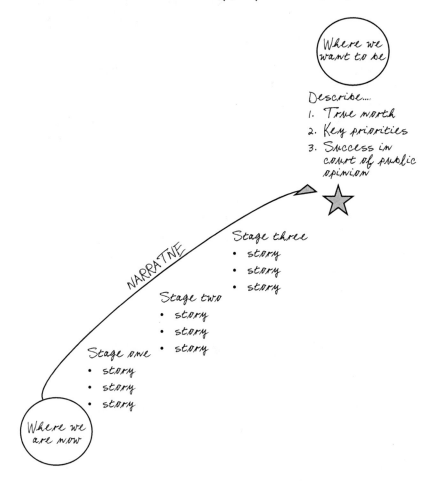

Where we want to be

Describe....
1. True north
2. Key priorities
3. Success in court of public opinion

NARRATIVE

Stage three
• story
• story
• story

Stage two
• story
• story
• story

Stage one
• story
• story
• story

Where we are now

the charter and sub-charter of vessels as part of the group's shipping and logistics activities.

GM&T has achieved more than a decade of growth, from a small office in London with just a few people to a truly global presence today. The growth has been extremely rapid, and the challenges for Vitaly and his leadership team have been considerable.

One of the challenges has been that of recruiting people into the business and bringing them up to speed with the culture and business plan as fast as possible. To do this, Vitaly decided to write a book with the help of his staff, one that explained the history, culture and strategy of the business.

Entitled *The Energy to Succeed*, the book sets out to create a vivid snapshot of GM&T today. As Vitaly says, its purpose is 'to help people understand where the company has been, where it is going and what it is going to take to hit our targets fair and square'. He explains:

> 'We decided that we would get people from all over the company to tell their own stories about how we have developed, how they see the culture, and how they see our unique, multicultural, global business... We wanted everyone to participate and work together to create a valuable tool that would explain why we play such an important role in the world, how energy is a critical factor of success for all our clients, and why we aim to provide energy in ways that are more flexible and innovative than anybody else.'

At 109 pages, the book describes the company's True North, its strategic priorities and the key needs of all of its customers, and provides a platform for staff to talk about the values of the organization, bringing them to life with stories and examples that show how the culture drives effectiveness. It literally is a corporate narrative, populated by a lot of different stories narrated by members of staff for members of staff.

How storytelling changed a CEO's leadership

This is the story of a leader in crisis who discovered authentic storytelling to gain an 'emotional edge' that helped to create motivation, buy-in and belief where before there was none.

Hannah was the London-based CEO of an international conglomerate of manufacturing companies. The origins of the company were male and British colonial but Hannah was European and grew up in the Middle East. Nevertheless, she rose fast; Hannah did not fit the company archetype but succeeded because she was driven, commercial and always kept the bottom line in sharp focus. In short, she delivered results.

When her parent company radically changed its business model, it moved much of its manufacturing to the developing nations from which it once took only raw materials. Hannah was tasked to drive the change from London against tight deadlines while simultaneously downsizing the London office. It was a big ask. 'I had people I needed to do hectic and important work. They all knew that if they were successful they basically worked themselves out of a job.'

When I arrived, I found Hannah's people understood the project; they could see it was rational. But from senior executives down, they were detached, confused and fearful about the future. Hannah needed to deliver 'people' results – discretionary effort in adverse circumstances – but her customary focus on the bottom line was not connecting. The work began to grind to a halt. Her people needed more.

It was when we dug down together into Hannah's strengths that we made the key discovery. 'Since I was a child fairness was very important but I've never really associated it much to the business. I always believed my private person was other than my business person.' Hannah's 'split personality' was a revelation to her:

> 'As we went through the process, it suddenly hit me that you can't split one person out of the other. Because I found that basically even with all my commercialism, at the end of the day the things I would chose to do in business are about doing the right thing – giving back something better than I got, being fairer.'

I showed Hannah that her 'two selves' were actually compatible. Mapping her strengths onto the needs of the organization produced a powerful fit since she genuinely believed her company was 'doing the right thing'. It made a huge difference to her communication style. 'I started sharing with people. The story was still the same story – we were doing this because it was more commercial, but it was also the right thing: the resources belonged to these countries. But the way I engaged with people, I got into the emotional more.'

Hannah began to listen more and use many more stories to celebrate and inspire:

> 'I used all sorts of stories from other people in the company. Lots of examples of people behaving with integrity, behaving according to the values, some of them very small but making it much more human. Some were stories that I'd heard many times before, some came because as you start talking to people you hear more.'

Hannah saw her new story-driven approach produce measurable results:

> 'Beforehand I was much more businesslike. But giving time for talking to people about things which are not just "One, two, three, here's what I wanted to tell you" created buy-in to the vision. I saw people relate to the change. They connected to the stories, looked at the issues and thought much more out of the box. Before it was about "We have to do this, but I will do what I have to do and that's it", now they are actually willing to try and find better, more creative solutions.'

Achieving this 'emotional edge' delivered benefits to Hannah's organization at every level. Her staff were motivated, her senior executives engaged in ensuring best-practice change management. Everyone could answer the inevitable question 'What's in it for me?'

> 'I got them energized, committed and realistic, willing to look beyond "I'm going to lose my job" into "Well how am I going to do it best." It was pride – people had pride in what they were doing. It made life so much better.'

There were direct benefits for Hannah too:

> 'I had a corporate communications department where I was signing things off half-awake. I am giving much more time and attention to communication now. I'm more attentive to detail and the small things, whether I'm chairing a board meeting, meeting ministers and presidents or talking to consumers and staff. The process of being true to myself, and telling more stories, gave me more confidence to do what I'm doing: it's a challenge and I love challenges.'

Stories are the superglue of messages

A storytelling organization is a healthy organization. Stories are incredibly powerful ways of getting messages across, and are the superglue of messages. Great stories have legs and travel far; they can define you or your organization. Choose them with care and always make sure they reflect your point of view.

PART IV
The leader outside

Use a potent point of view to power your leadership

How to develop a persuasive standpoint to win friends and influence people

> *What you stand for matters more in a transparent world. For this reason, the best leaders always have a potent point of view to influence people and win the day. But how do you choose the right one, and how do you structure it to be compelling? Here are the four essential ingredients of a powerful point of view.*

Leadership *is* persuasion. This is a crucial truth of leadership. Every day we have to persuade people to believe in our cause, to believe in the future we see.

To achieve that future, we have to persuade employees to work smarter and faster and more efficiently in pursuit of our goals. We have to persuade our financiers to give us more money. We have to find ways to persuade customers to buy our products or services. We have to persuade our bosses to give us more resources or allow us to embark on a particular project. We have to persuade colleagues to collaborate. The list is endless.

To be persuaded, people need to understand how we see the world, what we believe in, and what benefits will derive from what we are proposing. They need to feel the force of our passion and our belief. Without a compelling point of view, it can be exceedingly difficult to persuade, especially when there are competing views or there is strong opposition to our plans. Stories definitely help, but to be of maximum use they have to stem from and serve a potent point of view.

But what is a potent point of view? How is it different from an opinion? What elements should be in a point of view to make it powerful? How can you supercharge your point of view to be more persuasive?

What is a point of view?

First of all, let's examine what a point of view is. I often get asked about the difference between a point of view (POV) and an opinion. When I use the phrase point of view, I have a very specific meaning in mind. And a formula.

The dictionary defines '*point of view*' as 'a manner of viewing things; an attitude; a position from which something is observed or considered; a standpoint'.

It defines '*opinion*' as 'a judgement formed about something, not necessarily based on fact or knowledge'.

Exactly right. To me, a point of view and an opinion are fundamentally different. Your point of view will seldom change – because it is based on the things you believe in, on the things you are prepared to stand up for and on your view of the world from the position you occupy. Presumably, the leadership position you occupy and your basic beliefs and values will be constant for some time. An opinion is subject to change, and is much more about your view of a subject based on how much you understand about it now – which could change with more information or insight.

You are going to be much more constant with your point of view, especially when it is in opposition to that of your critics and detractors. We will see later in this chapter why that matters, and how and why it can win you the day. We will also see how a point of view can power thought leadership, and why that matters too.

A key part of the definition of a point of view is the word 'attitude'. Attitude is described in the dictionary as 'a complex mental orientation involving beliefs and feelings and values and dispositions to act in certain ways'. A point of view should embrace *all* of these things. It should be an expression of what you think and believe about the world you operate in, it should describe how you behave every day as a result of those beliefs, it should take a stand on issues that are important, and it should call on others to act and behave in the ways you believe necessary.

Essentially, a point of view is an expression of what you stand for, and in a radically transparent world where everyone is connected and can express their own views, it is increasingly important to have one, and make it public.

There is no longer a 'mass audience'; instead we are dealing with a majority of minorities, an ever increasing number of niche interests needing to be addressed. For example, fast-food chains have to deal with obesity groups, health groups, anti-litter groups, farmer's groups, consumer groups and so on. Middle-ground consensus is no longer possible because your issue gets aired in a thousand different debates and discussed at the edges the whole time. Your actions will be praised and pilloried at the same time. You and I, in the middle, hear wildly contradictory views – a juxta-positioning of extremes.

One of my favourite quotes comes from Michael Eisner, a leader in the US entertainment industry and for 10 years CEO of Walt Disney Company. He said: 'The best leaders always have a potent point of view. What amazes me is that it is always the person with a strong point of view who influences the group, who wins the day.'

And that's a key point. You have to have one, already formulated, about the issues of importance to you. You can't make one up on the hoof. Once you have one, it is like carrying with you a loaded gun. You may not need it, but when you do it is already loaded and ready to be fired at your target.

Only one point of view? Or do you need many?

I believe you should have an over-arching point of view – one that explains your purpose, as well as points of view on crucial issues that relate to your purpose. Your main point of view explains why you exist, whether you are the leader of, a business, a charity or a public sector organization.

Earlier on in this book I gave you my meta-point of view. To remind you, it was this:

'I believe in leadership. I believe that in the modern working environment, leadership has been undervalued, over-criticized and underappreciated. Yet great leaders can make a huge difference in people's lives. Great leaders can make great places to work, they can help organizations grow and prosper, and they can alter the destiny of our lives. Great leaders can secure the wealth of nations and make a positive difference to many thousands of people. We need to encourage and liberate the responsible and inspiring leader in everyone.

Because of this belief, I have made it my mission to make leaders more effective by making them better, more inspiring communicators. I do this by one-to-one coaching, by training and by writing books that can help leaders everywhere. By doing this, I hope that I can make a significant difference to many thousands of people, not just the leaders I can make more inspiring, but also the many more followers of the leaders I help.

Every person who is or aspires to be a leader has it in them to be an inspiring leader. They simply need to learn about what it really means to be inspiring, and abandon their preconceptions about inspirational leadership.'

There are four essential ingredients in this point of view, which I will explain in detail later.

You already know the 12 other strong points of view I hold on effective leadership communication – they are expressed as the 12 principles in Chapter 3. Underpinning this are the values I live my life by, and their relevance to leadership. All of these I can present as points of view.

You may also need points of view on the key issues that may affect your business or your customers.

All of these POVs should be interdependent. How many you need depends on your circumstances. Once you have a meta point of view, you can much more easily form related views, using my formula, as we will see later with the example of global security company G4S.

There is another reason you need powerful points of view – and that's because of the negative effect of *not* having them.

The toxic effect of not having a point of view

Many leaders I know run the risk of being bland, remote and apparently rudderless. They opt to champion the inoffensive and innocuous, at least in public, by remaining silent on every issue lest they draw attention to themselves. What they don't appreciate is that having no point of view can be more toxic than having a controversial one.

People don't respect leaders who don't have a point of view. Leadership often means having to take a stand for what you believe, converting people to your cause and getting them to think and act differently.

Not taking a stand leads to a lack of clarity and direction, or to people not making decisions. It causes high levels of ambiguity. Ambiguity can paralyse teams. People lose confidence in leaders who are unwilling to make a clear and decisive stand. People will spend all their time trying to second-guess what the leader really wants.

Taking a stand while withholding emotional commitment is equally confusing. Agreeing something intellectually but not committing emotionally leads to being seen as disingenuous, inauthentic or even disengaged. If you do not show the required commitment, then why should others? A point of view is impotent without the passion of visible values.

When you do witness someone taking a stand, with powerfully argued logic backed up by passionately held beliefs, the result can be completely compelling. It is leadership in action.

The four essential ingredients of a powerful point of view

People trust the motives, judgement and competence of leaders less now than just five years ago. They see so many failures, so much media criticism, so much apparent focus on ruthless profit, and they hear so much logical argument about what is good for business and growth, what is good for the organization but not its publics, and so little about how good leaders are good for society, that they have come to believe that most leaders are exclusively self-motivated and therefore not to be trusted.

Winning trust is essential to effective leadership, but people will not trust those they do not feel they know. To convince people to your cause, you need to let them know more about who you are, what you believe in, what you stand for and how you see the world. In my view, this has never been more important. Yes, you need logic and facts, but you especially need passion and conviction in today's transparent, hyper-critical world.

Expressing your *beliefs* is therefore a crucial part of a convincing point of view.

It is all very well talking to your beliefs, but people will still be suspicious if they feel you are simply speaking empty words. They need to be convinced by your actions too. You don't always have time to let people see your actions speaking louder than your words, so you have to give them evidence of your behaviours, and link those behaviours to your beliefs.

Your *behaviours* need to be expressed in a potent POV, alongside your *beliefs*.

All behaviours have a consequence, so your behaviours need to be beneficial if people are to be converted to your cause. You need to explain how your beliefs drive your behaviours, and how your behaviours deliver *benefits* – benefits specific to the people you are addressing.

If you are able to express these elements powerfully and concisely, you have a strong POV – but now you need one more element: the call to *action*. After all, the reason you are expressing a point of view is to convert people to your cause and influence their behaviours. Unless you specify the behaviours you desire, how will they know what to do?

My formula?

POV = BBBA (BELIEF, BEHAVIOUR, BENEFIT, ACTION) (See Figure 12.1.)

It means being certain about how you think, about how you see the world from your position, what you believe as a consequence, how these beliefs drive your own (or your organization's) behaviours, the benefits derived as a result, and how you think others should behave.

A powerful point of view is one of the most important tools of inspirational leadership. As I have said, leadership is often about taking a stand.

FIGURE 12.1 POINT OF VIEW

Belief	...the things you believe about the world, based on your unique perspective and experience
Behaviour	...the things you do as a result of those beliefs
Benefit	...the benefits your stakeholders get from your behaviours
Action	...the things you'd like stakeholders to do as a result

This means being courageous and speaking up about what you believe in, and persuading people to your cause so as to get them to act differently.

Speaking out on what you believe in shows your followers that you have a moral compass and are worthy of their trust. It gives them the confidence to follow you. As a leader, you are going to have to stand up and give your point of view time and time again. A powerful point of view generates trust: it shows people where you are coming from and allows them to align with you.

Too few leaders think about developing points of view, yet when well-articulated a point of view can help you win friends and influence people, and gain a stronger voice in shaping the future. Once you have them, they are liberating: you will be able to use them on all sorts of occasions and you will look for occasions to use them. Leaders should be talking to important issues more often, with more transparency, more conviction and, yes, passion. Having a point of view is an inseparable part of building a personal brand and determining what your leadership will be about, what issues you will lead on and even come to champion.

It's what others are looking for and why they will listen when you speak.

A point of view in action

Let us now deconstruct a point of view, using the formula BBBA. You are familiar with what I see as my purpose in life – but how does my purpose manifest as a POV? The truth is, it *is* a point of view. Here's how it is constructed.

- *Belief*: I believe in leadership. I believe that in the modern working environment, leadership has been undervalued, over-criticized and underappreciated. Yet great leaders can make a huge difference in people's lives. Great leaders can make great places to work, they can help organizations grow and prosper, and they can alter the destiny of our lives. Great leaders can secure the wealth of nations and make a positive difference to many thousands of people. We need to encourage and liberate the responsible and inspiring leader in everyone.

- *Behaviour*: Because of this belief, I have made it my mission to make leaders more effective by making them better, more inspiring communicators. I do this by one-to-one coaching, by consulting and training, and by writing books that can help leaders everywhere.

- *Benefit*: By doing this, I hope that I can make a significant difference to many thousands of people, not just the leaders I can make more inspiring, but also the many more followers of the leaders I help.

- *Action*: Every person who is or aspires to be a leader has it in them to be an inspiring leader. They simply need to learn about what it really means to be inspiring and abandon their preconceptions about inspirational leadership.

Let me give you another example of a POV in action. In Chapter 4 I talked about the importance of being yourself better, and I gave examples of my personal values. One of them was *curiosity*. How would I express this value in a POV?

- *Belief*: I believe that if you are not learning every day, you are dying.

- *Behaviour*: That means that I take time every day to learn something new, and give free rein to my curiosity, especially about other people. I never let a question go unasked and unanswered, no matter how stupid it might sound.

- *Benefit*: What I get out of this is unexpected opportunities, new relationships, new perspectives, constant delight and, hopefully, a wiser view of the world. I find I am luckier than most, because I am discovering opportunities and making connections all the time.

- *Action*: I think that you should learn to liberate your curiosity, ask more questions and take more time to find the answers to questions that come to mind. You'll find that serendipity will work in your favour too.

When you take away the scaffolding of *Belief, Behaviour, Benefit, Action*, a point of view comes over as a short, sharp and coherent story. It gets attention, it makes people think, it exhorts them to behave differently.

Deconstructing a company's point of view

Now, let's look at an example of a point of view developed for a previous client of mine, G4S, the global security services company (formerly Group 4 Securicor). G4S is headquartered in Crawley in the United Kingdom and is the world's largest security company. It has operations in more than 120 countries and employs more than 620,000 people. (It is one of the world's largest private employers) In the UK, during the 2012 Olympic Games, it suffered reputational damage by falling short on the provision of security personnel for the Games venues. Nevertheless, G4S is still a highly successful, international security outsourcing business with few peers.

We built a strong POV for G4S long before the Games scenario, with a specific purpose in mind. At the time, the business was one of the largest in the world, but also one of the least well known. People saw G4S uniforms everywhere, and simply thought 'security guards'. The company, however, does far more than guarding. It provides security solutions in scenarios where security and safety risks are considered as strategic threats. At the time, not enough people understood enough about why G4S was important to them. The company stated that its purpose was: 'Securing your world.' But what did that mean, and why was it important?

The answer is simple: because everyone's welfare and prosperity depends on having a safe and secure environment in which to work and live. For this reason G4S has a vital role in society.

Also, people saw security and risk management as a cost, a necessary evil. They did not see it as a value – adding revenue-generating service – so they pushed it down the line and procurement of risk and safety services was disaggregated and decided at low levels in client companies. Few recognized the potential benefits that could be unlocked from a more holistic perspective and more integrated security solutions. We had to flip perceptions of security on their head to engage and educate at the top level of client companies. The strong POV also had to:

- enable enhanced relationships at all levels, but increasingly at senior levels, in customer organizations;
- help people to see G4S as a 'critical' partner for clients;
- achieve competitive differentiation;
- transform meetings into sales opportunities.

After a root and branch research exercise, several workshops and final approval by the leadership team, this was the G4S POV:

- *Belief*: Our welfare and prosperity depend on us being able to operate in a safe and secure environment. Sadly, in a world increasingly full of risk, we have to focus even more on our security challenges. When we do, however, most of us focus on the downside. At G4S, we believe that in every security challenge there is an opportunity to unlock hidden benefits that can help us to thrive and prosper.

- *Behaviour*: The key to releasing wider benefits for our clients is to always look at the bigger picture and consider solutions that transform performance. To do this, we deliver world-class project management that brings together our expertise in logistics, technology and managing the world's biggest force of security personnel, and the knowledge derived from providing security solutions in diverse regulatory environments in 120 countries around the world. By doing this, we offer governments and businesses secure solutions that deliver more than the sum of their parts.

- *Benefit*: Clients that see the challenge of securing their world more holistically are able to protect critical assets more efficiently, generate extra revenues, reduce costs and deliver a better experience to the people they serve.

- *Action*: Recognize that the most secure and beneficial solutions come from understanding the whole problem and the interdependence of parts. Let us help you to see the opportunities that exist in the challenge of securing your world.

This meta-POV was then translated into market sector POVs and specific customer areas within markets. The company's communications director, Debbie Walker, toured the company's markets, teaching senior management everywhere how to use the POV, how to storytell with a POV as a base, and how to translate the POV into their specific circumstances. She observes:

'It made a dramatic difference to our confidence as an organization, and our ability to communicate more effectively with our customers. When people realized it focused them on talking about the client's issues first, it gave them more confidence to build relationships at the senior level. It gave us a point of pride and differentiation as well...

The real benefit was the ability to make a POV specific to client opportunities, or explain how we were relevant to markets. It allowed our sales teams to hold more conversations with clients about their needs, and that translated into sales. It also helped to engage better with other key stakeholder groups in a way that was meaningful to them.'

Turning a point of view into a sales pitch

Here is an example of how Debbie worked with one team to develop a strong POV for CEOs of hospitals, founded on both the company POV and using the *Problem–Solution–Benefit* method I outlined in Chapter 11.

This was the structure we insisted on them using:

- What was the client problem? Illustrate the downside costs of not taking action. Translate this into clear needs. (*Problem.*)

- What was the G4S solution? What were the features and advantages? (*Solution.*)

- What was the benefit? (As described by the G4S customer.) (*Benefit.*)
  Was third party validation available? Could actual results and numbers be used? Set the context.
  Always use the line: Transforming challenges into opportunities.

And here was how they translated it into an opportunity in hospitals. By recognizing the wider picture, the high-level needs of the customer, and linking this to the G4S POV, it enabled them to elevate their conversations to board-level decision makers:

- *Challenge?* (They didn't like using the word *problem*.) For the healthcare sector, work-related violence is a serious occupational hazard. And the human cost – physical/psychological pain – brings real cost in monetary terms. Question marks over staff and patient safety undermine productivity and reputation. With it, the sustainability of a hospital itself can come under scrutiny. But measures to deter acts of violence and aggression must address the root causes of the problem: prevention rather than cause. And they must balance the operational requirements of a hospital with proper care for its patients.
  Here they are addressing the issues and needs of the board of the hospital – reputation, future funding and effectiveness. All based on the G4S POV that we can only thrive and prosper in a safe and secure environment.

- *Solution?* G4S knows that managing violence and aggression involves a range of actions at key touch points; it is more than just security. Measures to reduce violence are based on sound risk assessment to identify 'incident triggers' – a complex combination of personal or situational reasons such as fear, anxiety, frustration, medical conditions, drugs or alcohol. All against a backdrop of increasing patient expectations. Staff deserve dedicated training to deal with triggers and to encourage reporting – with effective systems and processes in place to ensure learning. And those affected should have adequate access to support such as counselling, to better deal with the consequences. This is a wider approach that comes from experience.

Smart – this part demonstrates that the simple solution of guards at a desk will not be enough to deal with the problem; it requires a much more integrated approach.

- *Benefit?* A realistic reduction in incidents by 20 per cent and in the impact of aggression by 10 per cent can see a hospital rank amongst the safest. For staff, a safer environment brings improved confidence and morale, less occupational stress and the ability to get on with the job in hand. For patients and visitors, action to reduce the routes of frustration means improved levels of care and reassurance in often difficult times. And for the hospital itself, optimum productivity, fewer compensation claims, reduced staff absenteeism and replacement costs, and improved retention make for a better bottom line. And a far healthier reputation.

    Again, smart. This moves the conversation to the future sustainability of the hospital – the main concern of the CEO, not the procurement department or the head of security.

- *Call to action?* Improved management of health and safety risks is vital in a dynamic healthcare sector. By focusing on the opportunity in every challenge and starting with the bigger picture, we offer solutions that deliver more than the sum of the parts – ensuring the safe and secure workplace that staff deserve, the service the public rightly expects and the performance that stakeholders demand. Let us help you see the opportunity in the challenge of securing your world.

    Call us – we can help you satisfy all of the people to whom you are accountable.

Point of view, storytelling and powerful conversations are all connected, as you have seen in this example. From their POV, G4S was able to construct more compelling stories that enabled higher-level conversations with prospective clients. A POV can help in other ways, too. Giving expression to a POV can, for example, provide clarity around a sense of purpose.

How a POV powered the purpose of a public sector organization

Eddie Morland is CEO of the Health and Safety Laboratories near Buxton in Derbyshire. The HSL is an agency of the UK's Health and Safety Executive and is a global centre of excellence for health and safety research and incident investigations. Whether it is a train crash, an explosion or trying to understand the root causes of accidents, the HSL is the equivalent of crime scene investigation in detective work. However, in order to continue its mission while (like every other public sector organization) suffering from decreasing funds from government, Eddie and the leaders of HSL decided they needed to increase efforts to win business from the private sector.

But how was it to express its purpose in a way that was more attractive to the commercial sector, and not be seen as a regrettable cost of doing business?

We used the BBBA methodology to arrive at the purpose. We discovered, working with the leadership team, that their strongly held *belief* was that the well-being and prosperity of Britain relied on being able to make progress in a safe, healthy environment. Sadly, too many people saw H&S as a hindrance to progress. At HSL, they believed that by learning from health and safety experiences, they could enable individuals, organizations and the nation to make sustainable progress that benefited all.

Their scientific approach, knowledge and experience helped them to understand the complex interactions between people, plant and processes. Their unmatched depth of scientific talent, combined with extraordinary lab facilities and proximity to the regulator, allowed them to offer joined-up, practical solutions to clients that benefited workers, employers and society. (*Behaviour.*)

Organizations that followed their advice enjoyed improved predictability through less downtime of people and plant, giving a faster return on investment and an improved bottom line. At the same time, they created a better working environment, leading to greater employee commitment and an enhanced reputation. (*Benefit.*)

Their call to *action* was to ask leaders to appreciate that moving from compliance to excellence in health and safety brought benefits that would directly and positively influence an organization's results. They wanted decision makers in H&S to work with them to enable their businesses and organizations to work better.

This led to the powerful purpose statement that proudly sits on the front page of their current website: 'Enabling a better working Britain.' The statement works so well because it resonates at many levels with internal and external audiences, whether they are workers, employers, business owners, shareholders, public sector organizations or regulators. It was born of a better expression of their point of view.

How a point of view can power a Thought Leadership programme

When you are a leader, people are looking, listening, waiting – what do you have to say? There is little point in having a powerful point of view and then not expressing it widely. Translating your point of view into Thought Leadership – via think pieces, research and studies – can be a powerful way of delivering leadership – for you, your firm or the organization you lead.

Why? Because Thought Leadership, delivered on your own website, at conferences and other speaking opportunities, in the media or any other platform you can think of, will help you to:

- win business;
- build brand awareness;
- win supporters;
- be better understood;
- build your personal profile;
- attract like-minded people;
- influence the markets you serve;
- shape regulatory environments;
- lead public and even national debates;
- turn employees into your advocates;
- be sought out;
- be *seen* as a leader.

Why wouldn't you do this?

With a powerful POV, all you have to do is expand it/them into presentations, speeches and articles. When you have a passionate POV, you are much more likely to be attractive to the media, because they *love* people with a strong point of view. It makes for better copy. You also get sought after for talks, so you will appear on more platforms, which will get reported. Even if you only express yourself in a blog, with a strong and interesting POV you will be much more likely to attract a following.

To succeed in this critical media environment, you need to make sure your POV is compelling to your key audiences. It must be expressed in *their* language, relevant to *their* agenda, and based on an understanding of *their* issues. If you also communicate tangible benefits for *them*, you will be able to champion causes that truly set you apart.

How a point of view can equip you for the hyper-critical media environment

Recently I spoke to the CEO of a leading NGO who was questioning the effectiveness of her performance in a televised debate and whether the point of view she had expressed was convincing or indeed appropriate. The fact is she was worrying needlessly; in the context of that debate, the merit or otherwise of the fine detail expressed in her point of view came second to the expectation that she air a point of view honestly and forcefully. The point is that leaders in every walk of life are expected to have a point of view – indeed it is demanded of them. You don't get to lead people in any sphere unless you have something to say – and say it.

Many leaders I have interviewed talk of the importance of having views on issues long before they are called on to give them. As Moya Greene, CEO of The Royal Mail Group, says:

> 'Being a leader in a transparent world can be very difficult. The media can be quite cruel and can be pretty indifferent to the truth at times. Whether you are talking to the media or talking on some public platform, you have to have thought through your position on issues before you get called on to give them.
>
> These days, you simply don't have time to think about formulating your point of view in the heat of a discussion. You must have done it beforehand. When you were at school, you'd be very foolhardy to walk into an exam without having cracked open a book. When talking publicly, you have to make sure that you have anticipated the issues and are not in a situation in which you urgently have to search for the answers that support the position you're taking. You have to have it all mapped ahead of time.'

All of the leaders I spoke with were acutely aware of the demands placed on them by the modern media environment. They commented that they seem always to be on the defensive, and want to find more ways to get on the front foot. They know that they need to find more points of resonance with customers and shareholders and stakeholders, and tell them things that help them to understand better what they are trying to do and why they should be supported.

The media's job is to represent the interests of their readers – their constituents, who support them by buying their publications every day, week or month. That means they will challenge you whenever they think you are not acting in the interests of their readers. Simple. So your job is to have a point of view that clearly identifies with the needs of their readers.

The better you can argue your case from their readers' point of view, the better a hearing you will get.

We hear a lot about bad leadership, about poor decisions and about mistakes and their consequences. But who speaks up for leaders, if not themselves? The fact is, there are many, many more great decisions taken, and great leadership displayed, than ever gets written about. We simply do not hear enough about why business is good for society, nor about how inspiring leaders enable progress in business, the public sector and the Third Sector, nor how leadership requires conviction and courage in a world where there are so many opposing points of view and so many baying critics.

The truth is, you simply cannot satisfy everybody. Not in a world where everybody has a point of view and everybody can express a POV on a blog or in social media, and be quoted in a voracious world of modern media. Most journalists now seem to believe that a 'balanced debate' is the articulation of two extremes, when we all know that the shades of grey in the middle are often where the real argument lies.

To win you have to make sure you satisfy your supporters, as well as those likely to support you, and give a convincing case to the undecided – the *real* audience most of the time. As I will show later, you are unlikely to be able to convert your opponents, so trying to persuade them is likely to be a waste of time.

You have to concentrate on the people who are still 'winnable', and reinforce the support of those already on your side, while not showing aggression towards your critics. Respecting their point of view while posing an alternative is assertive rather than aggressive behaviour. It also allows you to acknowledge their point of view, so that those watching you see a respectful but assertive person in command.

The persuasive power of an equal but opposite point of view

The trick lies in reframing the argument by posing a different, values-based point of view – equal in power but completely opposite, if necessary (see Figure 12.2). Whenever we get attacked, it is usually because a critic has adopted a moral high ground and attacked us from that summit. That is the ultimate 'point of view' – the view from a moral high ground! If you now try to defend yourself against those attacks, you will look and sound defensive. You will be arguing with a critic who will never be persuaded. The people who can be persuaded, however, those who have not yet made up their

FIGURE 12.2 TAKING THE MORAL HIGH GROUND

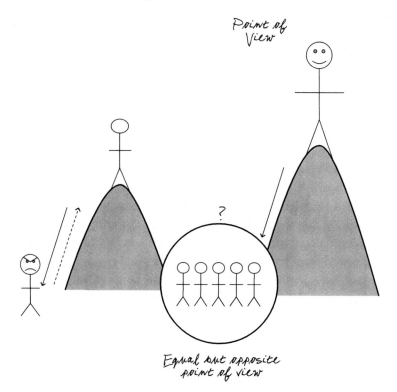

Equal but opposite
point of view

minds, are watching you in this debate, and what they see is a defensive, reactive person being led, unsure of what is coming next and struggling to marshal arguments.

The meaning people take from things often depends on the context – so you need to control the context. We create meaning not just from the facts given in an argument but also from the elements that surround it. To provide an equal but opposite moral high ground, you have to pick out the relevant core values of an issue, then relate your value system to it. Articulate the facts and issues within this moral framing, defining 'their argument' in one way and yours in another ('us' and 'them'). You can then articulate your point of view with a moral authority that enables you to win hearts and minds.

When working for the chemical and pharmaceutical firm Bayer I would often have to defend the company against animal testing. Critics would adopt the ultimate high ground, showing photographs of rabbits or other household pets bleeding from the eyes, then ask a mother with baby, walking in the street, to sign a petition against animal testing. Who could argue against that? Who thinks it is fun to torture animals for dubious gain? Not I, for one. And I would hate to try to justify it on that basis. No facts would help in these circumstances, either.

'We only use 2,000 animals a year, under strict, government-controlled conditions,' I might say. Although true, the problem is that the response to this fact would be a horrified reaction. 'What?!! You do *that* to 2,000 animals every year?' Straight away, I've lost.

So, best to reframe the argument from a different moral high ground. Don't talk to the animal rights activist (who, remember, you will never persuade), address the mother with baby. Perhaps we can still persuade her? Say: 'It is a horrible thought when expressed like that, testing on animals. I agree. However, what you are being shown is not wholly true. It is not our choice, entirely, that we do such tests. The government legally requires us to test medicines on animals, under very strictly controlled humane conditions (not the way shown here), and there is a very good reason. Untested medicines could have a potentially lethal effect on humans, so we have to do everything we can to guard against that. In our company, we believe that our products should be safe and effective, and of the highest quality. We can't do that without testing. It is a matter of choice. Your choice! Would you prefer us to test on animals, or give your baby a medicine untested and potentially lethal? What would you have me do?'

Facts, emotions and symbols

Now you have completely reframed the argument, requiring a different moral perspective, and made a direct appeal to the audience you have in mind. You are not being aggressive to the attacker, but you are taking charge of the discussion. In this case you have used facts, emotion and symbols, just as your opposition did. Facts were used to reinforce the legitimacy of your point of view, emotion was used to reinforce the morality, and the symbol of a dying relative was used to focus the discussion from a different perspective.

As leaders, we are most often communicating change, which creates opposition to change. People will reframe our arguments, using their values or position, and often try to make it a personal attack. If our POV is clear, our goals are clear and our core values associated with that goal are also clear, then we are in a strong position to reframe the discussion.

I chose to illustrate an extreme case, but the truth is often our arguments are not that polarized. In these cases, it is powerful to show that you understand and accept an opposing opinion, while asserting your right to voice your own. By not insisting on 'being right' you can create a platform for constructive debate – and enable a powerful and positive conversation. By not making someone else wrong, you may be able to enable an atmosphere of co-operation, without agreeing with the opposing opinion!

The three types of argument, and why you should stay in the one about the future

When arguing over a point of view, you are going to find yourself in one of three types of argument. What happened (examining an accident, for example), your values (do you support animal testing, nuclear power etc), or choices for the future. These are the three types of rhetoric.

Today, rhetoric has a bad reputation. It is used as a word to describe meaningless, insincere argument. Actually, it was a Greek word to describe effective or persuasive speaking or writing. The Greek art of rhetoric held that there were three types of argument: forensic, demonstrative and deliberative.

The *forensic* type was about arguing with facts, or what occurred in the past. It was used in, for example, court cases. It was used to determine blame and guilt.

Demonstrative rhetoric was about the present – which camp or tribe you belong to, based on your values. Good or bad, hero or coward, ally or enemy? Today it is much more about which community of interest you represent.

The prime purpose of *deliberative* speech was to move people towards future action – new laws or policies that would affect society.

You could say these three types of rhetoric were about the past, the present or the future. As a leader, you are *all* about the future, so the rhetoric you want to espouse (mostly) is deliberative. Notice that in the case of the woman with child and the controversial subject of animal testing, I moved her to the future by suggesting this would be a choice she would have to make, rather than spend time arguing the facts or values with my attacker.

You can oh so quickly get snarled up in forensic discussions and never make progress. Unless you are powerfully persuasive, arguing over different value sets is also difficult. Much easier is to move to a discussion on choices for the future.

Are you discussing a poor track record of recruitment? Move this discussion quickly to: 'What are we going to do to stop making poor decisions?'

Are you dealing with poor sales figures? 'What are we going to do to move forward, and build our pipeline?' This stops the debate getting caught in quicksand, allowing you to get your point of view across and focus on the more positive choices that will allow you to solve the problem.

In summary

The purpose of articulating a point of view is to align others to you and allow it to impact on their behaviours and beliefs. Leaders must articulate values that are deeply held and that have the power to change not everyone's mind, but rather the minds of 'the undecided' (in political parlance, the swing-voters) and plant seeds of doubt in the minds of those who oppose them. In fact, the act of clarifying ideas in this way is liberating in itself and contains its own dynamic – it most often manifests itself in an increase in your passion and power. This is how leaders come to be seen to have leading (and winning) personalities – their strong viewpoint helps people around them to behave in ways they consider valuable and rewarding in themselves.

Points of view are empowering and liberating because they allow you to deliver your perspective with confidence and passion; they ensure you are highly relevant to your audience, and they establish you as a leader because they will be about the issues and causes that really matter to you.

Try it – it's powerful stuff.

Winning in the court of public opinion

Why you must always prepare properly for public platforms

> *Representing your organization externally needs a completely different set of communication skills. You should never do so without proper preparation. Understand who you're talking to and what they need to hear, know your objective, train your voice and body to perfection, and always rehearse your answers to the tough questions that will inevitably come your way. Here are seven things to remember before taking to the stage, and 12 ways to make your material more compelling.*

As a leader, not only do you have to inspire your followers, but you also have to influence positively the opinions and behaviours of people outside your organization. Why? Put simply, it's because a better reputation will help you to achieve better results. You wouldn't be a leader if you weren't all about achieving better results.

The more senior you get, the more often you will have to represent your organization externally. The problem is, once you step outside the organization you lead, you need a completely different set of communication skills. The openness and informality that make you a good internal communicator need to be contained and tempered when you are on external platforms.

I would go as far as to say that you should actually avoid accepting a public platform unless you can clearly explain how such an appearance will benefit your organization. If it is simply about flattering your ego then you are in great danger.

You need to be absolutely clinical in assessing why you are appearing on a public platform – whether it is on stage giving a speech or in the media doing an interview – and accept that you need to put in a great deal of effort to make the most of such a public opportunity. Most of the leaders I have coached have rolled their eyes at the mention of training and rehearsing for speeches or media interviews. Somehow, the idea of practising becomes an annoyance that takes second place to the real business of running the business or organization they lead.

However, you need to remember this – every time you step in front of a microphone you not only risk your own reputation, but also that of the organization you lead. *Never wing it.* Training and preparation are absolutely vital.

Whether you are making a speech, giving a media interview or giving a presentation, there are seven basic rules that apply.

1 Know exactly what you want to achieve.
2 Make a speech or media interview your own – authenticity matters.
3 Prepare fastidiously for questions and answers, and rehearse your script to perfection.
4 Ensure you have a strong voice and a positive image.
5 Select and then stick to a key theme.
6 Find ways to make your material more compelling.
7 Take great and creative care with the pictures or graphics you use to illustrate what you want to say.

Know what you want to achieve

Have a look again at Chapter 8 in this book. Every time you go on stage or appear in front of the media, work your way through this planning process:

- What do you want to achieve?
- Who do you need to influence?
- What do you want them to do and why should they?
- What are they doing now and how do they think, feel and act at present?
- What stories can you tell to illustrate your key points?
- How does your point of view influence what you're going to say, and how can you work your beliefs and passions into your messages?

Very often, delegates in the conference hall can all have a common interest – and it might be that they want to know more about your expertise and experience so that they can learn from what you have to say. However, you might be in a much broader-based audience, with a variety of needs, and you will need to think through what different views you may have to address.

You may be going in front of a radio interviewer, and really want to deliver a message to government, your customers or your suppliers. Remember that the journalist is not your audience, it is the people that he or she represents that you are really talking to. Plan your messages for them, and don't allow yourself to be dictated to by the journalist. Make sure your stories resonate with the audience you have in mind and will be appropriate to them.

Own your material

If you are writing your own speech or media soundbites, then you have already achieved this objective. But, if the material is being prepared for you, you must find ways to make it your own.

Have you been given a speech to read? Rewrite the opening and the close, or rehearse them so much that you can give them without having to read the script. Always read what you've written aloud. The written word – perfect on the page – can sound wrong or be uncomfortable to read aloud, and you won't know it until you've tried it. By rehearsing, you work out beforehand where you're likely to trip up.

Find and tell personal stories to illustrate your points, ones you've directly experienced or are confident telling.

People will detect when you are inauthentic or are simply parroting a party line, so make sure you are comfortable with what you are saying.

Rehearse well and prepare for tough questions

In the end it always comes down to how well you have prepared. I have never seen a speech get worse as a leader has practised. I have met only a very few gifted leaders who are able to speak brilliantly without some considerable amount of rehearsal. You are very unlikely to be one of those people. Invest time and effort in rehearsals. Never wing it.

Apart from anything else, rehearsing gives you confidence and helps you to look like you are a 'natural' who doesn't need practice. People who don't rehearse are the ones most likely to look wooden on stage or on camera. If you don't look and sound passionate about your subject, why would you expect anyone to be persuaded by what you say? It is only with confidence that you can really display your passion, so don't shirk on the rehearsals.

If possible, always videotape your rehearsal. Watch yourself with the sound turned off. This is the only way you will be able to see whether you look convincing and believable. These days, videoing yourself and then watching it privately is far easier than you might imagine. I'm amazed at how many leaders suggest that they don't have a video camera to do the rehearsal. Don't be ridiculous – you have a mobile phone with a video camera on it and you have earphones to use to listen to yourself while watching your rehearsal on the phone. Filming yourself is easy. Even if you do have friends or colleagues to advise you on your performance, you will improve simply by observing yourself.

I would not advise over rehearsing your speech or interview on the day itself, as this can make you a little stale. But do rehearse once, especially at the venue if possible. Many of us have to travel when giving presentations, so your hotel room is of course the ideal place to put in some practice. I don't advise practising in front of a mirror, however. You need to watch yourself on video to get the best benefit. That's the only way you will have the vaguest idea of how your audience might feel watching you.

Video yourself to encourage muscle memory

I often smile to myself when my client says they have rehearsed the presentation or speech in their minds. That may have helped them to get more familiar with the words, but it won't have helped them to tune their bodies and voices to the presentation. And if they don't do that, then the words won't matter. Your body needs muscle memory that comes with rehearsal so that you are not having to multi-task and to think about all those body things while also concentrating on the flow.

Some of the funniest and most productive rehearsals I have held with clients have come when I forced them to keep silent while rehearsing a speech. I ask them to speak the words only in their minds while rehearsing their facial expressions and hand gestures. Although hilarious at first, they soon get the point when they see their performance on screen. You convey a huge amount with your face and hands, and expressiveness is crucial to being convincing and inspiring. Yes, it is true that this in effect is rehearsing your emotions, but it is your passion and strength of emotion that people will remember. Your own enthusiasm and passion for what you do is what will make it appealing to others. Being cool and detached does not sell them on you.

Rehearsing on video, whether it is for a presentation, a speech or a media interview, is probably the single most important piece of advice in this chapter. If you do nothing else for your next appearance, try this. When you are comfortable with how you look and sound, you will know that you can wow the audience and that will show in your performance.

I do not trust computers. I have been let down so many times that I always, always, always check that presentations are up and running the way I anticipate they will. This is one of the most important parts of your rehearsing on the day – checking exactly how you will manage slide transitions, your own presence on the stage and how you will walk about and command the stage, and whether or not your lapel mike is functioning properly. Rehearsing well allows you to overcome these glitches when they do occur, as you will still be able to speak even if the technology fails.

On one occasion recently, I was talking to more than 300 people, with five giant screens around the hall. Half of each screen was a close-up of my face while I was talking and the other half was given over to my slides. Midway through my presentation, the slides went blank. I paused for the technicians to try and fix the problem but soon realized that it might take some time, so I pressed on with my talk. After about five minutes, my slides resumed and the technicians managed to get the slides to the same point that I had progressed to. The rest of the presentation went smoothly. Afterwards, talking to some members of the audience, I asked whether the problem with my slides had distracted them at all. Almost uniformly, they said they had not noticed that my slides had disappeared. They were so busy concentrating on my face that they weren't paying any attention at all to my lovingly prepared graphics. Since then, I have made my presentations very light on slides, if I use any at all.

Tough questions, robust answers

If you have thought hard enough about your audience, you should be able to anticipate the questions people will want to ask. *Never wing it.* Remember that in public every word counts, and can count against you, so you need to weigh every word carefully.

Most importantly, prepare a concise answer to the 'so what?' question. Be ready to explain, in very simple terms, what it is you are really saying.

I'm amazed at how often CEOs and leaders cannot answer simply the most basic questions about their organizations. 'What does your company do?' That is a question I've seen floor CEOs in the past. The problem is they're so close to their own companies and situations that they literally can't see the wood for the trees. They fall into the trap of thinking that because they're immersed in their own organizations and its issues, they should be able to answer questions at any time from anybody. But it is these simple questions that can often cause the most trouble. Difficult questions have probably already received some thinking time. Make sure that you can answer the basic questions, and trial them on friends and relatives. Make sure they give the thumbs up and that your answers are simple, clear and direct.

Think very hard about probable audience attitudes and try to see the world the way they see it. What tough questions might they put to you and what would your key messages be for each? If some of these questions are likely to distract from your key themes, then learn how to answer the questions briefly and bridge back to your main messages. Make sure the questions are potent, and if possible practise with somebody else lobbing you these difficult questions in a hostile manner.

Very often, I have seen executives formulate much better answers that they have then incorporated into their speeches, when undergoing this kind of 'hostile' practice. It is these tough questions that have the power to concentrate the mind and get you to focus on the real issues. Not only must your response be accurate, honest and forthright, but you must look honest and confident when delivering your answers.

This is especially true when you are live on air being delivered hostile questions by a journalist. You have to remember who your real audience is, and not appear shifty and guilty. You're not speaking to the journalist, you're speaking to people out there. Remember that they are watching you and they will be making judgements not only on your words but on your appearance.

Practise giving the answer to these questions out loud in front of colleagues or friends, and get them to tell you how convincing you sound when answering these tough questions. Video yourself and check whether you look shifty, uncomfortable or distracted.

Go it alone if you must, but I highly recommend getting help from professionals before dealing with the media. Media training is essential in today's world, and you need to make sure that you can deal with radio, television, pre-recorded sessions, on-location sessions, studio sessions, remote locations or radio cars – all of them have special features and you need to be familiar with them all if you want to be comfortable and confident.

Why your voice and image can be more important than words

The call came at about 9 am. The local radio station wanted to do a live interview with one of the executives of AEA Technology, of which I was an executive director. The company had been split out of the United Kingdom Atomic Energy Authority and was soon to be floated on the London stock exchange under controversial circumstances. The Tories wanted to press ahead with privatization, the Labour Party was opposed, unions and many staff were opposed. The local radio chat show host wanted an executive to defend the privatization live on air in the next 30 minutes. No one else was available, so I accepted the invitation. I was to go to the local community centre, where the station had a room that was used for 'down the line' interviews.

I arrived at the community centre and was walked to the room. We passed the main hall, where a group of some 30 women were in the middle of an aerobics class. The sound of their feet on the wooden floor was definitely going to be a problem. I was put in the room and an engineer did sound tests. The noise from the aerobics class was too great. 'Go and tell them to stop,' he said.

'Not a chance,' I said, envisaging having to confront 30 hot and sweaty exercising women next door. 'You send someone.'

A few minutes later, rather ominously, the thumping stopped. We were ready to commence the interview. I was sat in a small room in a comfortable chair, and the microphone was on a small coffee table lower than my knees. I had to lean forward and down to ensure my mouth was close to the microphone. I had a pair of headphones on so that I could hear the radio show host, and the people phoning in with questions. The interview commenced and I was live on air. The chat show host and the phone-in guests gave me a tough time, but I knew my stuff, I had a crib sheet in front of me, and

I stuck to my guns. I was respectful of everybody's views, but assertive in putting mine forward. I used stories, I had a burning platform to talk to about why the changes were necessary, and I painted a picture of a future in which all of us would thrive, to the benefit not only of staff but also of local communities.

At the end of the half hour I left feeling pleased that I had delivered all the key messages and acquitted myself well. (I have to admit, I did slink past the aerobics hall so as not to have to confront any of the irate women who had had to stop their exercise.)

When I got back to the office I asked my press and publicity manager to get hold of a transcript of the interview. It arrived the next day and I gave it to my then CEO, Dr Peter Watson, a no-nonsense northerner who was leading the organization through the change programme into a new commercial future. He was pleased with the interview and suggested that I circulated it to all other Executive Directors so that they could learn from it. He also asked me to get a tape of the interview and circulate that as well.

The next day, the tape of the interview arrived and I was horrified. I sounded just like a chipmunk, my voice tremulous, high-pitched and squeaky. There was no authority in that voice at all. The tape has never been seen again, but my lesson was well learned.

By leaning forward in my chair to get close to the microphone, I had stretched my neck and put myself in a cramped position where I couldn't breathe properly. The effect on my voice was disastrous. The more passionate I got, the more high-pitched was my voice. I was mortified.

Words can sometimes be the least important part of your communication

Your voice is one of your most important tools, whether it be in informal conversations, giving a speech or giving a media interview. Some people say that words can often be the least important part of communication, and that what people remember is your presence, which is dictated by your image, your voice and your confidence. (I don't believe that's true, but I do believe a strong presence enhances your words considerably.)

As I have said throughout this book, effective communication is based on trust, and if we don't trust the speaker we are not going to listen to or believe what they have to say. That means that you have to make good eye contact with your audience, you have to have a warm tone of voice, you have to have expressive hand gestures and a warm facial expression. You need to seem be relaxed and confident, and you need to be slow and deliberate in what you say. The combination of a strong voice and a confident image is very powerful.

Your degree of confidence is reflected in your body language and your voice, and if you sound stressed you will send messages that will lead to people distrusting you. Observers will think there is something wrong. They will see dissonance and they will not be convinced.

One of the most frequent mistakes I see from leaders when on stage, or doing radio or television interviews, is to forget to breathe. They speak too quickly, and in not breathing their voice begins to quaver. The signal is that they are overly nervous, even if they are not. It is the lack of oxygen affecting their voice, not their nerves.

Breathe properly. Pause frequently in order to recharge your voice. You're going to need it for the important, passionate moments, and for the big finish.

My mistake in my infamous radio interview was that I was both stretching my throat and not breathing properly. Even today, when giving speeches, I find my voice starting to quaver and I realize that I have to slow down and breathe deeply before I can proceed.

Having mastered using your voice, you also have to master using your body to create the right impression. Even if you don't feel confident, you have to practise walking and standing in the right way. Always ask someone to video you during a rehearsal if possible, in order to see how you look. If you can't be videoed, then have someone you trust give you feedback about the way you look. Stand tall and smile often (smiling is really a secret weapon for it not only helps the audience to warm to you, but it also gives you more confidence – remember my story about the Russian weightlifters?) Being aware of how you are presenting yourself physically, and how you sound, is incredibly important.

Remember, your presence strongly influences how your message is received by an audience, and whether or not you create the right connection with that audience.

The importance of remembering your theme

One technique I give my clients, very often just before they are going on stage or in front of the camera, is to remind them of the one word that defines the theme of their speech or their interview.

For example, one of my clients recently had to appear on a national television business show, talking about the investment his company was making in graduates. We had been doing a question-and-answer rehearsal with him and I feared that he might now be overloaded with information and lose the essential message. Just as he was about to go live, I reminded him that his story was about 'Growth, Growth, Growth. Everything you say tonight must illustrate that you are growing the company and that growth is important not only to you but to your staff, your customers, your suppliers and local communities.'

This thought helped him to focus and he delivered a brilliant live interview, always remembering to return to the theme even after the most distracting of questions.

Twelve ways to make your material more compelling

Think hard about how you're going to make your material compelling. This is done by using a strong 'hook'; the start that hooks people in to what you have to say. There are so many tricks you can use to draw people in, whether it's a live audience or readers of a publication. Here are 12 techniques to prompt your thinking when planning your next public appearance. They are all proven ways to 'hook' your audience in by intriguing them to listen well.

1 *Present a mystery with a surprise revelation.* 'Who is the most famous man in the world who collects *Spider-Man* and *Conan the Barbarian* comics? Answer – President Barrack Obama.'

2 *Use a switch on a common theme.* 'So you think men are the unfaithful ones? Try this. Recent studies show that women are just as unfaithful as men but are a lot more likely to lie about it and a lot less likely to get caught. Simply put, it seems that women are better at having affairs than men.'

Offer a startling statement. 'The greatest threat to our health and well-being today is sensationalist journalism that makes us paranoid about eating anything.'

4 *Ask rhetorical questions.* 'If you had £20 million and the chance to do something about crime prevention in your city, how would you spend the money?' (Then you are into the classic problem–solution–benefit mode.)

5 *Look for and use milestones.* 'This time last year we had built just 100 widgets. Today we build our 1 millionth widget.' (I was at British Airways at the time of its 10th anniversary of privatization. To celebrate the anniversary, which absolutely nobody was interested in, we devised a global campaign called 'Concorde for a Tenner'. The idea was that to celebrate the 10th anniversary British Airways, over 10 nights, would offer up tickets on Concorde for £10 a seat to the first 10 callers on an 0800 101010 number. This generated 33 million telephone calls from around the world over the 10 nights. It was the ultimate case of turning a milestone into something far more memorable.)

6 *Predict the future.* Everybody loves a futurologist. And it's a lot simpler than you think. Simply try the technique of extrapolating trends to see what might happen in future. (I remember once talking to a chief executive who was involved in analysing house prices and mortgage trends all over the UK. He extrapolated house price trends in the North for the next 10 years, and compared the same trends in the South. What he saw was an increasing North–South divide in house prices, with prices in the North growing at a far slower rate than those in the South. He predicted that this gap would become so wide that it would have a major negative impact on workforce mobility. It generated national and regional news coverage by the truckload.)

7 *Use fascinating facts.* 'In 1985, the first mobile telephone call was made in the UK. Today more than 95 per cent of adults own a mobile phone.' Or, try this: 'In 2011, there were 2.1 million violent crimes recorded in the UK. I was one of them.'

8 *Begin with a news item.* 'You may have seen in the newspapers this week that while nicotine is addictive, it isn't harmful. Really, it's the tobacco that will kill you.'

9 *Use the 'on this day in history' approach.* 'Today is July 29. On this day in 1981, crowds of 600,000 people lined the streets of London to catch a glimpse of Prince Charles and Lady Diana Spencer on their wedding day. The couple were married at St Paul's Cathedral before an invited congregation of 3,500 and an estimated global TV audience of 750 million people.'

10 *Invent a catchphrase.* 'Pooper scooper.' (To encourage dog owners to clean up after their pets.) 'Clicks, bricks and flicks.' (A business model where a business has an online presence, a high-street presence and a catalogue presence.)

11 *Ride on the wave of a current ongoing issue.* 'How are we going
to kick start the economy? We are all obsessed with the economy,
and rightly so because it is the one thing that impacts on each
and every one of us.'

12 *Make relevant or surprising comparisons.* 'The country with the
highest birth rate in the world is [Pause]... Niger! It has 51.26 births
per 1,000 people. The country with the lowest birth rate in the
world is... Japan, at 7.64 births per 1,000.'

Most importantly, remember that nobody, but nobody, thanks you for
a long presentation or speech. The shorter the better. You have to take the
time to distil what you want to say down to its essence. The shorter and
more simple you keep what you have to say, the more likely people will
retain your key messages. Clarity has many enemies, including jargon and
length.

Time and again I have seen leaders stand up, speak without notes and
without slides giving a short, sharp, passionate speech, and the applause has
been deafening.

Real confidence will come from telling stories that you love and using
those as the pillars of any talk. Draw on the stories to make the points you
want and avoid drowning the audience in facts. And always remember 'the
rule of threes'. People usually can only remember three points, so organize
your speech or your interview notes around three key points and use the rule
of threes when you make those points. This is a very general rule in speaking
and writing, which states that ideas presented in threes are more interesting,
more enjoyable and more memorable. The number three occurs frequently
in well-known stories – from the three little pigs, to the Three Musketeers or
the Three Wise Men.

Some of the most memorable quotes have involved threes – for example:

Up, up and away.
Faith, Hope and Charity.
Truth, justice and the American way.
Sex, drugs and rock 'n' roll.
Life, liberty and the pursuit of happiness.

I could go on, and on and on, but I think you get my point.

Pictures, please, if you must use PowerPoint

Perhaps the most common mistake I see when helping executives rehearse their presentations is too many words on their slides. What happens is this – the slide becomes a series of bullet points mainly for the benefit of the speaker, and not for the audience. In effect, the slide is their on-screen set of speaking notes.

At my company we must be pitching for new business several times a week every week. I see many of these pitches and can understand why they are so word-heavy. There is a strong belief that our audience needs to see what we are saying in order to understand our message. The problem is that members of our audience are very often squinting at the screen to try and read what's on display, and not listening to us at all. Slides like that can actually be hugely distracting and unhelpful to our cause.

We now have come to understand the difference between a presentation to be made to our potential clients and a leave-behind document that re-minds them of what we have said. The first will be dominated by interesting photographs, enlightening graphics or intriguing visuals that enhance the stories and narrative of our pitch.

Our speaking notes are kept off the slides, but we know that those speak-ing notes may well be useful to our potential clients, so we produce a second version of the presentation that has both the visuals and the words. That's the one we leave behind after the pitch.

My advice? *Dump the text. Use only images.*

The right image can not only transform your presentation, but also trans-form a media opportunity and its position in a paper or magazine. In this age of iPad editions, blogs and news websites, pictures are more important than ever before. There are more opportunities for pictures to be used these days, but remember that every picture you use needs to tell a story or enable you to tell your story better.

This is where getting some creative help in can pay enormous dividends. A good designer can give you ideas for great visuals that can make your speech or media interview much more memorable.

Strategy. Ownership. Rehearsal. Voice. Theme. Hook. Graphics. These are the keys to performing well on a public platform.

So, what about the words? I hear you ask.

When words really matter
Why some are simply much more persuasive than others

> *Sometimes a subtle change of words can reveal a truth not previously recognized. When you take care to find exactly the right word, the one that conjures up a whole new concept in people's minds, you can expand horizons and achieve more.*

When your followers believe they can achieve the impossible, they often do.

Your job is to persuade them both of the need to achieve, and their ability to do so. You achieve great things because of the way you make your followers feel.

Very often, you can change the way they feel, by changing the words you use.

Words really do matter, and no matter how much you hear about the mythical '55 per cent body language, 38 per cent tone of voice, 7 per cent actual words' rule, forget it. Of course how you look and how you say things will influence how the message is received, but what you say really matters.

Having studied communication for more than 40 years, I have seen so many situations where a change of words in a sentence has had a dramatic impact on outcomes. Time after time, for example, I saw experiments in direct marketing achieve huge uplifts in response rates with just a simple change of word.

What were some of those powerful words?

YOU. A simple way of personalizing what you have to say and making people feel you're talking directly to them. Probably the most powerful word in a leader's arsenal, and second only to the name of the person to whom you're speaking.

Another one, surprisingly, is BECAUSE.

The reason? To complete a sentence after the word 'because', you have to find a strong reason. Usually, you will be asking someone to take action, so the words after 'because' will have to contain a benefit statement, a WIFM (what's in it for me?) And we know how much I love WIFMs! Every time you create a causal relationship it is incredibly persuasive, even when you give a weak reason. In fact, a weak reason will always be more persuasive than giving no reason at all.

Another one is AND instead of BUT. This one is a pet hate of mine. I am almost phobic about not using the word 'but'. I will tell anyone prepared to listen that an apology never has a but in it. You can bet that when you say anything with a 'but' in it, the only thing that people hear will be the words that come after the 'but'.

'I think you did a great job with the new sales system, BUT it still needs some tweaks before it's perfect.' The person listening to you is guaranteed only to hear the need for more changes, and will completely miss the praise.

'I am sorry about what I said yesterday, BUT you always make me angry when you don't put the dishes away.' This person will definitely not hear an apology, they will simply hear another attack.

Ban the word from your vocabulary and replace it with the word AND. It is SO much more effective.

For example, try this: 'I think you did a great job with the new sales system, and I think a few more tweaks will make it even more efficient.'

Or this: 'I am sorry about what I said yesterday, and in future I will try not to get so angry when you don't put the dishes away.'

Both the sentences are vastly improved and far more likely to get a positive response.

The power of who, what, where, why, when and how

When I was a magazine editor, I devoured research on people's reading habits. I wanted to know what it was that attracted people to read stories, from how best to lay out the page to what words to use in headlines. This is where I came to this view that the most powerful words of all are who, what, where, why, when and how.

These six interrogative pronouns are powerful because they almost always mean the start of a question, and questioning is the very basis of great leadership. Simply ask people questions that help them to understand situations, or help them to get to the right answers themselves, or show you really care and are interested in what's going on, and you're halfway to being inspiring without doing anything else.

Perhaps it's because these words were drilled into me when I started my life as a journalist, but they have served me incredibly well.

Most problems at work have to do with miscommunication. We make assumptions instead of asking questions, and then we wonder why so many things go wrong. Asking questions is fundamental to building trust and relationships. For a leader, questions help you better to understand the people you're working with, what motivates them and what gets in the way of better performance, and they enable better-informed decision making.

I cannot stress enough how important it is to listen to and appreciate your staff. When you ask good questions, you show people around you that you really value what they think. I strongly believe that in a more open, collaborative and transparent world, in which top-down leadership models are rapidly disappearing, asking good questions is a more important skill than ever.

The more we use these six power words, the more likely we are to be good listeners. The more questions we ask, the better we will understand situations and the less likely we will be to want to talk about ourselves all the time. I don't believe that I have ever seen 'the art of asking questions' on the list of necessary skills of leadership, but I believe it should be. This is such a fundamental part of leadership.

Whether you are coaching an employee, seeking to find out how people feel, trying to understand a complex situation or even just networking at an event, I believe that these words, should you practise them enough, will become a secret weapon that can make you far more inspiring.

As Rudyard Kipling wrote:

I keep six honest serving-men
  – (They taught me all I knew);
Their names are What and Why and When
  – And How and Where and Who.

Why using these words in your headlines will improve readership

If you do write a blog or a weekly column in your staff newsletter, then remember how powerful these six words can be in your headlines. Research has shown that any headline that starts with one of these words will always result in a better-read story than those without.

(The eagle eyed among you will now notice how many of my chapters start exactly this way.)

'How John Smith won our biggest client' will always capture more readers than 'John Smith wins biggest client.'

'Why leaders always ask open-ended questions' is a much better headline than 'Open-ended questions get richer answers.'

The reason is that such a headline always leaves an unanswered question in the mind of the reader, which compels them to read on. Whether it is the headline on a PowerPoint slide or on your next blog, always think of starting with who, what, when, where, how or why.

Use words that deliver social proof

Talking about making small changes to a few words, I'd like to draw your attention to some work done by persuasion scientists, including Dr Robert Cialdini, Professor of Psychology at Arizona State University. His recent work is profound and simple. He says that when uncertain, overwhelmed and time-scarce people come to make decisions, they increasingly rely on just a handful of mental shortcuts to guide their decision making and behaviour.

One of these decision shortcuts is what the scientists call 'social proof'. With social proof, we tend to follow the lead of comparable others, if given a steer showing how large numbers of our peers do what it is we are being required to do.

For example, we will tend to prefer a restaurant that is busy, work late if everyone else is, and leave a tip in a saucer full of small change. We assume that if lots of people are doing something, then it must be okay. Putting this practice to use to achieve better outcomes requires very few extra words. Let me give you two examples.

For years, hoteliers struggled with getting guests to reuse their towels. Sending a towel to be laundered every day when the guest is staying several nights is not only expensive but also environmentally harmful. By simply changing a few words on a standard sign requesting guests to reuse their towels, hoteliers were able to decrease usage by more than 26 per cent, with enormous financial and environmental benefits. All they did was add a simple sentence telling guests that the majority of their fellow guests reused their towels (the social norms appeal).

In another experiment, this time involving tax, social proof messages in reminder letters saying that the vast majority of citizens paid their taxes on time improved response times by some 15 per cent and brought hundreds of millions more revenue to government coffers. If an understanding of the persuasion process could generate such impressive returns in these two cases, could not a few extra words of social proof work wonders for your business?

Through subtle changes in wording, leaders can open the minds of their employees and impact their behaviours, because better words, more carefully chosen, can actually induce a different state of mind.

Three different stories illustrate my point.

Turning passengers into guests

Recently I was talking to the CEO of a small local airport. He had been brought in to turn around the declining fortunes of this airport, which had seen passenger numbers halved over three years of mismanagement. He had a huge and multi-faceted job on his hands, not least of which was the culture of his organization.

Staff at this airport were both long-serving and dedicated. He did not believe that the issue was about trying to get them to work harder. They all knew there was a huge job to be done to restore the airport, and therefore the security of their own employment. There was no doubt they were willing to change. The problem was that they didn't know how. There was one significant barrier to change – and that was that they tended to think of passengers as 'hostiles' who needed to be herded as quickly and as efficiently as possible to their boarding gates. Families and relatives dropping them at the airport were to be managed out at speed so as to prevent the system from clogging up.

No matter what he did, he could make little headway in changing staff attitudes. He tried calling passengers 'customers', in the hope that this would signal to his staff that they were not sheep and that they were valuable to the airport. 'This caused my employees to pause for a moment, and I could see them wondering what on earth I was on about. But it had no effect on their attitudes and therefore no effect on their behaviours,' he said.

> 'We realized that we had to put staff through some training to help them become more customer-friendly, and we discussed with the trainers how we might do this. As we argued, one of managers suggested that the key issue was that we wanted our staff to be more hospitable. That was the breakthrough. What we really wanted, was for our staff to treat all visitors to the airport as they would guests in their own homes.'

This small but subtle change had a remarkable effect. 'Suddenly our staff realized exactly what we meant and many spontaneously began behaving exactly the way we would have wanted them to – without any training.'

Just one word provided the launch pad for a change programme that has – among other things – turned around the fortunes of the airport and once again enabled growth.

Treating customers as users

Discussing the issue of the importance of words, a marketing director referred me to a book that has heavily influenced the way he talks to his staff about his company's customers. The book in question is *Users, Not Customers* by Aaron Shapiro. He explained:

> 'Mr Shapiro made me realize that a single word can change attitudes throughout a company. The word customer defines a relationship in transactional terms – buying or selling. Yet we want our customers to keep using our products and keep coming back to us. We only do that if we solve their problems. The act of buying doesn't solve their problem. It is only when they use our product that their problems get solved.
>
> This takes you into the territory of what people need to meet their needs, which touches every part of the business because it makes our people realize that you're making products that people will use, hopefully for a long time.
>
> This is how you align the whole organization to the idea of a lifetime user. With that in mind you will think differently about quality, manufacturing, marketing and service. One word becomes transformational.'

From sustainability to thriveability

At a cocktail party in London, I was talking to the sustainability director of a well-known British retail brand. We were discussing the idea that CSR (corporate social responsibility) as a concept was dead. Even the word 'sustainability' was old and past its sell-by date.

Why so? Because, we agreed 'sustainable' is a defensive word. It suggests hanging on to what you've got. In my mind it sets up a picture of protecting and maintaining, or preventing further loss.

And yet, when I talk to business leaders today, I hear them talking about something very different.

They talk about finding ways to ensure that the total environment in which they operate is capable of sustaining everyone's growth. They talk about businesses not being able to thrive in a bankrupt society. They recognize the need to ensure that the economies of the communities in which they operate are thriving, or else they will not be able to thrive themselves. They talk about creating an environment in which everybody benefits, now and in the future. To my mind, they talk about 'thriveability', not sustainability, and I have started using the word more frequently.

Every time I now use 'thriveability' with people, it provokes a very interesting reaction. The reason? Straightaway, when you hear this word instead of 'sustainability', your mindset is different. You entertain a more positive, and a different, concept. It has led to far more positive discussions about how business can be a force for good.

Take care to find exactly the right word

In these examples, we were changing words so that they became a different metaphor in the minds of our followers. Instead of thinking of people as passengers, we were thinking of them as guests. This was a different metaphor – one that conjured up a very different way of feeling.

In each of these examples, a subtle word change revealed a truth that had not previously been recognized. Thriving, not sustaining. Lifetime users, not one-time customers. Guests to be respected, not passengers to be managed.

When you take care to find exactly the right word, the one that conjures up a whole new concept in people's minds, you can expand horizons and achieve more.

Why leaders should embrace social media

The six reasons you should be more engaged

> *Already, 1 billion people use social media. By 2020, it is believed that there will be 5 billion users of social media. And yet, only a small number of top leaders engage. Can you really afford to ignore it?*

There are many leaders who will read this chapter and ask themselves why I'm bothering to write about something that is now second nature to them. The answer is that – if you are one of those people – you are in the minority... by some margin!

Recent reports have suggested that just 7 per cent of the leaders in the top 350 companies on the London Stock Exchange have a digital presence. While I cannot vouch for that statistic, I do know that many of the leaders I work with either do not actively engage in social media or have a very limited presence. Of those that do, many have other people scripting their words for them.

My own attitude to social media dramatically changed on hearing a story from one of my clients. Until that moment I had very much believed the digital revolution was something every leader needed to understand, in order to ensure that our organizations were engaged with social media to the benefit of the brand, but I also believed that young people were natives to this and I never could be. I saw it as a way of communicating, not as a way of working.

My client told me of an occasion when, one afternoon, he was dramatically summoned to see one of his clients. The call had come from the CEO and there was no room to negotiate on timing. His presence was required immediately. As the senior partner of a global professional service firm, he was being held to account for a failure by his team.

This client was worth a seven-figure annual fee. The account was now under threat of instant termination. His team had let this client down badly, attempting to do a job for which they were not qualified. Their botched efforts were now in need of unusual skills to solve the problem. They had just one chance and just a few days to fix it... or else!

On his way back to the office, my client was distressed. Although he had 2,000 members of staff, he knew no one with the skills that could help solve this particular problem. How could he find such specialist skills in such a short time? In the taxi, on the way back to his office, he tweeted a 140-character plea.

'Before I had got back to the office I already had a dozen replies. With those people I was able to be more expansive so I e-mailed a full brief to them. In effect, I socialized my problem. By the time I got to my desk, I already had five CVs in my inbox from people who knew what to do. Four of them were my own employees and one was a freelancer who worked with us. That afternoon we gathered to talk about the problem.

Through the rest of the afternoon and late into the night, using wikis to enable virtual collaboration, texting and e-mailing each other, we worked on the problem. By the next morning, I was able to go back to my client with an outline solution. Ultimately, we managed to save the client – but only because I was able to act with such speed.'

Through the power of social networking, my client had saved several million pounds worth of income. He is definitely a fan.

Why leaders won't use social media

However, he is still in the minority among the many leaders I deal with. While nearly all of them recognize the importance of social media to their organizations, they still resist the use of social media themselves. They either don't know how to use it or they fear that they will lose control if they try.

They talk about how their tweets can be taken out of context and mis-quoted or abused in the media. They tell me it's too risky, that they can see no return on their investment of time, especially when it comes to blogging. They say that social media is really only for young people. They say that it exposes them to reputational damage or that it could allow privileged information into the public domain. Sometimes leaders do try twitter, then pull back from it after seeing their comments being criticized and shared on a mass scale online and in the media. They talk about how difficult it is to communicate complex issues in just 140 characters.

While I accept that these are the difficulties and dangers, I believe that these leaders are denying themselves powerful ways to collaborate, share knowledge and tap into employee skills that can be used for competitive advantage.

Leadership today is a product of our times and we have to embrace digital communications. Leaders who do that can communicate directly with their front-line employees, they can engage in conversations with customers, and they can tap into communities of interest, knowledge and news that will give them real benefits.

What is your attitude to social media? At one end of the scale, you get many leaders who see social media as a threat. They limit the amount of time employees can spend on social media, they don't believe that it pro-vides a useful channel to communicate with customers, and suspect it directly challenges their hierarchical command and control structures. There is a massive tension built in to this view – how do they maintain control in what appears to them to be such an uncontrolled environment? Their impulse is to build walls and protections that keep this unruly world well and truly out.

Those who are a little more adventurous tend to limit the use of social media to listening to customers and other stakeholders. It is a useful alter-native to more expensive market research.

At the other end of the scale you get leaders who are actively encouraging the organization to link employees to customers in all sorts of ways that improve customer loyalty, make the organization more efficient and drive up employee engagement. At this end of the scale, my experience is that these leaders are themselves active users of social media. They really 'get' the benefits.

Why leaders do use social media

Increasingly, many more leaders will take up blogging and tweeting. They will have little choice. In some sectors, leaders are being actively encouraged to take part. For instance, I have seen that CEOs in the British National Health Service (NHS) are actively encouraged to make use of social media and are being given online tutorials to enable them to take part.

Many other public sector leaders I know who do blog are enthusiastic. For example, Nick Baird is Chief Executive of UK Trade and Investment (UKTI), which is a government department working with businesses to aid their success in international markets. He says that tweeting and blogging have made the world more 'cheerfully anarchic':

> 'I believe that as a leader you need to tweet and blog, which I do all the time. It helps you to understand that as a leader you aren't in control of everything and it enables you to be informal yet frank. It puts an even greater premium on authenticity. There are times when I blog on a subject and sometimes all of the reaction to it may be people complaining or whingeing about issues only vaguely related to my subject. This is good, though, because it gives us sight of issues that are bothering people and which we can then do something about.
>
> I am not in favour of trying to put disciplined frameworks around the use of social media, because I think that we can adapt and adopt new ways of exploiting this cheerful anarchy that it offers us as organizations.'

Throughout this book I have been talking about how leadership is about showing more of yourself, revealing more of your character to your followers. I've talked about how leaders seek to make connections and actively listen. I've talked about the importance of conversations that create choices and a better future. I've talked about the importance of inspirational content in the form of a compelling vision and motivating stories. I've urged leaders to always look to form communities of interest and give those communities context and meaning. Finally, I've suggested that leadership is about encouraging collaboration in new and different ways to drive progress and create a more inclusive organization.

The six reasons you should be more engaged

Character. Connections. Conversations. Content. Communities. Collaboration. This is what leadership is about and this is what social media is about.

These are the six reasons you should be more engaged with social media (see Figure 15.1).

FIGURE 15.1 SOCIAL MEDIA

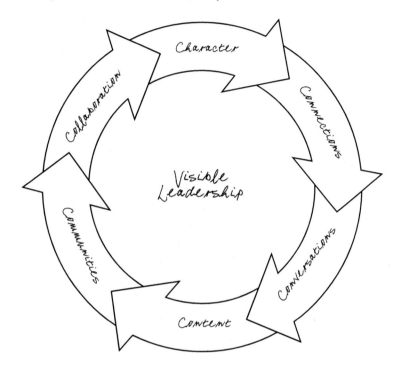

You can show more of your character to more people

Business leaders cannot stay aloof from a massive trend that all other parts of their business or organization are adopting. So much of leadership is about being a role model. If you want the organization you lead to engage in social media, then telling them to do as you say, not as you do, will quickly distance you from your staff.

There is no doubt in my mind that, where business leaders do engage in conversations with their customers and consumers online, all of those watching are more likely to trust the brand as a result. It is a great way for leaders to target different audiences, deliver key messages, and communicate about their beliefs, products and services. It is also a way of challenging stakeholder opinions and putting your side of the argument across to the public.

The adoption rate, however, is still extremely slow. Only a small percentage of leaders are active online. That does seem a huge missed opportunity to me. A leader's job is to inspire, and simply not showing up for – or in – social media will fail to inspire anybody.

Those leaders who are active on social media are thought to be more inspirational than leaders who aren't. Social media facilitates openness. It helps leaders to be more accessible, enables followers to understand who they are and what they believe in. Those followers will be much more likely to trust as a result.

The visibility of social media does place great stress on authenticity. Being authentic is critical to effective leadership, so tone really matters. My advice is that you should do everything in your power to engage with social media yourself, and not give it to someone else to do on your behalf. Only you can speak in your authentic voice. People have an acute ear for anything inauthentic. This is especially true of employees, who will quickly work out the 'falseness' of such a personal medium as a blog or tweet. They will know that this is not your voice and it will not help them to believe in you.

Those leaders who do use social media primarily target their employees. They feel more comfortable confining what they have to say to an internal audience. However, the number of leaders and CEOs who are engaging with customers is on the rise. I have seen some CEOs openly giving their e-mail addresses on television and radio to encourage feedback from customers, in spite of the worry that it might stimulate a flood of complaints. They see complaints as a way to take action and fix problems within the organization. Having done so, they are able to communicate back to customers to improve reputation and build loyalty. To them it is an opportunity, not a threat.

Many CEOs are now also targeting investors, the general public and news media with their tweets and blogs. Unlike meeting rooms or offices, social media has no physical or geographical boundaries. It lends itself to conversations and creates higher levels of engagement, because it allows leaders to communicate their ideas and enthusiasm about the future of their organization confidently and informally, in a way that is engaging and inspiring to others.

You can make connections more easily, be more accessible and listen better

The world is changing. The convergence of digital, social and mobile is enabling connections between customers, employees and partners in all sorts of new ways. Leaders must recognize that a more connected world is changing the way people engage. We are living in a continuous feedback environment. When news and views are spread around the world at this sort of speed, the only response is to build the organizational agility that enables you to respond at speed.

Being active on social media shows that as a leader you are listening. It is a great way to get news and views in a timely, cost-effective way. It enables leaders to flatten hierarchies and get things done. When leaders are online and listening, they are far better able to influence the conversations that matter. They can learn things first-hand about how customers perceive their services – things that they can take back into the organization and actually do something about.

Leaders today are rightly focused on getting better customer insights, and are constantly seeking a better understanding of individual customer needs in order to find ways to improve services and products. With so much at stake, why allow others to do all the listening for you? It's only when you're involved in the interactions yourself that you will be able to get a real sense of what needs to be done. After all, market research is simply data unless it provides insights. Insights enable action. By being actively engaged in the conversations that matter, you will be treated to a treasure chest of insights.

Some leaders I spoke with use these insights to drive action and awareness in their organizations. They become passionate about solving problems and inspiring employees to deliver solutions. They just love to go back to customers online and tell them about what they've done in response to what they've heard. When consumers or employees see that you are responding to what they say and acting on their suggestions, you inspire greater loyalty.

Ben Verwaayen, the immediate past Chief Executive of the telecommunications business Alcatel Lucent, told me of how he had encouraged 80,000 staff around the world to e-mail him directly when he first arrived to lead the organization. He said he received thousands of responses, and replied to every e-mail himself. As a result, he said, he knew more about what was going on in the organization than nearly all of his managers.

You can engage in more conversations and be more influential

Leadership takes place in the thousands of conversations you have with your followers and supporters. The web is the ideal place for conversations and encouraging participation. The web *is* dialogue. Most successful ideas and social media are the ones that embrace conversations and encourage participation, often from the most unlikely sources, as seen in the example of my distressed client at the beginning of this chapter.

My only warning is that social media is where leaders do have to learn to exchange control for participation. I'm often amused by the idea that, somehow, if you don't hear what people are saying then they aren't saying something about you. As amusing as this idea is, it is this head-in-the-sand attitude that prevents many leaders from engaging in these conversations. Whether you like it or not, these conversations are taking place, and the worst thing to do is to ignore them and not try to influence them. When you can find out what people really are thinking, feeling and doing, you can begin to have a positive influence on those beliefs and behaviours.

When leaders learn to enable discussions between customers, employees and suppliers, everybody wins.

You can create content that brings to life your vision, and share more stories

One of the great advantages of social media is that you can speak directly to audiences. Not too long ago, leaders had to rely on print and broadcast media to get their message out to external publics. Today, you can easily reach those audiences without having to run the risk of having your words distorted or wrongly interpreted.

Leaders can communicate their vision in an unambiguous way to a wide and varied audience. They can be much more consistent in their communication with multiple stakeholders, unmediated by third parties who can twist or reframe points of view.

'But, I simply don't have the time,' say those who are still resisting.

'So, how do you communicate then?' I ask.

'I send out a weekly e-mail/newsletter.'

At this point, those who are alert will spot the trap. 'So what's the difference between writing something for a weekly e-mail and blogging?'

Most leaders I know make a point of talking directly to staff, usually through a personal e-mail column company newsletter. If they can take the time to do this, then why not simply deliver it in the form of a blog? If you want to limit access to the blog you can do so, just as you can restrict who has access to your tweets. The only difference is that the medium is different – the content is likely to be the same.

When online in public, it's really important to remember that you need to add value to the conversations taking place. If you simply want to peddle the party line in an unsophisticated and blatant way, you will soon be very unwelcome.

Telling stories, sharing insights or giving an expert view are much better ways of getting your messages over.

You can create communities of interest, network better and learn more easily

By creating online 'places', where people with common interests can 'hang out', leaders can create mutually beneficial networks. Within those networks, leaders can ask for help and advice and enable others to do the same. They can post content, articles, information and news about topics of interest to their community. They can create forums and newsgroups, or enable instant messaging for more immediate communication. The possibilities are endless.

Creating these communities is easier than you might think, and the benefits are enormous. Not least of which is staying current with developments in your marketplace by tapping into a regular flow of 'insider' news and Thought Leadership that stimulates thinking and inspires ideas.

You can promote collaboration by demonstrating a collaborative leadership style

The huge trend in leadership today is to build more open and collaborative cultures, in which employees are encouraged to connect with and learn from each other in order to thrive in a world of such blistering speed. This is a powerful way to enable the innovation and imagination of staff – who, after all, are the people who actually deal with customers every day.

When leaders demonstrate collaboration through their online activities, it is a potent signal of the need to change the organization's culture.

The very nature of social media is collaborative. Leaders who use it to their advantage build social capital with all stakeholders.

Why you simply can't ignore it any more

Researchers say that the use of social media has now exceeded 1 billion users worldwide. As I write this book in 2013, indications are that the growth rate is accelerating. By 2020, it is estimated that there will be 5 billion users.

Facebook is still the most popular place online for users to get connected worldwide. According to a study conducted by the Global Web index, daily active users of Facebook have reached 665 million. Twitter, on the other hand, is still the fastest-growing social network by active users. More than 1 million accounts are being added to Twitter every day.

LinkedIn is now the undisputed largest professional business network on the planet and has been growing during the early part of 2013, though not as much as Twitter and Facebook. There are more than 200 million LinkedIn users, with two new users joining this business social website every second.

Another social website enjoying growing popularity is Google+, which has attracted the attention of 359 million monthly users and is currently the second-largest social network.

Social sites such as Instagram and Pinterest are also rapidly growing in popularity and have attracted huge online audiences due to the unique way they allow users to interact, write posts and upload amazing photographs to their platforms.

Mobile phone usage of the internet has grown by 60 per cent in the past two years, meaning that use of the internet will be even more easy and popular as the months go by, opening up social media rapidly to users in developing markets worldwide. While they may not have television sets in their homes, they increasingly do have mobile phones, which they use for everything from torchlight to telephony.

The argument that social media is for young people only is rapidly being debunked. Twitter's fastest-growing age demographic is 55 to 64-year-olds, with 79 per cent growth. People over 45 are the fastest-growing demographics on both Facebook and Google+.

The fact that social media is now becoming universally popular is one of the reasons so many world leaders are adopting Twitter, with – at last count – more than 264 leaders from countries in the United Nations now active on it. These world leaders have sent more than 350,000 tweets to more than 52 million followers in 42 different languages. Of these leaders, research says that only 30 do their own tweeting. The most popular of them all is President Barack Obama in the United States with 15 million followers.

These are growth trends that leaders simply cannot ignore.

Perhaps my main point was best articulated by The Work Foundation, a leading independent, international authority on work and its future. It recently published a White Paper on harnessing social media to improve workforce effectiveness.

It concluded that too many organizations were running scared of social media, terrified that 'the Barbarians – a ravenous hoard of reviewing, judgemental and vocally opinionated consumers' were at the gates and about to overrun organizations. Those organizations were adopting a myriad of defensive strategies to keep the barbarians out.

The problem is that the barbarians are already through the gates – because those social media savvy consumers are also the vast majority of organizations' employees, who don't leave their social media capabilities at their front doors when they leave for work in the mornings.

Recently, our firm's head of innovation, Amelia Torode, organized a unique day for me and all of our group's company MDs. We were taken to learn how to do coding on a digital training day. It was an eye-opening experience as we went from having no skills and little understanding to being able to code our own apps – in just eight hours!

For a business that advises clients on their digital presence in the marketplace, it is essential we understand what's possible. Knowing how the web works, and understanding what's possible, opens up a whole new world of ideas and strategies, and we have all benefited from our 'coding' day, even though I will likely never myself produce an app.

And, I guess, that's the real point. How can you begin to understand this new world of digital possibilities and maximize the opportunities if you don't engage with it yourself?

PART V
Bringing it all together

What is your leadership inspiration quotient?

How to make the intangible more tangible

To join the small community of leaders who understand what it is to be inspiring, you have to ask yourself the right questions – the ones that can help you to improve your performance as an inspiring communicator. If you can do that, you will more easily make a difference that changes poor performance into exceptional results. These are the 13 questions you must ask yourself if you want to benchmark and improve.

Leadership – and the ability to inspire – is the greatest intangible asset of all.

Great leaders make organizations profitable and successful. They help to drive enormous value from all of the other 'soft' assets of an organization

– culture, knowledge, reputation and relationships. They create great places to work and they enable their followers to grow and develop and perform. They inspire success. The skill of inspiring people is of enormous value.

So how do you begin to make such a valuable intangible more tangible?

The only way is to put in place some measures. Try to begin to understand how inspiring you are as a leader by assessing your own skills, and then corroborating your views with those of your employees or direct reports. What's important is not the absolute mark that you give yourself, nor the mark your employees give you – it's the gap between those marks. It is in that gap that you have to improve, and if you do improve you will also improve the quality of your leadership, and thereby increase the chances of achieving your goals.

To join the community of leaders who understand what it is to be inspiring, you have to ask yourself the right questions – the ones that can help you to improve your performance as an inspiring communicator. If you can do that, you will more easily make the difference that can change poor performance into exceptional results.

These are the questions that really matter – the ones to ask yourself. Against each one rate yourself on a scale of nought to 10.

1 Can I say that I genuinely inspire our people by communicating with passion and integrity? (Does my leadership team do the same?)

2 Am I confident that everyone (at all levels in the organization) has a clear view of our values and our purpose so that all the decisions they make are aligned with these?

3 Do all our people understand what each of them needs to do to help achieve our overall goal, and are they inspired by it?

4 Is everyone in the organization committed to constantly improving our key relationships – with each other, our suppliers, partners, stakeholders and, most importantly, our customers?

5 Are we having enough meaningful conversations with our employees so they feel engaged, motivated and committed to what we are doing? Am I recognizing good work when I have those conversations?

6 Can I truly say that I understand what things are like for our people so that I can talk about issues that are important to them?

7 Do I make it a priority to get feedback and input from our people across the organization and respond to their concerns? Am I a good listener? Do I make it easy for people to bring me bad news?

8 Can people in the organization look at me and say that I speak out strongly and clearly on the issues that are important to me and to our organization?

9 Am I known as a leader who inspires and engages people by using stories to communicate the messages I want to convey, or do I only use charts with facts and figures?

10 Am I confident that the way I act, and the signals I send, communicate the right messages to our people?

11 Am I and all of the leaders in the organization properly prepared and trained for speaking publicly so we can ensure that every word we say counts?

12 Is communication a fundamental leadership priority within the organization, ensuring that we develop all of our leaders to become inspiring communicators?

Above all, am I doing everything I can to ensure that our people, our customers and all of our stakeholders trust who we are and what we do?

This questionnaire is based on *The Language of Leaders*' 12 principles, and was formulated with help from Sinead Jefferies of Opinion Leader Research, a UK research company. You can now do this Leadership Inspiration test online at **www.languageofleadersbook.com/thinking**. This online test not only shows where your strengths and weaknesses lie, but also offers relevant practical tips on areas where you can improve.

Many hundreds of leaders from around the world have already done this test, and gave themselves an average rating of about 7/10. These leaders came from all over Europe, the USA, South America, Australia and the Far East.

Interestingly, the area in which these people felt least able to perform was on their ability to 'engage', scoring themselves lowest against the comment 'My leadership team are having enough meaningful conversations with our employees so they feel engaged, motivated and committed to what we are doing.' (Most employees would agree with this assessment!)

Surprisingly, the next lowest mark they gave themselves was on the ability to articulate an inspiring vision – an area that countless surveys of employees around the world have shown is one of the most important attributes of leadership. This is a significant gap, and a worrying one.

Across the board all leaders appreciated that they need to develop and improve, but it appeared that the fewer people a person said they led, the less confident they were in their skills. Managing a small team would imply potential for much greater influence, but perhaps for many the training and support in communication does not 'kick in' until responsibility increases to far higher levels in the organization's hierarchy?

The skill these leaders felt was their strongest was their ability to articulate a strong point of view, and they also rated themselves highest against the comment 'Do I make it a priority to get feedback and input from our people across the organization and respond to their concerns? Am I a good listener? Do I make it easy for people to bring me bad news?' This is, perhaps, the biggest gap between the perceptions of leaders and employees. Most employee engagement surveys show that employees regard listening as one of the poorest skills of their leaders.

How do workers rate their bosses?

Intrigued by these gaps, I commissioned some research to understand more about how employees felt about whether their bosses were inspiring them. The study was conducted by YOUGOV, an internet-based market research firm, for the company I chair, The Good Relations Group, one of the UK's leading communications agencies. We surveyed a nationally representative sample of more than 4,000 workers in Britain and found that only 21 per cent rated their bosses as very good at inspiring them, with just 5 per cent rating their boss as 'extremely inspiring'.

That's only one in 20 employees who give their leaders the top score for inspiration. At the other end of the spectrum, 33 per cent rated their bosses uninspiring with a further 12 per cent rating them as 'extremely uninspiring'.

It was clear that the older you get, the more demanding you are of your leaders. Nearly 40 per cent of people over the age of 55 regarded their bosses as uninspiring, which is a third more than those aged 25 to 34.

Significant variations in inspiration appeared across industries. Employees from the media, marketing, advertising and public relations sector were most likely to rate their bosses as inspiring (31 per cent rating them 8 or higher on the scale) followed by those in the IT industry (28 per cent). Only 20 per cent of employees in government rated their bosses as inspiring. Two-fifths of employees (40 per cent) who worked in travel and transport said their bosses were uninspiring (giving them a rating of between 1 and 4 on a scale of 1 to 10), suggesting this is an industry with the least engaged workers (see Figure 16.1).

This research shows there is a huge inspiration deficit, one that leaders and managers everywhere ignore at their peril. An inspiration deficit leads directly to an engagement deficit (see Figure 16.2 overleaf). And that leads to failure.

FIGURE 16.1 WHERE ARE THE INSPIRING BOSSES?

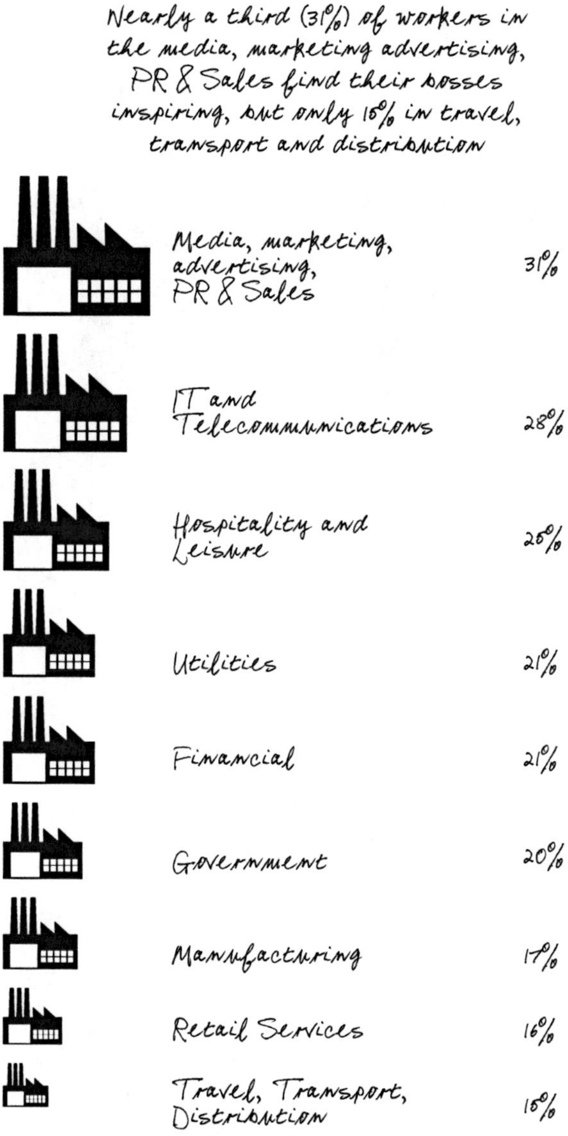

Nearly a third (31%) of workers in the media, marketing advertising, PR & Sales find their bosses inspiring, but only 16% in travel, transport and distribution

Media, marketing, advertising, PR & Sales		31%
IT and Telecommunications		28%
Hospitality and Leisure		26%
Utilities		21%
Financial		21%
Government		20%
Manufacturing		17%
Retail Services		16%
Travel, Transport, Distribution		16%

FIGURE 16.2 HOW INSPIRING?

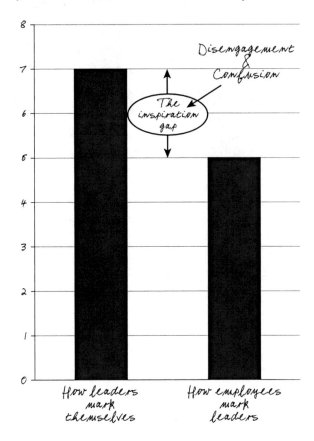

On the other hand, as we have already seen, engaged employees drive greater growth and profitability. Employees who are engaged and inspired perform better on almost every conceivable measure:

- *Profit*: organizations with top-quartile engagement scores have twice the annual net profit of those in the bottom quartile.

- *Revenue growth*: those with top-quartile engagement scores have 2.5 times the revenue growth of those in the bottom quarter.

- *Customer satisfaction*: those organizations with top engagement scores enjoyed 12 per cent higher customer advocacy.

- *Productivity*: top-quartile organizations have 18 per cent higher productivity than those in the lowest quartile.

- *Employee turnover*: high-performing organizations have 40 per cent lower turnover of staff than those with low engagement scores.

- *Health and safety:* organizations in the lower quarter have 62 per cent more accidents than those in the top quartile.

(Source: www.engageforsuccess.org)

What leader in their right mind would set out deliberately to underperform in any of these areas? Engagement may be hard to measure and therefore seen as a soft intangible, but it impacts directly on profitability or service outcomes. It is not an optional extra. Workers are only engaged when they have inspiring bosses.

This was one of the main insights I gained from the many hundreds of hours I spent interviewing leaders, and then examining the transcripts of what they had to say, for *The Language of Leaders*. It was from their wisdom that I drew the 12 principles, and it is worth repeating some of the things they told me here.

In relation to each of the chapters in this book, these are their views...

Chapter 2: On relationships and trust...

General Lord Dannatt, former Chief of the General staff of the British Army. 'It comes down to the personality of the leader, and that is all about character and integrity. Success in the enterprise will be defined by the followers, the workers, the foot soldiers, who will look at the leader and decide whether this is the kind of person that they're attracted to, whether they're the kind of person that they want to follow. Their understanding of that person's integrity will actually determine the degree of enthusiasm with which they follow that person. Is that person to be trusted? Is that a person who's got their best interests at heart or is he or she only interested in short-term success or getting the right figures on the bottom line? So communication and character are both really important.'

Tom Enders, CEO of EADS, a global aerospace and defence business. 'Leaders must stand up and speak out about things that really matter. This is what will give them credibility. It takes courage. You have to lead from the front. If you really want to motivate people, you have to give them your trust. In a book about the power of trust in organizations, I found a quote that pretty much captures the way I try to operate: "I'd rather trust and be occasionally disappointed, than not trust and be occasionally right." It doesn't mean blind trust, obviously, but you have to give trust to unleash the enormous creativity in your company. When you delegate responsibility, when you truly trust people to do a job, they are wonderfully motivated.'

David Morley, Senior Partner at global law firm Allen & Overy. 'If you are going to get your message across and influence the way people behave, which ultimately is what leadership is all about, then there has to be trust in you as an individual and in what you say. When trust goes, cynicism takes its place and it's very difficult to influence cynical people, or people who are cynical about you or your motives. Then it doesn't matter how brilliant a speaker you are – if people don't trust you, you may as well not be talking.'

Chapter 4: On learning to be yourself better...

Lord Victor Adebowale, Chief Executive of Turning Point, a health and social care organization. 'The difference between leadership and management is that leadership involves emotional investment in the task whereas management requires intellectual investment. Good leaders understand the importance of this. Sadly a lot of leaders don't communicate in this way at all, because they are actually terrified. They fear that they will be found out and people will see that they do not have an emotional connection with what they are trying to achieve. They want to avoid exposing themselves. They don't want to take the risk because all communication involves risk. The fear is that you will be exposed as inauthentic, or worse, that your authentic self will be rejected. I believe that the act of communicating is itself a risk, but the act of being inauthentic is an even greater risk.'

John Hirst, Chief Executive of the Met Office, the UK's national weather service. 'If I want to inspire others I have to remember that I can't do that if I am not inspired myself. If I am not convinced I will not convince others. And if I'm not comfortable in my own skin I won't be able to win people's trust.'

Chapter 5: On purpose, vision and values...

Sir Anthony Bamford, Chairman of JCB, the world's third-largest construction equipment brand. 'There is a difference between a purpose and a vision. Purpose is what you do all the time. It is why you exist. A vision is about how successful you will be at what you do, and this will be expressed as a five-year business plan. The plan will be translated into annual goals, and even monthly and weekly goals. The plan has to work in tandem with your purpose.'

John Connolly, past senior partner and CEO of accountancy firm Deloitte, and Chairman of global security company G4S. 'You have to talk about what the future looks like, how you are going to achieve it, and you have to explain the case for change. You have to talk with people about their role in achieving the vision, and make sure they see how they fit in. You have to make sure they understand what you stand for, why what you are doing is important, and how everyone will benefit from success. Human beings work best when they believe in who they are, what they are doing and in the way in which they are doing it together.'

Chapter 6: On bringing the outside in...

Sir Stuart Rose, Chairman of online grocer Ocado and former Chairman of Marks & Spencer's. 'We live in a world which is so fast moving you have to have your antennae permanently switched on 24 hours a day and they have got to be literally quivering. You have to bring that into the company.'

Paul Polman, global CEO of Unilever, an international consumer goods company. 'Bringing customers in helps everyone understand the purpose of the company. All you have to do then is ignite the flame that links the passions of your people to a great sense of purpose, you are up and running. That's what makes a high-performance organization.'

Chapter 7: On engaging through conversation...

Sir Christopher Gent, Chairman of global pharmaceutical company GSK. 'To get people engaged and fully supportive of decisions, you have to go through a process of vigorous debate. This conversation may take longer than you would like, but in the end you will implement faster and more successfully if you do take the time.'

Peter Cheese, CEO of the Chartered Institute of Personnel and Development. 'Empowerment is about giving others the space to succeed, trusting them to perform within the boundaries that you have set, and aligning them on broader objectives and goals. Empowerment therefore requires trusting delegation and a huge amount of conversation to enable success.'

Colin Matthews, Chief Executive of BAA. 'The communication between employees and their direct managers is critical. If you think of communication as a cake, then corporate communications from the top is the icing, and the real substance is in the discussion between front-line supervisors and employees. Too much icing, without the cake, can make you ill. Leaders should ensure that those front-line managers have the tools and skills to have quality conversations with their staff. Leadership isn't something you do by yourself at the top; you have to have leaders everywhere in the organization.'

Sir Nicholas Young, Chief Executive of the International Red Cross. 'It is really important to get our volunteers and staff along with changes, so we take the time to go out and ask them, and discuss ideas with them. It really makes it much easier to inspire people if you know where they are coming from, if you know and understand what their issues are. It is only through these conversations that you can encourage and support and inspire others to achieve.'

Chapter 8: On connecting with your audience...

Lord Colin Sharman, former Chairman of global insurance company Aviva. 'If you really want to communicate, and make a connection with your audience, you have to understand what it is that they need to hear, where they're coming from, and you'll need to address those issues upfront. You will also have to talk with them with the right tone. Unless you do both of those things, they are unlikely to hear anything you have to say. You might give a brilliant speech, but you won't have communicated.'

Judith Hackitt, Chair of the British Health and Safety Executive. 'Preparing for the communications session means trying to understand where people in your audience are coming from. Will they be feeling antagonistic? Are they in a state of fear or uncertainty? Unless you acknowledge that early on then there will always be difficulty in connecting. Rather than battling my way against negative feeling in a room I always try to acknowledge it. That can be really powerful because it shows people that you clearly understand where they are coming from.'

Jane Furniss, Chief Executive of the United Kingdom Independent Police Complaints Commission. 'You have to be really clear about who is in the audience, what you'd like them to do or think as a result of what you say, and what benefits they'll derive if they do.'

Chapter 9: On being a better listener...

Dame Amelia Fawcett, Chair of the Guardian Media Group. 'The ability to listen well is probably one of the most powerful tools of communication that a leader can possess. Those that listen well listen with real intent. They are hearing not only the words, but also the meaning beneath what people are saying.'

Sir Maurice Flanagan, Executive Vice-chairman of the Emirates Airline and Group. 'Leaders gain respect by showing respect. One way you show respect is to really listen. You get respect when people feel that you are taking their views into account. Good listening is not just about understanding what people want to tell you, it is also about the expression on your face when you are listening. People must feel you care about what they have to say.'

Ayman Asfari, Group Chief Executive of Petrofac, a global oil industry facilities business. 'It is crucial to encourage people to bring you bad news. You must never stop the flow of bad news, because if you do that, it will be the beginning of the end. You have to create an environment where people can challenge you and you must be prepared to listen to those challenges. I know from long experience that when people have had a chance to be heard, they might then rally behind a decision even if it is not what they initially voted for.'

Chapter 10: On sending signals...

Richard Gnodde, Chief Executive of Goldman Sachs International. 'Leadership communication can be defined very broadly as everything we say, everything we do, how we conduct ourselves, and what body language we display. Good leaders instinctively know when to talk, when to shut up, how to hold themselves and how to behave. People have always looked to the top for signals and leaders have always been in a fishbowl. The bowl is more transparent than ever today with the internet and 24/7 scrutiny.'

Antony Jenkins, CEO of Barclays Bank. 'If I walk the floors in Barclays and I'm frowning the whole time, hunched over with my hands in my pockets, concern will pass through the building like wildfire. But you have to be very sensitive to how you present at all times. Managing your emotions and channelling them in the right way, as opposed to just letting them run wild, [is] really important.'

Judith Hackitt says that being visible can sometimes send very specific signals. 'When you talk to most senior managers, they will tell you that health and safety is very important to them, but you can pick up signals that clearly show this is not the case. If you ask how long it has been since they last went out into the plant and the answer is "um… um…" then everything starts to unravel. The words and the actions don't match. So leaders must take time to visibly send the signals that they want people to receive.'

Chapter 11: On telling stories...

Sir Nicholas Young of the Red Cross. 'A storytelling organization is a healthy organization. I just love stories. They are incredibly powerful and potent ways of getting messages across, far more powerful than statistics or analysis, the death-by-PowerPoint approach. Stories move me and they move people in the organization.'

Sir Maurice Flanagan of Emirates Airline Group. 'A good story combined with strong logic and supporting statistics can go a very long way. Logic gets to the brain and stories get to the heart.'

David Morley of Allen & Overy. 'Messages sink in better when people work things out for themselves. There's something about the discovery process which helps people to remember better. When they conclude things from your story, it is so much more powerful than if you try to tell them in a series of dry points.'

Chapter 12: On articulating a powerful point of view...

Michael Eisner, former Chief Executive of the Walt Disney Company, after which he founded the Tomante Company, an enterprise that invests in media and entertainment businesses. 'The best leaders always have a potent point of view. What amazes me is that it's always the person with the strong point of view who influences the group, who wins the day.'

Natalie Ceeney, CEO of the Financial Ombudsman Service. 'People don't respect leaders who don't have a point of view.'

Moya Greene, CEO of the Royal Mail, the national postal service of the United Kingdom. 'Leaders need to have views on issues long before being called on to give them. Being a leader in a transparent world can be very difficult. The media can be quite cruel and can be pretty indifferent to the truth at times. Whether you are talking to the media or talking on some public platform, you have to have thought through your position on issues before you get called on. These days, you simply don't have time to think about formulating your point of view in the heat of a discussion. You must have done it beforehand.'

Chapter 13: On preparing for public platforms...

Sir Stuart Rose. 'Leaders have to become competent in all forms of media. You have to be able to do radio, you have got to be able to do TV, you've got to be able to do a pre-record, or handle being on a location, or on a studio set – they are all quite different approaches and senior people must know how to handle all of them. And it can't just be the CEO; the top team needs to be trained.'

Sir Clive Woodward, former English rugby union player and Head Coach of the 2003 Rugby World Cup winning side, then Director of Sport for the British Olympic Association. 'Preparing properly is the key to getting your message across. My whole experience tells me that the more thought I have given to my message, the better I will communicate it. It is like any aspect of sport: if you prepare well you will communicate well. And, always think about what questions you might get, and prepare for those as well.'

Chapter 14: On the power of words...

John Stevens, Baron Stevens of Kirkwhelpington, was Commissioner for the London Metropolitan Police from 2000 until 2005. He is now Executive Chairman of Monitor Quest Ltd, a strategic intelligence and risk-mitigation company. 'Leaders in high-profile positions need to assess every word they utter. When I was leading the Northern Ireland collusion enquiry, which lasted two decades and led to the conviction of 90 people, it was the highest-profile criminal enquiry of its time. I soon came to realize that every word mattered and echoed throughout Northern Ireland.'

Philip Green, formerly CEO of water company United Utilities. 'Whether you like it or not people hang on your every word and the words have more impact than you realize, arguably more impact than they should have, but it takes great skill to talk with passion and still be on message and careful. Not only great skill but a great deal of rehearsal and practice.'

Chapter 15: On social media...

Dame Amelia Fawcett, Chair of the Guardian Media Group. 'Most communications are just not fit for purpose in the Facebook, Twitter, blog and 24/7 news world. One correspondent on the *The Guardian* has a following on her blog of 750,000 people. *The Guardian* has a circulation of 365,000. If you know how to engage with that sort of network it can be very powerful.'

Kevin Beeston, chairman of Taylor Wimpey, one of the largest British house-building companies. 'These days, everybody's got a camera with them. Everybody's got a mobile phone with a voice-recording system or a video camera, so you cannot drop your guard. Make one mistake and you will not get away with it. But, the opposite is also true – if you manage this environment well you have more ways of getting your message over and building your brand. And a strong brand is probably one of the most significant competitive advantages a company can have. So if you manage it effectively, it could be a big driver of shareholder value.'

Chapter 16: On striving to get better...

Sir Christopher Gent believes there is far too little emphasis placed on communications training in business. 'Not only does a leader have to make sure that they personally are capable when it comes to all forms of communication, but they should also make sure that senior people around them are also getting the right professional assistance. They should also be ensuring that they are making their whole organization a better-communicating organization. Good communication is crucial to success.'

Sir Clive Woodward has a saying he calls 'T-CUP' – thinking correctly under pressure. 'It applies to sport or business, to communication, to everything you do. It is the best definition of a champion – someone who thinks correctly when pressure is at its greatest. That takes practice.'

How these experienced leaders rated themselves

When I interviewed these 70 leaders for *The Language of Leaders*, I was very conscious that these were some of the most experienced people I had ever met, many of whom were at the end of careers spanning five decades. I asked each of them to rate their communication skills, on a scale of 0 to 10. Inevitably they rated themselves (on average) around 7/10, the same as the hundreds of leaders who have done my Inspiration Quotient test. Such a mark is, I believe, unhelpful. It says: 'Modesty forbids me from rating myself higher, so I should allow some room for improvement, but nevertheless give myself a good score.' This meant I had to probe a bit deeper: 'Are there occasions when you'd mark yourself very low or very high, and what made the difference?'

Now, I got much richer, more meaningful answers. Almost universally, they said there could be a wide variation from day to day. On some days, they would rank their performance as low as 2/10. On others they would give themselves 10 out of 10. So what was it that made such a big difference?

On the occasions when they gave themselves 2/10, they may have delivered their lines perfectly, with all the professionalism and theatrics they had been trained to use, but they walked away with little response or engagement from the audience. On the other hand, on those occasions when they gave themselves 10 out of 10, they may have stuttered, spat on the front row, or even repeated or fluffed their lines, but they felt an almost metaphysical connection with the audience. They resonated with the mood in the room, they addressed the issues that mattered and they persuaded people to their cause. They could see that their words were positively stirring the emotions of the people they were addressing.

The lesson? Great communication is not about perfect oratory. It is about resonance and connection and engagement. It is about moving people. It is about how you make those people feel. It is not about monologue, it is about dialogue. It is not about being seen as inspiring – it is about making people feel inspired.

On this basis, I believe every leader has it in them to be a great deal more inspiring. To do this they need to articulate a clear sense of purpose that provides a 'true north' for their leadership. They must also learn to listen more attentively, become more proficient conversationalists, bring more of their personality to their leadership, be more audience-centric and learn how to tell stories.

These 70 leaders I interviewed knew – as I hope you do too – that you don't communicate simply to provide information.

As a leader, you communicate to inspire.

So you should strive to be brilliant at it.

WITH GRATEFUL THANKS

First, I would very much like to thank you for buying this book. I hope it helps to make you a more inspiring leader. (If you were one of the many thousands of people who also bought a copy of my first book, *The Language of Leaders*, double thanks.)

Thank you to all the leaders who gave me their time and their views, both for the first book and for this one. I hope I have done you justice.

Thanks go to my daughter, Kirstin Kaszubowska, for finding me the font that has been used to create the figures in this book. (To my amazement, it is my own handwriting. If you're interested in these sorts of things go to this site and create your very own at **www.myfonts.com**)

A big thank you also to Natalie Smith for her patience and creativity in translating my hand-drawn charts into those you see in this book.

A special thank you must go to Jonathan Adler, who has read every chapter and provided terrific advice and counsel on what was working and what was not. His perspectives came from the experience of actually working with me, using some of these methods, to advise the leadership teams with whom we work.

Special mention must go to Richard Spence for his help, especially in working with me to begin articulating my coaching methods years before these books were produced.

Thank you to all at Kogan Page for their continued faith, with special mention to Matthew Smith, Helen Kogan and Nancy Wallace.

Thank you again to Vicky Swales, my tireless and endlessly patient PA, who has provided such invaluable help (once again) with the manuscript.

Finally, to my wife, Liz, thank you for your support, encouragement, proofreading and for taking so much of the load while I was being ruthlessly selfish with this book. You are now, and always will be, my inspiration.

MEET THE AUTHOR

Kevin Murray has been advising leaders and leadership teams on communication and reputation issues for the past three decades. He has worked across a wide variety of sectors and geographies, often having to advise leaders on how to deal with significant issues and sometimes, with crisis communications. He has also provided personal coaching for many of these leaders, helping them to become more effective as communicators.

Kevin is author of the best-selling book *The Language of Leaders*, and is himself the leader of a successful communications and CSR business, The Good Relations Group, which is part of Chime Communications plc.

He has 40 years of experience in communications, first as a journalist, then in corporate communications, and now in consultancy.

Previously, Kevin was Director of Communications for British Airways, and before that Director of Corporate Affairs for the United Kingdom Atomic Energy Authority (AEA). He started his career as a crime reporter on *The Star* newspaper in Johannesburg, South Africa, in 1973.

INDEX

CPSIA information can be obtained at www.ICGtesting.com
Printed in the USA
BVOW01s2007140114

341756BV00002B/2/P